Muslim Rebels

Muslim Rebels

*Kharijites and the Politics
of Extremism in Egypt*

JEFFREY T. KENNEY

OXFORD
UNIVERSITY PRESS

2006

OXFORD
UNIVERSITY PRESS

Oxford University Press, Inc., publishes works that further
Oxford University's objective of excellence
in research, scholarship, and education.

Oxford   New York
Auckland   Cape Town   Dar es Salaam   Hong Kong   Karachi
Kuala Lumpur   Madrid   Melbourne   Mexico City   Nairobi
New Delhi   Shanghai   Taipei   Toronto

With offices in
Argentina   Austria   Brazil   Chile   Czech Republic   France   Greece
Guatemala   Hungary   Italy   Japan   Poland   Portugal   Singapore
South Korea   Switzerland   Thailand   Turkey   Ukraine   Vietnam

Copyright © 2006 by Jeffrey T. Kenney

Published by Oxford University Press, Inc.
198 Madison Avenue, New York, New York 10016

www.oup.com

Oxford is a registered trademark of Oxford University Press

Library of Congress Cataloging-in-Publication Data

Kenney, Jeffrey T. (Jeffrey Thomas), 1954–
    Muslim rebels : Kharijites and the politics of extremism in Egypt / Jeffrey T. Kenney.
        p.   cm.
    Includes bibliographical references and index.
    ISBN-13 978-0-19-513169-7

    1. Kharijites—History.   2. Islamic fundamentalism—Egypt.   3. Islam and
politics—Egypt—History—20th century.   4. Egypt—Politics and
government—20th century.   I. Title.
    BP195.K4K46   2006
    297.8'3—dc22   2006003677

9 8 7 6 5 4 3 2

Printed in the United States of America
on acid-free paper

To Lauren . . . who changed everything.

Acknowledgments

This book has had a long gestation period, and I have accumulated many professional and personal debts along the way. I would like to thank Amanda Porterfield for introducing me to my editor at Oxford University Press, Cynthia Read. Amanda's friendly encouragement got the process started, and Cynthia's interest and patient reminders ("Any news on the manuscript?") helped me bring it to a close. Two readers deserve special thanks. Jim Piscatori and Bill Shepard took the time to read and comment on the entire manuscript; their insightful remarks have improved the final product in ways too numerous to mention. The flaws that remain are entirely my own. For their assistance in passing along material, both medieval and modern, I would like to thank Juan Campo, Chase Robinson and Michael Cook. In Cairo, I benefited from the help of many people: Akram Kadr made the city a more friendly place; Fahmy Huweidy generously loaned me an illegal book; workers in the Xerox room at AUC provided unsolicited opinions; and the booksellers of Cairo patiently shared their knowledge.

Finally, I would especially like to thank family and friends whose support made this book possible. Susan Hahn read and commented on an early version of the manuscript; she did not see the book through to the end, but much of her is still in it. Terrie Kenney provided quiet inspiration from the sidelines. Lauren

Kenney made the world a nicer place. I wish Ruth and Frank were here to see it.

I am grateful for the research funding I received from two institutions: Indiana University–Purdue University, Indianapolis, and DePauw University.

Contents

A Note on Transliteration

I have adopted a simplified version of the transliteration system
employed by the *International Journal of Middle East Studies*, one
that indicates the Arabic *'ayn* (') and *hamza* (') but omits other dia-
critical marks. Instead of the phonetically accurate Khawarij, I have
relied on the spelling most prevalent in academic writing: Kharijites.
I have also, in keeping with trends in the writing of Middle East
history (both classical and modern), adopted the neologism
"Kharijism" to capture the phenomenon of the movement(s) as
a whole.

Muslim Rebels

Introduction

This book is a study of the discourse surrounding Islamist violence in Egypt from the 1950s to the 1990s. Its analytic focus is the emergence and evolution of discursive references to the Kharijites, a seventh-century militant Muslim sect, as a way to denounce religiously justified violence and those who resort to it. My interest in this topic began while I was a graduate student in Cairo during the early 1980s, not long after Islamic Jihad had assassinated Egyptian President Anwar Sadat but significantly before al-Qaʻida carried out its now infamous September 11, 2001, attacks on New York City and Washington, D.C. Familiar with the historical role of the Kharijites, I was surprised to find the sect so prominently cited in both the popular press and books about religion and politics in modern Egypt. The Kharijites, it seems, despite their centuries-long absence from the historical stage, were very much alive in the minds of Egyptians. And as I was to discover, concern about the importance of historical symbols such as the Kharijites in the public discourse of Muslim societies was very much alive in the minds of scholars.

Any first-year student of Islam has heard or read about the Kharijites. An overview of their activities and ideas is an essential feature of introductory textbooks on Islam, and they are a recurring subject of discussion in more specialized works on the first several centuries of Islamic history. Historically, the importance of the Kharijites lies in the challenge they posed to Muslim ruling authorities throughout the Umayyad period and into the Abbasid and in the political and theological debates to which the movement gave rise. Assured of their own religious purity, the Kharijites judged other Muslims—those outside the Kharijite fold—as unworthy of the name Muslim and set about creating, through violence, an ideal community of the saved. The Kharijites emerged out of the period of Islamic history known as the first civil war or *fitna* (656–661 C.E.), a time marked by the murders of the third and fourth caliphs, 'Uthman and 'Ali, the first killed by (Egyptian) Muslims disaffected with his socioeconomic reforms and the second by a Kharijite seeking revenge. It is out of this same political maelstrom that the two major expressions of Islam, Sunni and Shi'a, began to take shape. Based on the image of the sect fostered by the Islamic tradition, the name "Kharijite" summarily defines a Muslim as an overly pious zealot whose actions and ideas lie beyond the pale of normative Islam. Modern Egyptians, then, saw in the Kharijites a traditionally sanctioned anti-model of rebellion—one that provided a means of critiquing and, ideally, controlling outbursts of Islamist violence.

The capacity of the Kharijites to serve this purpose is a function of the mythic structure of the Islamic tradition and the interpretive play of this structure in different historical contexts. The mythic image of the Kharijites was constructed by medieval thinkers more concerned with establishing and preserving a system of authority than with accurately telling history. Hence, in early sources, the name "Kharijite" came to denote both the original group that protested against the caliph 'Ali and *anyone* who rebelled against a leader or his appointed representatives. The myth of the Kharijites communicates a moral lesson on the limits of protest against authority: a good Muslim may not rebel against a legitimate ruler. In the Sunni tradition, however, authority is not just something to obey. According to another mythic strand, it must be earned, since a caliph or political leader is obliged to protect and uphold the law of God. And still another myth empowers Muslims to act against any wrongdoing they encounter in the world (with their hands, tongues, or hearts), including the wrongdoing of the caliph. Despite the potential tension between them, each of these myths is, by definition, true. But they are truths reflective of different times and circumstances that have become part of the tradition's collective memory.

> Their continued existence together poses a problem only for modern historians who tend to isolate one element from the narrative structure in the desire to create coherence out of the historical record, and for those who wish to remythologize.[1]

The contestation between Islamists and successive Egyptian regimes over political power and authority brought all these myths, and others, to the fore.

But the political and cultural world of mid-twentieth–century Egypt forced them into new configurations. From its first appearance in Egypt, discourse about the Kharijites differed markedly from that found in classical sources. Whereas in the medieval period the label Kharijite could be applied to *anyone* who rebelled against the legitimate ruler, in modern Egypt it was reserved exclusively for Islamists. Medieval writers tended to gloss the motivation for rebellion behind the all-encompassing phenomena of Kharijism, while modern Egyptian commentators distinguished between religiously motivated militants (= Kharijites) and others engaged in political violence. The historical contrast here reflects medieval versus modern attitudes toward religion and politics. Institutionally, the classical Islamic world witnessed the emergence of separate spheres of authority, a class of religious-legal scholars ('ulama') and the political office of the caliph (the Calilphate). Culturally, however, religion and politics continued to blend in Muslim thinking. In modern Egypt, the myth of the Kharijites was rationalized to suit the framework of the scientific nation-state, where the secular holds sway over religion, or at least where this issue is being worked out.[2] This is not to say that Egyptian intellectuals adopted a secular outlook identical to that of the West. They had, however, since the nineteenth century, wrestled with "how to be Muslim and modern," and this included debate about the proper relationship between religion and politics. Islamist attempts to (re-) Islamize society and politics rekindled that debate, and militant outbursts made the Islamist agenda impossible to ignore.

Why is Islam's mythic history, including the Kharijites, relevant to the development of modern Egypt? Here a parallel case may help clarify the issues at work. In his study of the intellectual and cultural ferment leading up to the 1979 Iranian revolution, Roy Mottahedeh observed that "[a]ny consensus on the meaning of the Iranian past has been torn up by the deeply felt disagreement among Iranians over the meaning of the Iranian present."[3] His point was that the past had become the battleground on which modern Iranians fought out their differences, and because their differences were so profound, what had been points of historical agreement were now subjects of intense dispute. That the religious past could play such a formative role in thinking about current issues is not surprising. After all, students of history are well aware of the continuous reinvention of tradition, which maintains the relevancy and plausibility of a cultural worldview over time. However, as Iranians, Egyptians, and Muslims of other modern nations have resorted to the Islamic past to meet the challenges of modernity, serious questions have been raised about whether their thinking is truly modern. The concern, of course, is that religious thought is not compatible with building a progressive civil society and instituting democratic rule, that religion and politics do not mix. Thus the Western developmental model, which equates modernization with secularization, casts a long shadow of suspicion on the Islamic idiom that has characterized Muslim political discourse.

The discourse under examination in this work, then, contributes to on-going scholarly efforts to analyze the creative potential of the Islamic idiom. The lines of debate on this matter are clear. Those who look favorably upon the potential of reinvented tradition have argued that through it Muslims are empowered to negotiate an authentic path to progress. Instead of following the modernization-equals-secularization model of development dominant in the West, Muslims, are said to accommodate social change by interpreting modernity through the lens of tradition.[4] Critics, by contrast, have maintained that notions of reinvented Islam obscure the universal processes of modern-ization and secularization that are buffeting Muslim societies behind a cloud of eternal essences. The result is that progress is impeded because Muslims, and some Western analysts, mistakenly see an unchanging Islam, rather than the underlying processes, as the driving force of activism and change.[5] As I will argue in the following chapters, reinvented Kharijism in Egypt has, at different times, fit the assessments offered by both proponents and critics. But a word here about my own analytic assumptions is in order before continuing.

First, while the Islamic idiom is rooted in past social and historical ex-periences, it is the present context that drives the application and under-standing of the idiom.[6] This observation is true across time. Early believers were reacting to their environment, just as modern believers are. But the experiences of early believers, including their differences, became codified as normative, which accounts for the mythic tension in the collective memory of the tradition noted above. The general point about the ambivalence of reli-gion, then, is actually a point about the dichotomous uses to which adherents put their tradition in all times and places.[7] Second, given that believers and their understanding of tradition are historically grounded, essentialist think-ing is never as narrowly essentialist as critics maintain. No matter how in-sistent a believer may be about a given God-ordained truth and its universal application, that truth has been selected and interpreted under particular historical circumstances. And the task of scholars is to unpack this idealized interpretive process. All this is consistent with the operation of reinvented tradition mentioned earlier, but it stills leaves open the challenge posed by those critical of essentialist discourse: Does it obscure the social, economic, and political forces that shape a historical context behind ambiguous, other-worldly language? My answer is that it certainly can, and it sometimes does, but the same must be said of any cultural discourse. Essentialist rhetoric such as the kind that has developed surrounding the Kharijites may appear sim-plistic to academics who prefer reasoning grounded in social and historical facts, not myths, but it has profound meaning and consequences. Moreover, it is not restricted to Muslim societies or the developing world. In the West, secular discourse on democracy, liberty, and the free-market system is also subject to ahistorical, essentializing trends because developed nations are in just as much need of the cultural authenticity that essentialism confers as those nations trying to catch up. Essentialism is part of the "culture-talk," to borrow Ernest Gellner's term,[8] that drives discourse in a society . . . any soci-ety. Specifically, it is a way of identifying or defining something across time, and definitions are basic to communication.

If my comments here suggest that I am blurring an already blurry subject behind some postmodern commitment to the relative merits of all meta-narratives, let me be clear. Communicating through a symbolic language such as the Islamic idiom is replete with problems, not least of which are the restrictions it places on those outside the cultural fold. But participants in a national public discourse need not become full-fledged historicists, acknowl-edging the modern basis of their cultural idiom and the context in which they are applying it, in order to communicate meaningfully. More important to successful communication are the social and political conditions that govern it, and the conditions in Egypt have not always been conducive to honest and open public debate. Known for its long-standing commitment to corporatism and (mild) authoritarianism, the Egyptian state has never made freedom of expression, political or otherwise, a high priority. During those periods when state-restrictions on public expression were eased, however, discourse on the Kharijites has tended to be richer and more dynamic. That the creative po-tential of reinvented tradition in Egypt was linked to intellectual and political openness should come as no surprise. The same could be said of the potential impact of culture-talk in any society. Of course, it does not follow that in order for such discourse to be meaningful it must occur in a democratic institutional structure. People living under restrictive or oppressive circumstances com-monly find ways to express their anger at and opposition to those in positions of power, even if it is only a quiet form of subversion.[9] Still, conditions do matter, and intrusive state-controls in Egypt have inhibited the free-flow of ideas and led to increasing popular dependence on the Islamic idiom. What this means is that the degree, and kind, of importance this idiom currently possesses for public communication is not simply a "natural" expression of Muslim society but rather a historical point in the trajectory of a nation.[10]

Numerous factors, starting in the nineteenth century and continuing to the present, have contributed to the rising importance of the Islamic idiom in

Egypt: opposition to imperialism and the related emphasis on cultural uniqueness by nationalist movements, government attempts to secure popular support by nationalizing religion, the challenge of Islamists, and the fluctuating
role of al-Azhar in public life. Many of these themes will be taken up later
in the book, but for now we need only indicate how the communicative
form of the Islamic idiom—with its traditional authority and orthodox-based
reasoning—was able to substitute for the unfulfilled promise of Egypt's modern political system. Pointing us in the right direction is Talal Asad's analysis of the deliberations of religious scholars as they work their way toward
orthodoxy:

> It is too often forgotten that the process of determining orthodoxy in
> conditions of change and contest includes attempts at achieving
> discursive coherence, at representing the present within an authori-
> tative narrative that includes positive evaluations of past events and
> persons. Because such authority is a collaborative achievement be-
> tween narrator and audience, the former cannot speak in total free-
> dom: there are conceptual and institutional conditions that must
> be attended to if discourses are to be persuasive.[11]

For Asad, the orthodoxy reached by a body of 'ulama' is a collaborative effort,
something to be negotiated; and the authorities who express it are bound by
recognized rules. Negotiating orthodoxy, of course, is not the same thing as
achieving a democratic consensus; but in the absence of a rule-bound political
system, it provides a protective cultural penumbra in which meaningful exchange and debate can take place. The Islamic idiom in Egypt creates this
cultural space for communication, though the range of participants is far more
diverse. It includes official religious scholars, state functionaries, politicians,
Islamists, secularists, and intellectuals of various persuasions. Scholars have
tried to type the range of opinions that have emerged in modern Muslim
societies such as Egypt, but it has proven a difficult and elusive task for reasons
that speak to the shifting ground of history and the identities that are being
forged on this shifting ground. First, it is not only religious positions that are
being categorized by a typology; political views are also part of the mix because
what is commonly measured are people's attitudes toward modernity, development, and the kind of polity in which they wish to live. So categories such as
traditional, neo-traditional, radical Islamism, modern, and secular reflect both
religious and ideological positions.[12] Second, as noted above, Muslim societies
are in a state of social and political flux brought about by modernity, and
Islamic culture provides the symbolic ground on which the future is contested.[13] This means that two identities, the religious and the political, are in a

state of motion and contestation. Moreover, whether Muslims *qua* Muslims can possess separate religious and political identities is part of the debate.

Thus the "orthodoxy" under negotiation in Egypt is not religious per se but more broadly political-cultural. Indeed, the Islamic idiom reflects this complex cultural reality, for it is as much a product of new, secular-based knowledge as it is of traditional religious knowledge; and it is found in settings not conventionally associated with Islamic authority. In the preface to his seminal study of the radical trend in the Muslim Middle East, Emmanuel Sivan wrote of his experiences in the bookstalls of Cairo, where he found modern Muslims searching for practical life guidance in classical commentaries. Struck by the "living reality" of the past for these readers, Sivan set out to understand "the transformation of medieval theology into modern Muslim politics."[14] Yet, while the bookstalls of Cairo provide one kind of insight into this transformation, another vantage point of discovery is that of popular magazine racks, where the dynamic between tradition and modernity reaches full disclosure. At these sites, readers will not find the multi-volume Qur'an commentary of the medieval scholar al-Tabari, but they can purchase a single-volume abridgement of his wisdom decocted for the busy masses. And this pocket-commentary mixes with very different genres: modern periodicals, romance novels, journalistic exposés, Islamist booklets, weight training manuals, political commentary, film guides, *fatwa* collections, horoscopes, and science journals. Foreign information is also available, as Egyptian daily newspapers and weekly magazines share space with *Le Monde, Die Zeit, The International Herald Tribune, The Economist, Time, Elle,* and *Vogue.* Traditional knowledge is part of this complex cultural array, but it is competing for space and the attention of readers. It is also blurring and fusing with knowledge bases with which it appears to be at odds. For those seeking life guidance at these magazine racks—microcosms of Egypt's complex culture—tradition has been reinvented for modern, if not postmodern, consumption.

Among the various symbols that inform the Islamic idiom in Egypt, Kharijism raises some of the most sensitive questions about modern Muslim identity because it explicitly evokes the dichotomy of good Muslim versus bad Muslim. It also directly connects this religious identity with a political one. A Kharijite is not only a misguided believer but a dangerous citizen as well. Here we are at the most basic level of an essentialist Islamic current that equates an early example of Muslim rebellion with one presently threatening Egyptian society: a bad Muslim is a bad Muslim for all time. A symbolic name such as Kharijites holds special communicative power because it carries with it an authority to act: "An epithet assigns substance doubly, for in stating the character of the object it at the same time contains an implicit program of action with regard to the object, thus serving as a motive."[15] The presence of Kharijites in the Muslim community, according to the Islamic historical record, authorizes Muslims to act to eliminate them, to remove this threat to the well-being of the community.

The chapters that follow will examine the motives of those who have leveled the accusation of Kharijism at Islamists in Egypt and those who participated in the wider cultural debate about this accusation. My intent is neither to defend the integrity of the Egyptian state against extremist predation nor to apologize for the radicals by historicizing and thus debunking the accuracy of the label Kharijite attached to them. Rather, it is to explore the power of discourse to shape historical events and understanding and the power of events to shape discourse. An underlying assumption of this project is that "[t]he political struggle to impose a definition on an action and to make it stick is frequently at least as important as the action per se."[16] The Egyptian struggle to define Islamist militants as Kharijites was part of the national effort to work through the Weberian axiom that the modern state "is a human community that (successfully) claims the *monopoly of the legitimate use of physical force* within a given territory."[17] The debates that ensued in Egypt over the Kharijites were not evidence of Egyptian indifference to Islamist violence or indecision about the need for a strong state. Quite the contrary: the vast majority of Egyptians were quick to reject the extremists and support the state. But at the same time, people were concerned about the kind of state that they were affirming in their rejection of Islamist radicals, and they recognized that political violence occurs in a context for which the state itself must take some measure of responsibility.

What an analysis of accusations of Kharijism clearly shows is that Egyptians grew increasingly sophisticated in their use of culture-talk to identify problems of state legitimacy and efficiency, especially in the areas of political participation and economic development. These problems are common throughout the Middle East, where integration into the modern world of nation-states and the global economy has proven more challenging and less satisfying than regional leaders and their populations initially anticipated it to be.[18] Identifying problems related to modernization is certainly not the same as offering solutions—a point that materialist critics of culture-talk have rightly emphasized.[19] However, substantive solutions have in fact been expressed within the culture-talk related to Islamist extremism, and these solutions reflect some of the same materialist understandings of modern Egyptian (and Middle Eastern) society that critics claim are key to development.

Egypt, of course, is not the only country to experience Islamist violence. Other Muslim nations have had to deal with the challenge of militant Islamist movements. And now the problem has reached global proportions, with the emergence of a transnational group of jihadists who received their initial training in a CIA-backed proxy war against the Soviets in Afghanistan and then went on to attack American interests around the world, including symbolic centers of power within the United States itself.[20] Although the events of September 11, 2001, lie beyond the focus of this book, the response they generated in the United States has important parallels with our study of Egypt.

Soon after September 11, 2001, the United States government declared war on terrorism, sending its troops first to Afghanistan to bring the perpetrators of September 11 to justice and then to Iraq to wage a purported preemptive war against future terrorist acts. A war-like footing also emerged in the United States as the National Guard took control of security at many of the nation's airports and the President warned American citizens to be alert in their daily lives to further acts of terror. Indeed, the government eventually established a color-coded alert system that, like the daily pollution index and pollen count, advises people about the level of danger connected with public activity. In addition to these practical steps taken to confront Islamic extremism, Americans embarked on a search for knowledge about Muslims and Islam. Demand for books on Islam increased dramatically; even the Qur'an became a popular seller. Media coverage of Islam and Muslim societies also grew as Americans tried to understand the religious and political motives of the hijackers.

Thus the American response to September 11, much like the Egyptian reaction to its problem with extremism, has been a classical combination of power and knowledge. In theory, knowledge is supposed to inform the exercise of power. But the political pressures caused by such a dramatic historical event push a state to react militarily first, based on limited knowledge, and then the national culture follows up by filling in the intellectual gaps. As a result, the knowledge that is eventually produced has a tendency to legitimize the power that has already been demonstrated by the state. We are still too close to the events of September 11, too engaged in the war on terror, to make a final judgment about whether power will ultimately subvert American knowledge about Islamic extremism. Some interesting comparative patterns have emerged, however, patterns that confirm the normative role of culture and the cultural past in public discourse on extremism.

Like state functionaries in Egypt, Americans officials, with President George W. Bush in the lead, were quick to make a distinction between good Muslims and bad Muslims. This observation played well with a public that did not want the fight against terrorism turned into a religious war. As it turned out, however, good Muslims were not only expected to reject the kind of terrorist violence displayed on September 11; they were also supposed to agree with the administration's broader war on terrorism. Politically, good Muslims, at home and abroad, were *with* the United States, not against it; culturally, they believed in freedom, tolerance, and open markets.[21] Good Muslims were also, according to The 9/11 Commission Report, supposed to "distinguish politics from religion."[22] Not surprising, the moral judgment of "good" voiced by administration officials, and many public commentators, reflected American ideals and concerns. And when American and other Western observers tried to account for the radical impulse that made a bad Muslim bad, they also often resorted to explanations that suited the Western historical imagination. President Bush, along with many others, commonly attributed the al-Qa'ida attack to a hatred of America's freedom and democracy.[23]

A more sophisticated but no less Western-centric explanation was offered by Paul Berman in his much reviewed book Terror and Liberalism. For Berman, the Muslim extremists who carried out the attacks on September 11 were influenced by two distinct cultural sources: "the Arab past and the Western present."[24] Although both played a part in shaping Osama bin Laden and al-Qa'ida members, along with their radical precursors such as Sayyid Qutb, it was the West that interested Berman the most:

> I don't mean to deny or ignore for one minute the authentically Muslim and local roots of bin Laden's enterprise and of the many other Arab and Islamic terrorist organizations of recent times. Still, an amazing number of the Arab and Muslim terrorists do turn out to have second and even primary identities as Westerners. It's good to glance eastward, and at the history of the Arab and Muslim world from hundreds of years ago. But in trying to make sense of these people's very strange behavior, we ought to glance westward, too— not just at Western politics and policies, but at literature and philosophy, at the deepest of Western ideas, not just now but in the past, and in the long-ago past. In the West, we do have our own customs and traditions, some of which are perfectly horrible.[25]

Viewed one way, this appears to be a simple recognition of the West's own violent past. But here the Western past serves as a lesson about the threat of current Muslim extremism. What could one possibly learn about Muslim extremists by understanding a custom or tradition of the West? The extremists, according to Berman, both envied and feared the West. They had experienced it firsthand, living and studying there. Moreover, they themselves learned from the West, borrowing one of its political ideas to use to their own advantage—totalitarianism. The totalitarianism of which Berman writes is the same totalitarianism that gave rise to fascism and anti-Semitism in Europe and that led to a long and bitterly fought world war. It also contributed to anarchist trends in European history, including those that shaped post-World War Two political sympathies among the left.

By connecting Islamist extremism with totalitarianism, Berman tries to show that the fanatical ideas expressed by the September 11 terrorists and their willingness to sacrifice themselves for the glory of the cause are not strange phenomena after all. Indeed, this radical movement is all too familiar: "This is not exotic. This is the totalitarian cult of death. *This* is the terrible thing that got underway more than eighty years ago."[26] Berman's interpretation of Muslim extremists as Muslim totalitarians may or may not be good history, but it is certainly an effective mythic narrative for his audience. He reawakens a Western tradition that resonates with Western sensibilities and that contains a plan of action: Americans know what must be done in the face of totalitarian aggression; they met this challenge before on the battlefields of Europe, and they learned the hard way the consequences of not addressing the problem early in its development. Berman, then, essentializes Muslim extremists for a Western-American audience: he cast bad Muslims into a cultural mold that made sense to Americans, just as the Kharijites made sense to Egyptians. His leap of cultural interpretation, however, begs several questions. Is it possible to engage, meaningfully, in the culture-talk of a culture different from one's own? And if so, what are the conditions and limitations of such cultural interchange?

These are not simply theoretical questions, since cross-cultural normative statements about Islam have grown commonplace in the West. Islamist extremism is just one among many issues, such as the fight against communism, the Israeli-Palestinian conflict, and the place of women in Muslim societies, that has over the years inspired Westerners to borrow the moral language of Islam in order to influence either Muslim or non-Muslim opinion or both. And this trend in cross-cultural moral discourse will no doubt increase as Muslim populations in the West grow and as the international struggle against Islamist extremism intensifies. In fact, globalization has already led to the merging and blurring of cultural discourses. The recent case of Muslim girls wearing head scarves in French schools is a case in point. Despite protest from Muslim and non-Muslim citizens, the French government passed a law, which was to take effect at the start of the 2004–2005 school year, banning the wearing of religious symbols, including Muslim head scarves, in public schools. Before the first day of classes, two French journalists were taken hostage in Iraq, and one of the demands for their release was that the law be rescinded. Secular state officials responded to this situation by "focusing on the criminality of hostage-taking under Islam and explaining why the law should not be seen as anti-Islam." Representatives of France's Muslim population—a population that was largely viewed as un-assimilated into French society—came to the support of the government, claiming that the law was a domestic affair.[27]

This international incident resulted in a secular government deploying the moral language of the Islamic tradition and a minority Muslim community asserting its commitment to the democratic process. But there is a distinction to be made here. Although French Muslims may speak as both citizens and Muslims, the French government has no such dual capacity. Participation in the discourse of a tradition, whether a religious or political one, requires au-thenticity, a quality that insiders automatically possess to some degree and outsiders typically do not. This point is important to our understanding of the discourse at work in Egypt, for some non-Muslim scholars have fallen into patterns of anti-extremist rhetoric involving the Kharijites. In textbooks and academic articles, written after the emergence of Islamist extremism in the 1950s, scholars made comparative references that link Islamists with the Kharijites.[28] Some presented Kharijism as evidence of the deep roots of radi-calism in Islamic history, and as a zealot-like tendency to which modern Muslims sometimes return; others viewed it as a behavioral option that Mus-lims either adopt or inadvertently fall into. Both understandings suggest that Kharijism is, in some sense, an explanation for Islamist extremism. A few writers even charged specific groups with being Kharijites. Interesting enough, the Kharijites were also introduced into post-September 11 discussions about Islamic extremism in the United States—not in a sustained way, but a few commentators drew connections between the perpetrators and the medieval Kharijites.[29]

Such comparative references participate, intentionally or not, in the in-sider ethical-political discourse, the Muslim culture-talk, surrounding Islamist extremism; and they do so, typically, for what might appear to be legitimate, sympathetic reasons: to identify and isolate a minority group of bad Muslims that are distinct from the Muslim majority. Those writing from outside the tradition, however, lack the authenticity that is vital to an active engagement with the discourse of reinvented Islam. Simply by virtue of their insider status, Muslims are empowered to interpret and shape their tradition. They also, in their everyday lives, interact with the tradition as a living reality that must be understood and applied in particular social, economic, and political circumstances. Thus a Muslim may accept the essentialist definition of a Kharijite, but this definition becomes a point of departure, not the end point, for further participation in the ongoing discourse. Egyptian Muslims, then, unlike sympathetic outsiders, can take an essentialist symbol such as the Kharijites—a symbol that supposedly anathematized religious rebellion and upheld the status quo—and transform it into a tool to critique the political establishment.

Outsiders have also, with the best of intentions, seen a potential within the Islamic tradition that the Muslim imagination has not seen. One scholar, for example, has written of the Kharijites as a possible developmental model:

> Concepts of democracy very much like those in modern political sys-
> tems can be found in the earliest period in Islamic history in the
> ideas of the Kharijite sect, which broke off from mainstream Islam
> in the seventh century over the latter's refusal to agree to the Khar-
> ijite tenet that the successors to the Prophet Muhammad had to be
> elected by the community.[30]

While the Kharijite view of election to the Caliphate was more open than what became standard Sunni policy, the Kharijite sect is not remembered in Islamic sources as a proto-democratic movement that battled for a more "progressive politics" in seventh-century Arabia. More important, the image of the Khar-ijites was not reinvented in modern Egypt for its progressive potential. In fact, the Kharijites as a traditional anti-model of militant Islam have been cast as impediments to democracy in Egypt and the Middle East. Only a handful of leftist historians—dilettantes whose cultural inspiration was more revolu-tionary Marxism than Islam—viewed the Kharijites as a positive model of change.[31]

If we wish to understand the causes and consequences of Islamic ex-tremism, we must listen carefully to authentic Muslim discourses, discourses that reflect a native understanding of the political and cultural struggles at play. Scholars, journalists, and policy analysts have already made important contributions to our knowledge of the historical and ideological roots of Islamist extremism, especially as it relates to September 11. And Egypt has figured prominently in these studies.[32] Egyptian Islamists, starting with the Society of Muslim Brothers, have long been models of activism throughout the Islamic world; and the ideas espoused by leaders of this organization, particularly Hasan al-Banna and Sayyid Qutb, have shaped both moderate and militant thought. One such militant was the blind Egyptian cleric, 'Umar 'Abd al-Rahman, who provided the religious ruling (*fatwa*) that inspired Sadat's assassins, and whom the Federal Court in New York convicted in 1995 for conspiring in the 1993 bombing of the World Trade Center and a later un-successful plot to destroy various Manhattan landmarks. Two of al-Rahman's sons went on to join the al-Qa'ida operation in Afghanistan. Egyptian Is-lamists have also been influential in the Saudi education system, where Osama bin Laden received his initial schooling. Bin Laden learned a great deal from the Islamist tradition in Egypt, particularly from the work of Sayyid Qutb. Bin Laden's cause also benefited from Egyptian volunteers, who trav-eled to Afghanistan to wage *jihad* against Soviet aggression. Some of these volunteers stayed on, following the Soviet defeat, to join al-Qa'ida; a select few went on to participate in terrorist missions against the United States. A for-mer Egyptian army officer, Ali Muhammad, led the Nairobi portion of the African embassy bombings in 1998. Bin Laden's second in command in Afghanistan, and his most trusted advisor, was Ayman al-Zawahiri, an Egyptian medical doctor and former leader of Egyptian Islamic Jihad.

Egypt, then, has contributed to a shocking and dangerous pattern of Islamist extremism, both at home and abroad. But this pattern of extremism has been matched by determined efforts to oppose Islamist violence that is equally deserving of our attention. As a nation, Egypt has lived with extrem-ism since the 1950s. It knows the consequences of terrorism, having suffered serious slumps in its economy and threats to the nation's political liberties—issues the United States has also had to face. Egypt has also waged its own dual-front battle against Muslim radicals, deploying both the martial might of the state and the moral authority of its culture to counter the threat. And in this half-century fight, Egyptians have learned something about the nature of Islamic extremism. Indeed, after the September 11 attacks, the Egyptian Prime Minister, Atef Ebeid, offered to share his country's knowledge of terrorism:

> The U.S. and U.K., including human-rights groups, have, in the past, been calling on us to give these terrorists their 'human rights.' You can give them all the human rights they deserve until they kill you. After these horrible crimes committed in New York and Vir-ginia, maybe Western countries should begin to think of Egypt's own fight against terror as their new model.[33]

That terrorism must be met with a strong hand and a willingness to over-look breaches of human rights is certainly one "lesson" to learn from Egypt's historical experience with Islamist violence. But there are also other lessons—about the desire for stability and trust, about the moral limits of authoritarian rule, about anxiety-ridden modernity, about the search for modern identity, and about the ambivalence of culture—all of which are reflected in the dis-course surrounding Islamist violence that developed over the years. Attention to this discourse may not prevent further acts of Islamist extremism. It will, however, humanize the Muslim effort to deal with this problem and lay a firmer groundwork for future cross-cultural understanding.

Chapter 1 explores the historical, literary process by which the early Kharijites were transformed into a mythic symbol of rebellion. Its purpose is to show the constructed nature of the Kharijites in the classical Islamic tradition. Although it is possible to outline the operation of modern uses of the Kharijite image in Egypt without such background, the power of reinvented tradition can only be fully appreciated if one has an understanding of the narrative continuum of which it is a part. In chapters 2 and 3, I map out the modern context in which Egyptians began to introduce the Kharijites into their political discourse. During the 1950s and 1960s, Egypt seemed poised to realize the Arab socialist ideal of development promised by Gamal Addul Nasser's revolutionary movement. The most vocal and organized opposition to this ideal was the Society of Muslim Brothers, which offered a developmental model rooted in Islamic rather than Western culture. For Nasser and the Egyptians who placed their hopes in him, the Society's Islamist agenda represented an impediment to political, economic, and social progress; and the political violence to which members of the Society sometimes resorted posed an intolerable threat to the stability and success of the nation. Recourse to the Kharijite image was part of the intellectual response, largely state-driven, to challenge the extremists. Traditional and religious in its character, this image served an ostensibly modern and secular purpose: the legitimacy of Nasser's state.

Chapter 4 covers the political discourse about Islamist extremism during the Sadat years. Sadat established his reputation as president by steering a course away from the policies of his predecessor. His distinctive legacy was his economic and political opening to the West, which was preceded by an opening of Egyptian society. The Islamist trend, which Nasser viewed as a threat and systematically oppressed, was embraced by Sadat in a symbolic marriage of convenience. The honeymoon period, however, was short lived, for Sadat was no more prepared to institute Islamist social and political demands than Nasser had been. Discourse on extremism during this period bears the distinct markings of the political negotiations underway between Islamists and the state; and the Kharijites were a tool for the claims of both the authorities and Islamists. The final chapter treats the political discourse on extremism in the 1980s and 1990s, a time when Egyptians began to explore the causes of extremism in more critical and nuanced ways. Indeed, Egyptians seemed to develop a self-conscious understanding that Islamist violence was a complex problem for which Egyptian society in general must take responsibility, including the state. As a result, Kharijism was transformed from a traditional anti-model of rebellion into a symptom of much that had gone wrong with the difficult historical transition to modernity. Taken together, these chapters highlight the dynamic and integral role of Islam in Egypt's political culture.

I

Origins and Legacy of the Kharijites

An opinion piece in the semi-official Egyptian daily *al-Ahram*, on 15 February 1993, argued that those who compare violent Islamic groups with the Kharijites "leap over history and disregard its objective circumstances."[1] The events that gave rise to the Kharijites, the article claimed, were particular to that historical period and have not been repeated since, and it therefore follows that Kharijite ideas could not have reemerged among modern extremists. This was not the typical view of the Kharijites that most readers expected to find in the pages of *al-Ahram*, which probably explains the title of the commentary, "Origins of Extremist Thought: A Contrasting View." Since the 1960s, *al-Ahram*, along with other Egyptian newspapers and periodicals, had published countless opinion columns and news articles that mentioned or discussed the Kharijites in connection with radical Islamist activities. As a result, Egyptians had no doubt come to assume that the first sectarian movement in Islamic history was relevant, if not essential, to understanding the spasmodic religious violence that befell their country.

Thus, when the opinion expressed in the article advised writers and preachers to avoid evoking the Kharijites to confront radicalized Muslim youth, it was working against the grain of popular religious culture in Egypt. It was also working against the grain of both the religious authorities who informed popular opinion and the secular political order that cynically turned to Islamic ideas and symbols when it was convenient and salutary. Even many Egyptian

Islamists who defended militant tactics, and who themselves were sometimes tainted by the Kharijite label, regarded the Kharijites as a persistent force in Islamic history and a potential threat to modern Muslim society.

Behind this widespread perception of Kharijite influence stands the authority of the Islamic tradition. No mere invention of modern establishment functionaries, the symbol of the Kharijites is firmly rooted in the Islamic past. Its meaning for Muslims, however, extends beyond the time of its original referent, into both the pre- and post-history of the movement. In short, it is transhistorical. This is a function of the nature of tradition and the complex of symbols, codes, and styles that carry it along through time. One of the distinctive features of a tradition is that the past is never really in the past. Believers always encounter their tradition in an eternal present, but they do so by interacting with what has been passed on from previous generations— accepting, adapting, or rejecting. It is this ongoing process that defines tradition and that engenders in its members a sense of what Edward Shils calls "the presentness of the past."[2] Moreover, those who participate in a tradition never experience the past as an undifferentiated whole. Their sense of the presentness of the past is always of a particular past, one with a distinctive cast of characters, ideology, and ways of dealing with sociocultural constants, such as legitimacy, authority, and rebellion. It is through these particulars that a tradition creates continuity between past, present, and future, thereby maintaining identity through periods of change.

The Kharijites are one such particular in the Islamic tradition. They represent, or were fashioned to represent, an attitude toward authority and violence that the ascendant Sunni orthodox wanted to preserve as a negative paradigm. Islam, like other religious traditions, provides its adherents with moral and ideological guidance; and it does so, like other religious traditions, through positive and negative models that evolved out of its mythic time of origin. Muhammad, for example, is the paradigm of human virtue for Muslims. And his career as Prophet and communal leader, including the reigns of his immediate successors, the four rightly guided caliphs, marks the limits of Islam's idealized past—a past that has become a battlefield for modern Muslims with diverse educational backgrounds and differing attitudes toward a politicized Islam. The Kharijites emerged during this same mythic time frame, and their influence in the political and theological life of the nascent cult has ensured their place in both critical and religious accounts of early Islamic history.

To understand the impact of the Kharijites on the discourse of a politicized Islam in modern-day Egypt, we first need to explore the medieval origins of the movement and its traditional image. The intent of this historical detour is not to fix the "true" nature of the Kharijites and then proceed to compare and contrast it with modern radicals. This is the work of modern Muslim thinkers who are the object of our study in later chapters. Rather, the purpose here is to establish why and how modern Muslim thinkers are able to evoke and use the image of the Kharijites. In part, the answer lies in our earlier discussion of tradition: individuals find themselves recipients of a theology/ideology that was ordered in, and is sanctioned by, the past. However, the "givenness" with which a tradition is received by later generations masks the fact that it did not spring from a founder's mouth fully formed. It required interpretation and codification. Put differently, the particulars of a tradition, such as those of the Kharijites in Islam, were made particular by a historical and historicizing process that is the very basis of the tradition. It is to this process in medieval Islam that we now turn.

Events and Meaning of Siffin

The traditional story line on the Kharijites begins with the battle of Siffin in 657, one of the culminating events of the first civil war that originated with the murder of the third caliph 'Uthman (656). Accused of nepotism and unfair fiscal policies, 'Uthman was besieged in his house in Mecca by disaffected Kufans and Egyptians who, after failing to convince him of his errors, broke down his door and slaughtered him. Following his death, 'Ali was elected caliph, but Mu'awiya, the governor of Syria and cousin of 'Uthman, refused to give 'Ali his allegiance until his relative's murderers were brought to justice. 'Ali could not accommodate this demand, as Mu'awiya seems to have known, because the support for his Caliphate, in part, came from those who had opposed and killed 'Uthman. Making no claims on the Caliphate himself, Mu'awiya was content initially to play the role of spoiler, confident of both the public reaction to his demand for justice and revenge, and the strength of the forces that he commanded as governor of a frontline province. The dispute between the two sides simmered for some time, coming to a head only after 'Ali put down another faction who opposed his rule—a Meccan force led by Talha, Zubayr, and 'A'isha, which was defeated at the battle of the camel. When the battle was joined at Siffin, neither side put on an impressive display of military prowess. In fact, it was the inconclusive results of the confrontation, both on and off the battlefield, that set the stage for the Kharijite rebellion.

After months of skirmishing and negotiating, 'Ali's forces, composed primarily of Kufan and Meccan fighters, gained the advantage. Concerned that they might be defeated, the Syrians reputedly thought of a ruse that would stem the offensive: they raised Qur'ans on their lances, thereby calling for peace, which seems to have been the major concern of both sides from the start. The fighting ceased, and it was agreed that an arbiter appointed from each side would meet to work things out, although precisely what kind of agreement these arbiters were empowered to reach seems to have remained vague. The essential stipulation was that the Qur'an would serve as final judge, hence the symbolic significance of Qur'ans on lances. In the course of the arbitration process, a document was drawn up that slighted 'Ali by not recognizing him as commander of the faithful (amir al-mu'minin). It also contained a reference to an additional standard of judgment, the sunna (tradition) of the Prophet. When the contents of the document were made known, a group of 'Ali's forces who had previously agreed to arbitration demanded that 'Ali renounce his decision to arbitrate and resume fighting the Syrians. When 'Ali did not comply, they turned against him and withdrew from his camp. Based on their rejection of the criteria for mediation established in the document, they took as their watchword "There is no judgment but God's" (la hukm illa li-llah). The initial band of protesters retreated to a site called Harura', where they were later joined by other defectors. The men among this force, which had separated itself from 'Ali's troops, were variously referred to as Muhakkima because of their slogan or Haruriyya because of their first camp. The more generic name by which they were to be known was Kharijites, literally "those who went out" or more figuratively "those who rebelled."

From Harura', the band of protesters proceeded to a site along the Tigris called Nahrawan, where their numbers supposedly increased as more fighters became disaffected with the outcome of the arbitration. Having rejected the authority of both 'Ali and Mu'awiya, the Kharijites began to commit a series of bloody attacks against fellow Muslims who refused to demonstrate agreement with their views. Although initially more concerned with Mu'awiya and his troops, 'Ali was eventually forced to move against the Kharijites at Nahrawan in 658. The rebel forces suffered a severe defeat, but they were not stamped out. Their remnants took to the desert from where they launched guerrilla-like raids. 'Ali himself was killed at the hands of a Kharijite in 661. His successor, Mu'awiya, the first of the Umayyad caliphs, suppressed numerous Kharijite uprisings during his reign (661–680), but he, too, could not put an end to the movement. Under various leaders, and with the support of different disenfranchised groups, rebellions continued throughout the Umayyad period (661–750) and into the Abbasid period. Shortly after their formation at the battle of Siffin, the Kharijites began to fracture into subgroups that differed on matters of moral and theological principle and methods of protest. The most violent of these groups, the Azariqa, named after its leader Nafi'b. Azraq, regarded those who did not take up arms in its cause as unbelievers. These unbelievers, so defined because of their opposition to the Azariqa, were subject to death, as were their wives and children, and their property was subject to forfeiture. In addition to the Azariqa, Muslim theologians cite the names of some twenty different subgroups among the Kharijites. By the ninth century, Kharijite bands had been all but eliminated from the central Islamic lands. Only scattered communities of Ibadiyya, so-called moderate Kharijites, survived.[3]

This is the traditional line on Kharijite origins or, at least, one version of it. Muslim sources transmit different accounts, with slight variations in the order of events at Siffin and Harura', though the outcome remains much unchanged. Although Western scholars have at their disposal a number of sources that relate material about Siffin, they have been frustrated with the content. There is, for example, a wealth of information about the size and composition of the forces that faced off on the battlefield and about the fighting itself. But little is said about the identity and motivation of those who became known as Kharijites. Why, for instance, did this group of people suddenly change their minds about arbitration? What is the meaning of the slogan that they shouted out when they rebelled? Were they identifiable by tribe, clan, or some other common alliance before Siffin? What kind of social, political, or economic considerations factored into their decision to rebel? In other words, the kinds of questions that a modern historian would raise about any group of rebels are, for the most part, left unanswered in the traditional sources. Not surprisingly, the fact that the sources are rather mute on these questions has not stopped scholars from reading answers into what information is available.

The history of Western criticism on the early Kharijites shares a common methodological division with modern research on Islamist groups. Scholars often split on whether to portray the motivation for rebellion as political or religious. This reflects, in part, a cultural bias of Western scholarship, which tends to view society, all societies, in categories of church and state, sacred and secular; it is also a function of the separation between religion and state that emerged in the early Islamic polity and that has come to be reflected in the ideological distinction between the ideal and the real Muslim society.[4] The first major treatise on the Kharijites appeared in the form of a German doctoral dissertation, submitted in 1884 by R. E. Brunnow.[5] His analysis of Kharijite identity wavers back and forth between the spiritual and political aspects of the movement. The Kharijite reaction to events at Siffin, Brunnow claims, demonstrated a religious response to a perceived injustice. Thus what distinguished those who "went out" from those who remained was "a high degree of religious zeal."[6] But, despite this emphasis on religion, Brunnow classifies the Kharijites as a political group. For him, their interest in the question of succession meant that they, along with the Umayyads and Shi'a, "were essentially political in nature and totally different from later theological sects."[7]

In a review of Brunnow's work, Julius Wellhausen, the famous Old Testament scholar and Arabist, takes the author to task for portraying the Kharijites as a political party.[8] His own account of the Kharijites, published some twenty years later, argues for the spiritual character of those who became Kharijites.[9] He does this by focusing on the *qurra'* or Qur'an readers who comprised a large portion of the early seceders. These qurra', Wellhausen claims, were ultra-pietists who had no interest in politics per se. Their commitment to God was stronger than their loyalty to tribe or nation. So, according to Wellhausen, when the community strayed into sin, when during arbitration Muslims supplanted God's judgment for their own, the Qur'an readers turned against the community, thereby becoming Kharijites. The Qur'an readers also figured prominently in several other Western interpretations of the Kharijites, but not because of their religious zeal.

Contrary to most historians, M. A. Shaban traces the word qurra' to a different root, translating it as "villagers" instead of Qur'an readers.[10] He maintains that these villagers were parvenu tribesmen who had risen during the reign of 'Umar, the second caliph, only to see their socioeconomic status threatened by 'Uthman's new policies. They had viewed 'Ali as someone favorable to their interests, someone similar to 'Umar. But their hopes were shattered by 'Ali's decision to arbitrate, especially after he put himself on equal footing with Mu'awiya, a first cousin of their original nemesis, 'Uthman. The Kharijites rebelled, then, because they believed their position in society had been jeopardized, not because they were pious zealots. A similar socioeconomic analysis underscores Martin Hinds's portrayal of the Kharijites. For Hinds, the qurra' were in fact Qur'an readers, but their protest stemmed from much the same set of circumstances outlined by Shaban.[11] Where he differs from Shaban is in his interpretation of the slogan "There is no judgment but God's." According to Hinds, this phrase expressed a religious protest, but in form only. The intent behind it was the socioeconomic status of the Qur'an readers. Thus Hinds attributes the seeming religious complaint of the Qur'an readers to a polemical maneuver, one that many Western scholars regard as commonplace among both medieval and modern Muslim thinkers: the tendency to cloak social, economic, and political issues in religious garb.

It has been difficult to reach a scholarly consensus about the motives of the Kharijites at Siffin because the people and events of early Islam in general lie hidden beneath layers of finely sifted tradition. The battle of Siffin took place in mid-seventh century (657). The sources that inform us of this date, however, are part of a corpus of historical works whose first tentative steps date to the mid-nineth century. To be sure, evidence of a written tradition predates this period, but it is scattered at best. Oral accounts form the raw material from which early history was written, but little is known of the transmission process and changes almost certainly occurred. The lateness of the compilation of our historical sources means that many social, political, and religious issues were encountered, and in some cases settled, by the time they were written about. The result is a back-reading of more refined theological/ideological views into the narrative stream of early Islamic history. Thus the early historical record probably reveals more about the attitudes and concerns of those living in the late eighth- and nineth-century Islamic polity than those living in the seventh-century polity.[12]

What we know about the early Kharijites, then, is what later medieval historians and traditionists (i.e., those who collected and passed on stories about Muhammad and his companions) decided was important; and their decisions about what to maintain and what to filter out of the accounts that reached them no doubt reflects the biases of an emergent Sunni orthodoxy. This goes a long way toward explaining the opacity of the sources: historical origins have been hidden behind polemical image. For this reason, the harshest critics write off the first hundred and fifty years of Islamic history found in Muslim sources as tedious and unreliable, an Islamic Heilsgeschichte driven by theological point-making rather than by historical accuracy.[13] Whether the historiographic situation is as bleak as this need not detain us here; scholars will be debating the matter for a long time to come. Instead, we must examine the polemic that the tradition has to offer, for this is what informs modern conceptions of the Kharijites.

The remainder of this chapter looks at the signs of this polemic in Muslim theological and historical sources. No attempt will be made to draw conclusions about the origins and fate of the historical Kharijites. The focus here is on the way the Kharijites have been presented in the tradition, the way that their ideas and practices have been framed by and for the dominant Sunni vision of Islam. At the outset, it is important to recognize that the blending of religion and rule in early Islam created a logical association in the Muslim intellectual tradition: "Orthodoxy meant the acceptance of the existing order, heresy or apostasy, its criticism or rejection."[14] Images of the Kharijites in the classical tradition often reflect this axiom of early Sunni ideology and lay the groundwork for the revival of Kharijism in the religious discourse of modern Egypt.

Proto-Origins of Rebellion

According to the Islamic tradition, knowledge about the Kharijites, about the dangers of Muslim extremists, predated the historical rise of the movement at Siffin. No less a figure than the Prophet Muhammad is said to have foretold of the civil discord that the rebels would sow. Preserved in the sunna of the Prophet—the practice and extra-qur'anic sayings of Muhammad collected into written form beginning in the latter half of the nineth century—are a number of reports or *hadiths* in which Muhammad not only seems to predict the emergence of the Kharijites but also calls on Muslims to eliminate them. The literary context of these hadith reports clearly indicates that Muhammad himself never mentioned the Kharijites by name. That was left to his companions who testify to the Kharijite-content of his comments. Despite the obvious gloss placed on Muhammad's statements, these hadith were and are commonly understood to refer to those who revolted against the caliph 'Ali at Siffin some thirty years after the death of Muhammad. In part, the popular acceptance of this material reflects the authority of Muhammad, the man in the tradition. But it is equally true that such anti-Kharijite hadith no doubt had strong appeal among later Sunnis who had emerged as the "orthodox" sect by overcoming "heterodox" opponents: Shi'ites and Kharijites.

A frequently cited hadith is one traced back to Sahl b. Hunaif. When asked if he ever heard Muhammad say anything about the Kharijites, Sahl replied:

> I heard [Muhammad] saying while pointing his hand towards Iraq:
> "There will emerge from [Iraq] a people who will recite the Qur'an
> but it will not go beyond their throats, and they will stray from
> Islam as an arrow strays from the animal [at which it is shot]."[15]

The analogy of an arrow straying from an animal (or gaming animal) appears in several hadith on the Kharijites, with different surrounding content. It is a regional expression used euphemistically to convey the superficial nature of Kharijite faith. That is, though conversant with the Qur'an, they did not take it past their throats and into their hearts, which presumably explains why they strayed and rebelled.

Another hadith transmitted by Sahl attributes to Muhammad a geographic reference similar to the one above: "There would arise from out of the

East a people with shaven heads."[16] As is typical, the statement lacks specific identifiers, but there is also an ex post facto ring of truth about it. Siffin, where the Kharijites first appeared, was located in Iraq, in an eastward direction from Muhammad's location in western central Arabia; so, too, were the cities of Kufa and Basra, major strongholds of the Kharijites during the Umayyad period. In addition, some Kharijites were known to have adopted ascetic practices, such as extended periods of intense prayer and shaving one's head.

Other reports ascribe to Muhammad both descriptive and prescriptive comments about the future Kharijites. 'Ali, the man who first fought the Kharijites and was later killed by one seeking revenge for the defeat at Nahrawan, is the source of the following statement made by Muhammad:

> During the final days there will appear some young foolish people who will say good things but their faith will not go beyond their throats, and they will go out from their religion as an arrow passes through an animal. So, wherever you find them, kill them, for whoever kills them shall be rewarded on the Day of Resurrection.[17]

Here we have another variant of the report passed down by Sahl, a common feature of hadith material. To this widely transmitted analogy, 'Ali provides additional information that, conveniently, justifies the very actions that he and later caliphs would take. Similar support for dealing with the Kharijites harshly is confirmed by other hadiths. One witness, for example, reports that Muhammad said that "a group would secede itself [from the community] when there was dissension among Muslims. Of the two groups [that existed at the time] the one nearer to the truth would kill them."[18] Again, the details here are lacking, but the error and fate of the seceders is made abundantly clear. And this fate matches the suppression of the Kharijites under the Umayyads and Abbasids.

One hadith recounts an occasion on which Muhammad suggested that one of his contemporaries—identified either as Dhu'l-Khuwaisira al-Tamimi or a man with a full beard, inset eyes, protruding forehead, and shaven head—was the Ur-figure from whom the Kharijites evolved. As reported, the incident occurred when someone challenged Muhammad over a particular division of the spoils. Following Muhammad's decision about the distribution, a man reputedly approached the Prophet and told him that he had not acted in a just manner. In response, Muhammad defended his decision and then made a foreboding announcement:

> From this very person's lineage there will appear a people who will recite the Qur'an, but it will not go beyond their throat; they will kill the followers of Islam and spare the idol worshippers.[19]

This hadith weaves together a number of themes passed on in other accounts of the Kharijites. It also provides additional information that appears predictive of the Kharijites. In the sources, the tribal name of Tamim, Dhu'l-Khuwaisira's tribal affiliation, is linked to a number of early Kharijites. Many of the Qur'an readers who abandoned 'Ali's forces, for example, were said to come from Tamim.[20] There is also historical evidence that links Tamim tribesmen and Kharijites in acts of rebellion, such as the overthrow of the governor of Basra in 684.[21] Thus, although not all Kharijites were tribesmen of Tamim, the numbers were probably significant enough to make the tribal connection feasible. As for taking the lives of Muslims and sparing nonbelievers, this behavior, too, came to typify the violent zealotry with which the Kharijites confronted the Muslim establishment.

Muhammad's insights into the future sectarian composition of the Muslim community were not limited to the Kharijites. According to the tradition, he foresaw the multiplicity of political and theological splits that would occur in the several centuries following his death. A famous hadith attributed to him lays out the numerical divisions of all the major religions in the vicinity of the Arabian Peninsula. "The Magians," Muhammad reportedly said, "are divided into seventy sects, the Jews into seventy-one, the Christians into seventy-two and the Muslims into seventy-three." Most versions of the hadith claim that only one sect would be saved, while the rest would die; a liberal variant reads that only one will perish, while the rest will be saved. This widely transmitted hadith provided the crude framework around which many Muslim heresiographers constructed their analyses of orthodoxy and heterodoxy.[22] Muslim sects were multiplied and manipulated to come up with an exact count of seventy-three. The vague wording of the hadith also allowed Muhammad's imprimatur to validate a number of divergent and competing orthodoxies. Thus Shi'ites and Kharijites wrote their own heresiographies in which they cast themselves as the one "saved sect" and condemned all others to perdition.

The need to put anachronistic ideas and positions into the mouth of Muhammad reflects a later stage in the evolutionary development of the sunna and the legal tradition, a time when Islamic authority began to win out over pre-Islamic custom. The pre-Islamic past, however, could assume an authority of its own as long as it was the past of (Abrahamic) monotheism and not Arab tribalism. Muhammad, for example, established his prophetic authority in the Qur'an by locating himself at the end point in the line of monotheistic prophets; and Muhammad's biographer, Ibn Ishaq, traced the Muslim Prophet's genealogy back to Adam, linking Islam's "perfect man" with the first man. Given the legitimating authority invested in the past, it is not surprising that sectarianism in general and the Kharijites in particular became subjects of further historical back-projection. After all, if the Kharijites could be placed into the thoughts of Muhammad, if a contemporary of Muhammad could be identified as the forefather of the Kharijites, then surely the movement's genealogy could be traced to its mythic, Adamic origins. We find an interesting case of this in the heresiographic work of the medieval Muslim scholar al-Shahrastani (d. 1153).[23]

Of the genres of Islamic literature, heresiography preserves perhaps the most systematic and tendentious portrayals of the Kharijites. Of the more famous heresiographers, such as al-Ash'ari (d. 935), al-Baghdadi (d. 1037), and Ibn Hazm (d. 1064), al-Shahrastani is commonly regarded the least polemical. He also comes relatively late in the development of the genre, which means that he had greater opportunity to refine the accounts of sectarianism found in the works of his predecessors. The body of his *Book of Sects and Divisions* contains much the same information provided by other heresiographers; this is to be expected since he borrowed heavily from other sources, notably al-Ash'ari and Ka'bi (d. 931).[24] His series of five introductions, however, presents a historical and philosophical explanation for the rise of sectarianism that is unique. It is his view of sectarian history that interests us here.

He begins, as many heresiographers do, by reciting the hadith about Islam being divided into seventy-three sects. This hadith is then connected or, at least, juxtaposed with a story/commentary drawn from Jewish and Christian sources. The story is about Iblis, the devil, and his role in the creation of doubt and discord. According to al-Shahrastani's unnamed sources, which he quotes at length, Iblis introduced doubt into the world when he refused God's command to bow down before Adam. This act of pride, which was the first doubt, gave rise to seven other doubts; and these seven doubts, al-Shahrastani claims, are the root of all false beliefs. Thus he writes that "every doubt that befell the offspring of Adam occurred because of the deception of the accursed devil and the temptations arising from his doubts."[25] For al-Shahrastani, then, these doubts form the deep structure of human history. Heretical groups, such as the Kharijites, are not mere epiphenomena of the seven doubts. Instead, they are part of a causative chain of sectarian formation, set in motion by Iblis but extending throughout prophetic history. Those who challenged the authority of Noah, Abraham, Moses, Jesus, and Muhammad "all imitated the first cursed one [the devil] in the manifestation of his doubts."[26]

This pattern of error and doubt, al-Shahrastani maintains, reemerges in each prophetic generation because of a human tendency to reject the command of those sent by God, a tendency which itself was engendered by Iblis. Al-Shahrastani focuses only on those errors that arose following Muhammad's call to prophecy, associating each of the major sects with its respective primal doubt. He traces the Kharijites to the third doubt introduced by Iblis: Why did God command the devil to obey Adam and make obeisance to him? To prove the existential link between the third primal doubt and the formation of the Kharijites, al-Shahrastani adduces two passages that, in his estimation, demonstrate the same sentiment of error. The first is the slogan adopted by the early Kharijites, "There is no judgment but God's." The second is a qur'anic citation (15:33), which quotes the devil as saying to God, "I would never bow myself before a mortal whom Thou hast created of a clay of mud molded."[27] For al-Shahrastani, just as the latter statement indicates a refusal to obey a lawful command of God, so the former indicates a refusal to follow a lawful human command. Both, he believes, exhibit the error of excessive pride, of unrestrained independence, of the failure to obey.

Another stage in al-Shahrastani's deterministic account of the formation of the Kharijites (and all Muslim sects) is his claim that, at the beginning of every prophet's era, there are harbingers of heresy. That is, not only do the errors of Iblis arise during each prophet's life, but they arise twice, once at the beginning and once at the end. The earlier manifestation of error is the precursor, and seeming immediate cause, of the actual later heretical movement. In the case of the Kharijites, their rebellion was foreshadowed by the actions of Dhu'l-Khuwaisira al-Tamimi. The man's questioning of Muhammad's division of the spoils was, al-Shahrastani argues, a clear example of rebelling against the Prophet. This point leads al-Shahrastani to draw a historical parallel that makes the label "Kharijite" applicable at the time of Muhammad:

> If someone who opposes the rightful leader (imam) becomes a Kharijite, then it is only proper that someone who opposes the rightful messenger should be called a Kharijite?[28]

In other words, if those who criticized 'Ali are called Kharijites, then the name should equally apply to Dhu'l-Khuwaisira who criticized the Prophet. Al-Shahrastani ends his proto-historical discussion of the Kharijites at this point in the introduction. But his final word on Kharijite identity comes in a separate chapter that rehashes the social and theological disputes over which the (Muslim) Kharijites split into subsects. He opens the chapter with a sweeping definition of a Kharijite that encourages Muslims to view the sect as a transhistorical phenomenon:

> Whoever rebels against the rightful leader agreed upon by the community is called a Kharijite, whether this rebellion occurred at the

time of the companions against the rightly guided leaders, or against
their beneficent successors and the leaders of any time.[29]

What is at work in this definition is an attempt to decoct the essence of a
Kharijite, to identify what makes someone a Kharijite in all times and places.
For al-Shahrastani, the particular events at Siffin appear to have little to do
with the essential nature of the Kharijites. Or, put differently, the events at
Siffin are merely one particular manifestation of a universal phenomenon that
unfolds throughout history—illegitimate rebellion. Kharijism, then, according
to al-Shahrastani, denotes the act of rebellion itself, without reference to the
reason or basis for the act. As we will see, al-Shahrastani's definition received
a good deal of attention from modern Egyptian Muslim thinkers who believed
they were witnessing another historical unfolding of Kharijism, or at least
wished others to believe it.

To arrive at his highly abstract and transhistorical notion of the Kharijites,
al-Shahrastani started from the same point of departure as other heresiographers: the Islamic tradition's historical experience of the Kharijites that
began at Siffin. Indeed, it was this experience that gave impetus to the tradition's construction of Kharijite proto-origins. The history of the Kharijites
after their defeat at Nahrawan is one of rebellion and infighting. Waves
of rebellion threatened the unity of the empire, while infighting led to the
formation of numerous subgroups. Extending knowledge of the historical
Kharijites into the pre-Kharijite past was one way of gaining intellectual
control over the kind of beliefs and actions that the carriers of the tradition
wished to proscribe—intellectual control being one of the softer means by
which the Sunnis maintained their power and authority. Thus the development within the tradition of Kharijite proto-origins reflects an effort to order
and Islamize the past in the name of Sunni orthodoxy.

Sins of the Ruler, Sins of the Ruled

What were the beliefs and practices attributed to the Kharijites that Sunni
authorities felt compelled to suppress? In his definition, al-Shahrastani
highlighted what has come to be perhaps the fundamental marker of Kharijism, rebellion against legitimate rulership. But he derived this universal
definition from the particular set of ideas and actions that reputedly characterized Kharijite uprisings in different locales and eras. We see evidence of
this on the page following his universal definition of a Kharijite, on which he
offers a more historically informed assessment of all Kharijite sects, one

clearly rooted in the events and aftermath of Siffin. "Common to them all," according to al-Shahrastani, "is dissociation from 'Uthman and 'Ali. . . . They hold, too, that those who commit grave sins are unbelievers, and that rebellion against an imam who opposes sunna is a duty and an obligation." Similar synoptic descriptions of Kharijite sects are provided by other heresiographers. Relying on the opinion of al-Ash'ari, his mentor, al-Baghdadi asserts that all Kharijites were united by a belief in denouncing 'Ali and 'Uthman, the two arbiters at Siffin, and all those who accepted the outcome of the arbitration; in labeling grave sinners as apostates; and in the obligation to rebel against an unjust ruler.[30] Ibn Hazm, the Andalusian theologian, characterizes Kharijites as people who believe in rejecting the arbitration at Siffin, damning sinners, rebelling against unrighteous leaders, the punishment of eternal hell fire for grave sinners and the legitimacy of a non-Qurayshi caliph.[31] It is interesting to note that al-Shahrastani's universal definition of a Kharijite could readily be inferred from any of the above accounts of Kharijite belief and practice. Heresiographers, then, seemed in agreement that, despite the splits that occurred among Kharijites over theological and practical issues, the various sects were united by a core of ideas. And many of these ideas touched directly on political affairs, on the role and function of the Muslim ruler.

In the framework of Islamic thought, the Kharijites are intimately linked to debates over political authority. Historically, the question of who has the right to rule the Muslim community was first raised upon the death of Muhammad in 632. But Islamic tradition, as well as Western scholarship, traces the origins of Islamic political theory to the challenges raised by the Kharijites, initially against 'Ali and Mu'awiya and subsequently against all non-Kharijite leadership. Of course, the first Kharijites were more interested in acting than propounding ideas, much like their major opponents, the caliphs, whose political turf they threatened. Later Kharijite thinkers, however, articulated a number of interconnected political and religious doctrines that legitimated the rebellious actions of their ancestors and that the Sunni tradition came to portray as untenable and dangerous. Of these doctrines, the most volatile was that a caliph could be and should be deposed, if he failed to follow and enforce the teachings laid out in the Qur'an. This position was based in part on a loose reading of a number of verses in the Qur'an, such as 5:48, which reads "Whoso judges not according to what God has sent down, they are the unbelievers."[32] Any deviation from the straight path by a caliph required the immediate intervention of the Muslim community. Muslims, in the eyes of the Kharijites, had a sacred mandate to call a caliph to account for his errors and demand that he repent. And, in theory, the Kharijites allowed only two possible outcomes in such circumstances. If the offending caliph recognized the error of his ways, his rule continued; if he failed to respond properly to corrective advice, then his rule was terminated. Hence the rebellion against 'Ali when he maintained the error of arbitration.

Kharijite political theory differed from that of other early Islamic factions in that it refused to accord the office of caliph, the Caliphate, special protective status. This is true for several reasons. First, Kharijites did not regard the Caliphate as the sine quo non of Muslim society. Kharijite sects did elect leaders who were given the title of caliph or imam, but the office itself was thought to be expendable. All that was required for good Islamic order, according to the Kharijite view, was the application of the *shari'a* or Islamic law. As long as believers could legitimately live under the shari'a and resolve their disputes amicably, there was no need for someone to oversee them.[33] Both Sunnis and Shi'ites, by contrast, held that the Caliphate or Imamate was divinely sanctioned and, therefore, a social and moral necessity, though they had arrived at this conclusion for vastly different reasons. For Sunnis, the caliph, the successor of Muhammad, was neither a divine nor especially pious individual; his status derived from the sacredness of the office, which had the responsibility, even if at times only symbolic, of enforcing the shari'a. For Shi'ites, the imam was an infallible, God-ordained figure whose divine guidance was essential to the Muslim community; he lent authority to his office, the Imamate, because he carried on the "mantle of the Prophet," representing God's proof (*hujja*) on earth.

The second distinctive feature of Kharijite political theory relates to the qualifications of the caliph. Unlike the Sunnis who restricted election to the tribe of Quraysh, Muhammad's tribe, and the Shi'ites who traced the line of imams down through 'Ali and his descendants, the Kharijites placed no conditions regarding birth or divine descent. Kharijites maintained that any Muslim—any Kharijite Muslim—could become caliph as long as he was of sound mind and character. Their egalitarian principle of election is said to be expressed in the prophetic hadith that they often invoked: "Obey whoever is put in authority over you, even if he is a crop-nosed Ethiopian slave."[34] Once elected, a Kharijite leader enjoyed the respect and obedience of his peers. But his status, the equivalent of first among equals, did not make him immune from moral scrutiny. Kharijite thought stipulated the overthrow and possible murder of a caliph if he was judged to be an unbeliever or infidel (*kafir*), and a caliph could be so judged if he was found to have committed a grave sin (*kabira*). Thus the authority of a caliph to lead and rule over his fellow Muslims "depended on his moral and religious probity."[35] And determining whether a caliph committed a grave sin, whether he crossed the line of moral and religious probity was an interpretive matter, for it required translating his political, economic, and social policies into the ethical-legal language of Islam. Here is where Kharijite moral theology bled into political theory with grave repercussions for both ruler and ruled.

Prior to its usage by the Kharijites, the term "unbelief" (*kufr*) was reserved for non-Muslims who lay outside the boundaries of the Muslim community. By pronouncing 'Ali and the Umayyad caliphs unbelievers (*takfir*), the Kharijites introduced this notion into the discourse and social life of early Islam. Moreover, because Kharijite egalitarianism made no distinction between ruler and ruled, all Muslims were subject to the same judgment and punishment as the caliph, which meant that any Muslim could be condemned as an unbeliever. This effectively divided a hitherto united faith community into two distinct and antagonistic factions: true Muslims made up of Kharijites and pseudo-Muslims who had rejected Kharijite Islam.[36] (It was for this reason that the idea of an unbeliever underwent a transformation within mainstream Sunni theological discussions. In addition to referring to infidels or non-Muslims, the word came to have the connotation of heretic or heterodox believer.[37]) But it was the means by which some Kharijites determined the factional categories into which their fellow Muslims fit that became the hallmark of Kharijite extremism. Kharijites were known to accost people and test their (Kharijite) Muslim bona fides by asking them their opinions about 'Ali, 'Uthman, Mu'awiya, and the arbitration process. An incorrect response resulted in death (*isti'rad*). No one was exempt from this religious vetting or its consequences. In some cases, the women and children of those judged to be unbelievers were also killed. Indeed, one of the theological issues over which Kharijites debated and divided was the legality or illegality of taking the lives of women and children. The most militant among the Kharijites, the Azariqa, followers of Nafi' b. Azraq, believed this was permissible. They also considered anyone outside of their own group an unbeliever by definition. Separation from sinful society, a *hijra* or migration to the true community of Muslims, was part of Azariqa doctrine. So when they came across someone outside their camp who said he was a Muslim, they would immediately kill him, but someone claiming to be a Jew, Christian, or Magian was spared. The Azariqa seemed to reserve their rage for an inner-directed Islamic battle: cleansing Muslim ranks, a trait that came to define the Kharijites as a whole.

It was the faith (*iman*) of other Muslims that Kharijites deemed insufficient and in need of reform. They reached this conclusion based not so much on what their fellow Muslims professed as on how they acted or failed to act. In other words, works were considered an essential component of faith in Kharijite theology. Such a position did not lead inexorably to extremist ideas or activities. However, when combined with a narrow, inflexible view of sin and its consequences, the insistence that works are required for salvation contributed to the larger theological calculus of militancy. For the Kharijites, works negatively affected one's faith when the works were major sins; and major sins put one outside the body of believers because they allowed no interpretive leeway whereby one could remain a faithful Muslim and a major sinner at the same time. The Kharijites, like all Muslims, viewed religion in communal terms. As the Qur'an itself suggests, prophets are sent to communities, and salvation is achieved within a community. But Kharijites went further than other Muslims by holding to a vision of the perfect community of believers, which is captured in their claim that Muslims constitute "the People of Paradise" (ahl al-janna), while others are "the People of Hell" (ahl al-nar). Inclusion of a grave sinner into the pure community of Muslims would, according to Kharijite reasoning, jeopardize the future reward of all Muslims.[38]

Reacting to the practical social consequences of the Kharijite view of sin, other Islamic factions—Mu'tazilites, Shi'ites, Murji'ites, and Sunnis—rejected the notion of excluding the grave sinner from the community of Muslims, although with varying degrees of theological leniency. The Mu'tazilites, for example, though socially tolerant of grave sinners in this world, agreed with the Kharijites that such sinners would eventually be condemned to hell in the next. The most liberal of the factions, the Murji'ites, refrained from making any moral decisions about their fellow Muslims, preferring instead to "defer" to God's judgment in the next world; and one Murji'ite subsect went so far as to claim that sin ultimately did no harm to believers who were sincere in their faith.[39] In contrast to the maximalist requirements of faith demanded by the Kharijites, the Sunnis advocated a minimalist approach, siding on this matter with the Murji'ites. For the most part, they separated works from faith. Thus, according to the reasoning of the Sunni theologian al-Ash'ari, a sinner could maintain his membership in the community of Muslim believers because he is "a believer by reason of his faith, a sinner by reason of his sin and grave fault."[40]

The very language chosen by al-Ash'ari and other Sunni theologians to describe the Muslim community demonstrates that conditions for membership were nominal:

> It is our opinion that we ought not to declare a single one of the
> people of the qiblah an infidel for a sin of which he is guilty, such as
> fornication or theft or the drinking of wine, as the [Kharijites] hold,
> thinking that such people are infidels.[41]

The phrase "people of the qiblah" refers to those who share the same direction of prayer, indicating that rather than purity from sin, a simple outward sign of assent was sufficient for inclusion within the Muslim community. But, though willing to overlook sin, al-Ash'ari was not willing to allow believers to deny the ethical authority that established what was and was not sinful: "we believe that he who commits any of these mortal sins...presumptuously declaring it lawful and not acknowledging that it is forbidden is an infidel."[42] Moreover, unlike some Murji'ites, Sunnis did not absolve the sinner, grave or otherwise, from the effects of sin. In the end, Sunnis concluded that rewards and punishments for one's actions would be settled in the hereafter, while a simple avowal of faith sufficed for good standing in the Muslim community.

Of course, the primary figures for whom this latitudinarian theology was developed were the caliphs. It was their putative sins, specifically those of 'Uthman, 'Ali, and Mu'awiya, along with the Kharijite reaction to them, that forced more moderate voices to take a stand. In the end, moderation won out. Al-Ash'ari summed up the Sunni policy toward the caliph in the following way:

> [W]e regard it as an error on anybody's part to approve "going out" [rebelling] against [the caliphs] when they have clearly abandoned rectitude; and we believe in abstinence from "going out" [rebelling] against them with the sword, and abstinence from fighting in civil commotions (fitnah).[43]

Thus, as portrayed in traditional Sunni theological sources, the contrast between the Kharijites and orthodox Muslims could not be more striking. Although the Kharijites preferred to cut off the head of the Islamic body politic rather than tolerate a deviant leader, the Sunni orthodox settled for a religiously sanctioned realpolitik. Although the Kharijites chose to lead the Muslim community into social unrest and possible anarchy rather than compromise their purist ideology, the Sunni orthodox opted for accommodation and social stability.[44] To the Kharijite demand for piety and purity, the Sunni response was moderation and communal unity. Nowhere is this latter point more evident than with respect to the issue of prayer.

Sunni tradition conceded that the Kharijites surpassed other Muslims in their dedication to and intensity of prayer. But along with this concession came the warning that enthusiasm may lead to excess, that piety and purity can be taken too far. This was certainly how Sunnis viewed the Kharijite refusal to pray behind non-Kharijite Muslims whose moral failings supposedly nullified the physical state of purity required by the ritual. The Sunni answer to this act of pious hauteur was that "Prayer behind every faithful man, be he of good or of bad behavior, is valid."[45] The social image of the Kharijites was that they were incapable of living alongside anyone whose beliefs differed from their own. Sunnis, by contrast, made diversity of views a doctrine of faith: "Difference of opinion in the community is a token of divine mercy."[46]

The line, then, between Kharijite belief and practice and that of the Sunnis was very clearly drawn in Sunni sources. That the line was sometimes drawn at the expense of historical accuracy should come as no surprise. Sunni writers, after all, had a mandate to distinguish between orthodoxy and heterodoxy, and the rhetoric of orthodoxy—no matter whose orthodoxy—entailed a degree of heavy-handedness. This explains why the Kharijites were presented in the sources as a coherent, identifiable group, why attempts were made to sum up the essential nature of the Kharijites. It was easier to aim one's critical eye at a single, stationary target with a distinctive set of behavioral and ideological characteristics than deal with the complexity of a fractured and amorphous movement. Moreover, a very effective way to ensure that the profile was distinctive was to portray the most radical faction of the Kharijites, the Azariqa, as representative of the sect as a whole. The cause of Sunni orthodoxy was better served, that is, the public was dissuaded from associating or sympathizing with Kharijite rebellions, the more frightening and dangerous the Kharijites appeared. Viewed historically, such an image of the Kharijites also provided a retrospective, theological legitimation for the martial actions that successive caliphs had taken against Kharijite uprisings. In short, under the pen of Sunni propagandists, the Kharijites became a foil for celebrating the triumph and supremacy of Sunnism. Not just the sum of its factional parts, Kharijism was portrayed as the epitome of what the Muslim community had come to reject. Interesting enough, the negative symbolism surrounding the Kharijites was not limited to the Sunni tradition. It also played an important role in the self-understanding of the Ibadiyya, the moderate branch of the Kharijites.

The Case of the Ibadiyya

The Ibadiyya emerged, in 684, when the eponymous founder of the faction, 'Abdullah b. Ibad al-Murri al-Tamimi, a Basran Kharijite, broke away from the Kharijite leader Nafi' b. Azraq over his extremist treatment of other Muslims. Ibn Ibad remains a nebulous figure in Ibadi history.[47] Although he is mentioned as the founder of the sect, Ibadi writers pay scant attention to him. Far more important to the formation of Ibadi theology, especially as it is distinguished from that of the Kharijites, are Abu Bilal Mirdas and Jabir b. Zayd al-Azdi. Abu Bilal prefigures Ibn Ibad in the Ibadi historical record. He was a survivor of Nahrawan who went on to become the center of the moderate faction of the Kharijites (i.e., proto-Ibadiyya) in Basra. He is regarded as the spiritual father of the sect and one of its first leaders (imams) because it is to his example that they trace their moderation: he rejected religiously justified murder (isti'rad), negotiated with the Umayyads, concentrated on peaceful propagation of the faith (da'wa), and adopted a quietist position vis-à-vis his opponents. A campaign against the Kharijites provoked Abu Bilal to revolt. He was killed in 680, and Ibn Ibad succeeded him. Jabir b. Zayd, who succeeded Ibn Ibad as leader of the Ibadis, was an eminent Ibadi scholar, referred to as the source of teaching (asl al-madhhab). Following in the footsteps of Abu Bilal, he took to task the extremist Kharijites who shed the blood of fellow Muslims. Moreover, his willingness to condemn certain behavior as radical put the Ibadis in good stead with the (Sunni) Umayyad governor of Iraq, al-Hajjaj ibn Yusuf, who permitted the sect to prosper, at least for a time.

The fundamental principles of the Ibadiyya read like an anti-Azariqa creed. According to Ibadi teachings, non-Kharijite Muslims are accepted as legitimate members of the Muslim community, and therefore they cannot be killed. Other penalties that the Azariqa inflicted on fellow Muslims are also rejected. For example, Ibadis maintain that the property of Muslims cannot be confiscated as spoils and that women and children cannot be killed or taken captive. Rejected, too, is the idea that believers are obligated to separate from the Muslim community when the ruler is a sinful tyrant. Under such circumstances, Ibadis advise dissimulation of faith (taqiyya) and caution.[48] Ibadis permit marriage with non-Kharijite Muslims and prayer behind them. In contrast to the negative model of the Azariqa, the Ibadis hold up the Muhakkima, those who first raised the protest against 'Ali with their slogan "There is no judgment but God's." Conspicuously absent from much of Ibadi positive theology is the name "Kharijites."

Although non-Ibadi authorities agree on categorizing the Ibadis as a subsect of the Kharijites, the Ibadi tradition itself is equivocal about its relationship with the Kharijites. As indicated above, the Ibadis were said to have arisen in response to the more extreme Kharijites, namely, the Azariqa. Given that the Kharijites formed prior to the militant activism of Ibn Azraq, and that Ibadis wanted to distance themselves ideologically from this radical faction, one might expect Ibadi thinkers to play up the purity of Kharijism prior to the advent of Ibn Azraq, to distinguish between orthodox Kharijites and heterodox ones. Some Ibadi authorities did precisely this, using for example the label "unjust Kharijites" (Khawarij al-jawr) to describe Azariqa belief and practice.[49] Others, however, attempted to disassociate the Ibadis from the larger sectarian rubric of the Kharijites—no easy task since the Ibadi myth of origin over-lapped with that of the Kharijites and, for that matter, with the Azariqite extremists whom they condemned. For these latter authorities, the concern appears to have been that the Kharijites had become identified with the characteristics of the Azariqa or, more accurately, that the name "Kharijites" had become so identified, much as it had in the Sunni tradition. So, to save the Ibadis from being tainted by the extremist behavior of some of their brethren and, *a fortiori*, the name that had come to symbolize this behavior, Ibadi propagandists had to recast the genealogical and historical relationship between the Kharijites and the Ibadis.

The work of the twelfth-century Omani scholar Abu 'Abdullah Mu-hammad b. Sa'id al-Azdi al-Qalhati provides some measure of the interpretive lengths to which an Ibadi writer had to go in order to cast off the burden of the Kharijites. His *al-Kashf wa 'l-bayan* is thought to be one of the earliest surviving Ibadi sources.[50] Part theological treatise, part heresiography, the *Kashf* mirrors the form and function of tendentious writing found in competing Sunni works. In fact, al-Qalhati is thought to have relied on al-Shahrastani's *Milal* for some of his material.[51] What did al-Qalhati have to say about the Kharijites? Initially, it seems, very little. The first section of the *Kashf* rehashes the early history of the Caliphate leading up to the events at Siffin. Particular emphasis is placed on the sins of the caliph 'Uthman, which justified his murder, and the eventual continuation of 'Uthman's deviant behavior by 'Ali. It is tempting to say that the *Kashf* offers a reading of this period from the perspective of the Kharijites. After all, who other than a Kharijite would legitimize dissent against 'Uthman and 'Ali and valorize those who rebelled at Siffin as "the best com-panions and leaders of the Muslims, their legists, Qur'an readers and schol-ars."[52] The problem, however, is that al-Qalhati never mentions the Kharijites throughout his entire narration of these events. Those who protested against 'Ali at Siffin he speaks of as "the Muslims," a reference favored by other Ibadi writers;[53] and once these "Muslims" left Siffin to gather at the site of Nahra-wan, he gives them the name "people of Nahrawan" (*ahl al-Nahrawan*).[54] Thus al-Qalhati champions the views and actions of that group of protesters who formally emerged at Siffin, but he avoids identifying them by the very name that they reputedly earned for "going out" from other Muslims—Kharijites.

Despite appearances, al-Qalhati did not completely deny the existence of the Kharijites. He was merely cautious about the context in which to introduce them, and, for him, the right context was a discussion of Islamic sects. This occurs in the second section of the *Kashf*, in which he provides an Ibadi heresiography structured around the prophetic hadith of the seventy-three sects. Al-Qalhati, then, relegated the Kharijites to a place where it was appropriate to deal with them as heterodox Muslims, as one of the unsaved sects of Islam. But, unlike other sects that could be dismissed out of hand as heterodox, the Kharijites required more attention. For the orthodox mantle that al-Qalhati traces down through the generations of Muslims—what he calls "the people of rectitude" (ahl al-istiqama)—at one time rested with the Kharijites. The matter becomes even more complex when the tactic is to link the Ibadis, the one saved sect (firqa najiyya), with the lineage of the people of rectitude without admitting an intermediate stage of Kharijite influence. The only solution to such a dilemma was interpretive legerdemain, of which al-Qalhati was an obvious master.

The circumstances surrounding 'Uthman's death, according to al-Qalhati, created three main divisions in Islam: the people of rectitude, who were responsible for 'Uthman's murder; the Shikak, or Doubters composed of those who opposed both 'Uthman and his murderers; and the 'Uthmaniyya, or those who continued to support the deceased caliph and sought revenge for his murder. Later, the events at Siffin led to a further split within the Muslim community, from which emerged four main sectarian divisions: the Shi'ites, the Kharijites, the 'Uthmaniyya, and the Shikak. Of these four, it is clear that al-Qalhati regarded the Kharijites as the orthodox remnant, at least ostensibly. It is also clear, based on his description of the Kharijites in this section, that they are identical with those whom he earlier referred to as "the Muslims" and "the people of Nahrawan." For al-Qalhati, the Kharijites lost this identification as a result of the divisions that developed within the Kharijite sect itself. Specifically, Kharijite purity came to an end when Nafi' b. Azraq

separated from [the Kharijites], dissolving their importance. He divided their community, opposed their authority and turned away from their belief, issuing commands with which Muslims and the people of rectitude differed.[55]

This action destabilized the community of Muslims and led eventually to the formation of sixteen different Kharijites sects, only one of which remained the people of rectitude. The border, then, separating orthodoxy from heterodoxy, which had set the Kharijites apart from the other three major sects, now passed through the Kharijites.

Even with this dramatic cleavage in the Kharijite sect, some portion of the Kharijites would, logically, continue to be the legitimate representative of orthodox Islam. Al-Qalhati admits as much by his use of the phrase "the kinds of Kharijites who are not the people of rectitude" to capture the fifteen wayward Kharijite subsects, those that followed the path of Ibn Azraq.[56]

However, the remaining orthodox Kharijites who are the people of rectitude do not in fact continue to be Kharijites in al-Qalhati's heresiographic schema. Instead, after he shifts them around in an interpretive shell game that essentially transfers to them the sole mantle of orthodoxy, he renames them the Ibadis. His first move is to cast the Ibadis as the original Kharijite sect, along with the Wahbiyya, the followers of the first "Kharijite" caliph, 'Abdullah b. Wahb al-Rasibi. Then he maintains that the Kharijites as a group moved away from the pure origins of their faith after the emergence of the Azariqa, leaving only the Ibadis with the legitimate title of the people of rectitude. Meanwhile, the practices that al-Qalhati had established as characteristics of the heterodox Kharijites (= the Azariqa) come to be equated with all Kharijites, making it possible for him to speak of a distinctive heterodox Kharijite doctrine, much like Sunni authorities. By the end of the work, al-Qalhati has relegated the Kharijites to the company of other erring sects, such as the Mu'tazila, Qadariyya, Sifatiyya, Jahmiyya, Riwafid, and Shi'a. And he feels confident enough about his reconfiguration of Islamic sectarianism to cite a chain of transmission for the Ibadi school with no reference to the Kharijites.[57]

As an example of the genre, al-Qalhati's *Kashf* fulfills the purpose of any heresiography: to portray a given sectarian group as the legitimate inheritor of Muhammad's authority and to demonstrate the error of others. Of equal importance to the Ibadis was avoiding association with the Kharijites, the sect that came to epitomize Muslim violence and rebellion. The Ibadi tradition offers its own reason for the anti-Kharijite polemic that it espouses. The "orthodox" Ibadis, as al-Qalhati points out, were the first to recognize and refute the depraved doctrines of the Kharijites.[58] Although perhaps satisfying for internal consumption, this explanation does not recognize that it was the name "Kharijite" more than the sect's origins and doctrines from which the Ibadis tried to distance themselves. And the Kharijite name had been anathematized by Sunni polemicists. As al-Qalhati's *Kashf* shows, the Ibadis also contributed to the process of making the name "Kharijites" synonymous with intolerance, murder, and mayhem.[59] With much of the discussion here focusing on rhetoric and propaganda, it is important to remember that al-Qalhati and his Sunni theologian counterparts did not create the negative image of the Kharijites ex nihilo. There were in fact groups of (Kharijite) Muslims whose actions and ideas threatened the then-existing Islamic leadership and the greater community; and this threat, not surprisingly, provoked both military and intellectual responses. Thus, at first, the negative image of the Kharijites may have accurately reflected the ideological content of the referent groups. At some later point, the image took on a life of its own, no longer merely representing what the historical Kharijites meant for Sunni orthodoxy but projecting onto others, onto non-Kharijite others, that representation. We shift now to look at how the Kharijites were used in the sources as a propaganda weapon in the arsenal of Sunni ideology.

Kharijites as Rebels, Rebels as Kharijites

Western scholars have pointed out that the name "Kharijites" was not exclusively applied in Muslim historical sources to individuals or groups who held to Kharijite doctrine.[60] By the Abbasid period (750–1250), it seems, Kharijite was often used simply to denote a rebel, someone who raised his sword, symbolically or otherwise, against caliphal or local authorities. The dating here is important, for it suggests that over time the original ideological content of the name gave way to other meanings. This is particularly true for the eastern provinces that initially were far removed from the political and cultural center of the early Caliphate. In one such province, Sistan, C. E. Bosworth notes

> Kharijism succeeded in transforming itself from a movement with its roots in the politico-religious vicissitudes of the early Arab Caliphate into one with some local foundations and with a concern about such grievances as excessive taxation and unjust tax-collectors. Because of this successful transformation, Sistan, in the early 'Abbasid period was virtually the sole major region of the east where Kharijism retained something of its earlier vitality and following.[61]

One does not need to travel as far east as Sistan or chronologically very far into the Abbasid period to find examples of this transformation of Kharijism, as Bosworth himself demonstrates in one of the volumes that he translated in al-Tabari's *History* series. In a brief passage from the year 806, a man, one Sayf b. Bakr from the tribe of 'Abd al-Qays, is described in the Arabic text as a Kharijite (*khariji*) who revolted and was subsequently killed by an agent of the reigning caliph Harun al-Rashid. In his translation, Bosworth renders the name "Kharijite" simply as "rebel," noting that in the context the name was "used in a general sense."[62] When Kharijite had developed this "general sense" and whether it has anything to do specifically with the transformation that Kharijism underwent in Sistan are questions that Bosworth does not address. We will return to the implications of his translation later, but for now we need to look at the latitude exhibited in the usage of the name.

The eleventh-century Nestorian Bishop Elijah of Nisibis, for instance, made a translation decision analogous to that of Bosworth. In his history of the world, written in both Syriac and Arabic, Elijah used the Arabic khariji to capture the Syriac word "rebel."[63] What makes this case so intriguing is that the rebellious events that Elijah was describing took place in the year 365/66, some three hundred years before the emergence of the Kharijites at Siffin. So generalized (corrupted?), then, had the original meaning of the name become by the eleventh century that a Christian historian could insert it into an earlier era, and a non-Arabian context, seemingly without fear of having committed an anachronism.[64]

The name "Kharijite" or one of its known equivalents—Haruri or Muhakimma—commonly appears in Muslim historical sources in ways that both identify and condemn rebellious acts, or, more accurately, condemn by identifying. An incident involving the governor of Basra, Ubaydallah b. Ziyad, in the early Umayyad period (ca. 680), highlights the latter situation. After a man had openly defied a command of Ibn Ziyad, he was ordered to be brought before the governor. A heated exchange led to Ibn Ziyad inflicting a severe beating on him. In the course of the beating, the man reached out for a nearby sword, whereupon Ibn Ziyad responded by saying: "Did you become one of the Haruri [Kharijites] today? If so, you have made yourself subject to punishment and thus killing you is permitted."[65] The surrounding text gives no hint that the man was in fact a Kharijite and offers no explanation of the legitimacy or illegitimacy of the charge. Several points about this incident, however, require emphasis: first, the readiness with which the name came to mind when violence was shown toward authority; and second, the logical connection between being labeled a Haruri or Kharijite and being worthy of punishment, of death.

The first point is reinforced in another story of plotting and assassination. In the year 700, a group of men from the tribe of 'Awf b. Ka'b b. Sa'd gathered to seek revenge for the murder of one of their tribe, Bukayr b. Wishah, the former governor of Khurasan. The man responsible for murdering Bukayr, Buhir b. Warqa' al-Suraymi, was in Khurasan when one of the plotters fell on him and stabbed him. Having witnessed the assault on Buhir, those in the immediate vicinity shouted out "A Kharijite!" The assassin failed in his mission and was himself killed. Some time later, this scene was played out again. A second assassin who had insinuated himself into Buhir's entourage attacked Buhir with a knife. And, again, the people shouted out "A Kharijite!"[66] As with the previous example, there are insufficient details to understand fully what the name means in this context. Were the people predisposed to view such assaults as those committed by the Kharijites? Were the people merely saying that the assassin was a generic rebel? Were they equating the assassin with a branch of the Ur-rebels from Siffin? Or is the introduction of the name into this story a typological gloss, a way that Sunni traditionists rhetorically identified the bad guys? That Kharijites could make easy scapegoats is clear from a different account of murder, one that has its roots in the politico-religious intrigue that was the Abbasid revolution. After the first Abbasid ruler, Abu al-'Abbas, was installed (ca. 749), questions were raised about the loyalty of Abu Salama, the man who held the office of wazir and who had previously opposed Abu al-'Abbas's claim to be Commander of the Faithful. A plan was set in motion, with the connivance of Abu al-'Abbas, to eliminate Abu Salama as a potential threat. Once the murder was carried out, one source relates, "They then said that the Kharijites had killed him."[67]

Despite the ambiguity surrounding these cases, they do share a common factor. The determination to label someone a Kharijite stemmed from the violent acts that were committed, not a set of beliefs that could be attributed to the actors. In some cases, the identity of the murderous actors remained unknown to those who brought up the name "Kharijite"; in others, the name was affixed to people who, although known to their accusers, never seemingly expressed beliefs for which the Kharijites were infamous. Acts of rebellion, then, were sufficient to evoke the name Kharijite. But this is not the same as saying that a Kharijite came to be the equivalent of a rebel. Before taking this step, we need to ask what kind of rebel? Was it the kind of rebel, as Bosworth argues, who no longer had ties to "the politico-religious vicissitudes of the early Caliphate"? And without these ties, was it the kind of rebel for whom the Sunni theological judgment of heterodox Muslim would apply? The question is rather moot since the surviving sources were written, for the most part, by the winners of the ideological contestation over Muslim orthodoxy, that is, by Sunnis; and Sunni identity, like the identity of any orthodoxy, rested largely on negative rhetoric, on defining themselves over and against their theological and political opponents. The Kharijites were one of those vying with the Sunnis for power, which means that their presence in the sources can never be totally generic or neutral. Read retrospectively, any reference to a Kharijite rebellion is in some sense charged with negative symbolism and is therefore pro-Sunni. Thus, when Bosworth translated "Kharijite" as "rebel," he divested the word of the heterodox connotations that it had earned at the hands of Sunni propagandists.

One possible way of justifying the translation would be to argue that Kharijism may have started out as a exclusivist religiopolitical movement, but it evolved into a social model of rebellion. That is, various disaffected peoples linked up with the Kharijites, literally or figuratively, at various times and places, to express their own particular discontent because the Kharijites provided a culturally recognized form of protest. Put differently, the Kharijites were both a model of and a model for rebellion. Accounts of Kharijite uprisings confirm as much. For despite the ideological and social purity that heresiographers claimed was characteristic of the sect, the Kharijites apparently compromised themselves on numerous occasions, joining forces with the unwashed in order to oppose the ruling authorities. For instance, some who fought under the banner of Kharijism were paid mercenaries.[68] For other putative Kharijites, loyalty to their particular leaders seemed to outweigh any commitment to a greater godly cause.[69] This is in keeping with the notion that regional bands of protesters with designated leaders and a particular set of concerns either associated themselves with Kharijite groups or rebelled in the name of Kharijism.[70] Viewed in this light, Kharijism, in its social reality, was more of a loose-fitting garment of protest that could be donned or cast off as the circumstances warranted. Perhaps this is the best explanation for someone like Shabath b. Rib'i who over the course of his life reputedly moved from Shi'ism to Kharijism to Shi'ism and back again.[71] Shi'ism, after all, was a competing form of protest alongside Kharijism. Such cases of dubious ideological purity lend credence to Bernard Lewis's observation about the nature of sectarianism in Islam, where religion and state are regarded as inseparable:

> Whenever a group of men sought to challenge and to change the existing order, they made their teachings a theology and their instrument a sect, as naturally and as inevitably as their modern western counterparts make ideologies and political parties.[72]

The contrast between the Kharijism presented in theological sources and actual historical examples of Kharijite rebellion is not altogether surprising. Theologians were in the business of arranging Islamic society into neat idealized categories—according to attitudes, beliefs, and doctrines. Such theoretical constructs fostered the sense that everyone was accounted for, that everyone fit somewhere within Islam's great chain of being. In other words, theological works were intended to order and control intellectually what was in truth a rather messy historical picture. The cases referred to above show how blurred a genre Kharijism probably was. The problem, however, is that these glimpses into the social reality of Kharijism are the exception not the rule. Rather than cut through the idealized view of Kharijism served up by Islamic theology, historical sources present layers of mystification all their own. Scholars who wish to test the argument that Kharijism was a social model of rebellion are faced more often than not with finely sifted accounts that make Kharijite history read like a series of patterned events. The letter of the Kharijite leader al-Mustawrid b. 'Ullifah to the Umayyad governor of al-Mada'in, Simak b. 'Ubayd, typifies the interpretive difficulties. It adduces a number of reasons for rebelling, but they are general in nature:

> On behalf of our people, we take revenge for oppressive judg-
> ment, suspension of divine ordinances, and the monopolization
> of the spoils. We call you to the Book of God, the example of
> His Prophet, and the rule of Abu Bakr and 'Umar; and to disavow
> 'Uthman and 'Ali for their innovations in religion and their de-
> parture from the judgment of the Book. If you accept, you will have
> regained your senses. If you don't accept, we can provide no more
> excuses for you and will declare war.[73]

The themes of this letter, if not the exact phrasing, are repeated by numerous Kharijite figures in both the Umayyad and Abbasid periods. They
hover above the events like clouds blocking our view of the social and political
reality. There are only so many times that one can come across a Kharijite
leader making a canned platform speech or dictating a form letter before one
realizes that one is not getting the full story. Did these Kharijites all, coincidentally, want the same thing? Did they all memorize the same Kharijite
catechism? Did they all follow the accepted form for expressing dissent? Or did
the historical sifting process have a tendency to harmonize expressions of
Kharijism/rebellion?

Although these speeches and letters offer little to go on, most cases of
Kharijite rebellion are even less informative. The sources are replete with brief
accounts of one or several Kharijites rebelling. These accounts, too, follow
patterns. For example, someone goes out from the community proclaiming
"Judgment belongs only to God." The phrase itself—the Kharijite watchword—
seemingly identifies the actor, but we are provided with no specific reason
or context for such a revolt. Or we are told that a certain Kharijite revolted
against a certain local leader, but the story goes no further. All these people may indeed have been ideologically committed Kharijites, or they may
have been Kharijites in the generic sense of rebels, or the two types may have
been indistinguishable at the time. To claim that one such event is clearly a
case in which Kharijite means rebel, as Bosworth did, is to suggest that one
has seen behind the historical patterns; and this leads logically to comparing
similar events. If the entire edifice of Kharijism is not to crumble, and it
should not, then a means must be devised for analyzing these patterns. To
date, no method has proven up to the task.[74] In the end, the historical tradition
leaves the reader to marvel at the intensity with which Kharijism seems to
have taken hold of Muslims in the first several centuries of Islam. The sheer
number of rebellious episodes attributed to the Kharijites underscores the

challenges—social, religious, and political—that Muslim authorities must have faced.

For our purposes, we need only draw attention to the fact that Kharijism was a complex social and religious movement whose roots lie in the partisan conflict of the first civil war (656–661), and whose rebellious and violent actions left their mark on the early Islamic polity and the history of Islamic thought. Notwithstanding historical critical questions about the motives of those identified as Kharijites in early historical sources, Kharijism has an unequivocal legacy in the Islamic tradition, one that cannot be easily reduced to that of pure rebellion. Like generic rebels everywhere, the Kharijites embody anti-establishment attitudes and behavior. But unlike a more universal notion of rebels, the image of the Kharijites is that they never rise up to defend a just cause or to denounce an unjust ruler.[75] They always separate themselves from both leaders and fellow Muslims who are worthy of respect, and they always kill those who truly deserve better. Most important, despite wearing their faith on their sleeves, they never really represent the principles of Islam for which they claim to fight. Though wrapping themselves in the mantle of religious devotion, Kharijite rebellions are more reflective of an unfounded pious self-righteousness and a fanatical commitment to an unrealistic and unobtainable social purity. In a very real sense, the Kharijites represent within the Islamic tradition all that the dominant Sunni majority came to reject, morally, politically, socially, and theologically. As has been suggested throughout this analysis, the image of the Kharijites is, in large part, the result of a Sunni-controlled vision of the Islamic past. And, for this reason, one must expect that the lessons to be learned from the past will be Sunni lessons, and they will come at the expense of Sunni opponents such as the Kharijites. We have already discussed the none-too-subtle lesson about Kharijism that al-Shahrastani attempted to teach in his heresiographic work. Other medieval thinkers also saw the Kharijites as a heuristic device that could communicate an important message about moderation in religion and respect for established authority.

The following story, which appears in numerous sources, notably those offering advice to rulers, demonstrates the extent to which the Kharijites were used as a foil for legitimating caliphal power and authority. It involves the actions of the Abbasid caliph al-Hadi during an encounter with a lone Kharijite who had been brought before him after being taken prisoner. The account as related by Mas'udi, in *The Meadows of Gold* (*Muruj al-dhahab*), is included under the heading "An Example of His Bravery" and seems to serve as a parable for the wise ruler. A brief character description informs the reader that while al-Hadi was known for being "hard-hearted, ill-tempered, [and] stubborn," he was also "well-bred, strong, brave, and generous."[76] Then the following story is related with no accompanying commentary:

> Ibrahim was actually with al-Hadi, who at the time was mounted on a donkey in a garden named after him in Baghdad, when the caliph was informed that a Kharijite had been captured. Al-Hadi ordered that the man be brought before him. As the Kharijite drew near, he grabbed a sword from one of the guards and continued toward al-Hadi. "I drew back," said Ibrahim, "and so did those around me." Al-Hadi remained motionless on the donkey, but when the Kharijite was almost upon him, the caliph shouted, "Cut off his head!" Though no one was behind him, the Kharijite was distracted and looked away. Al-Hadi then leapt upon him, knocking him to the ground; he seized the sword from his hand and sliced off his head. Ibrahim said, "We feared al-Hadi more than we feared the Kharijite, but, by God, he did not blame us for abandoning him. And from that day, he never rode his donkey and he always carried his sword."[77]

Whether apocryphal or not, the story is replete with symbolism and lessons to be learned for both ruler and ruled. First, there is the image of the rabid Kharijite who, seemingly unprovoked, takes hold of a sword and tries to attack the ruler. No explanation is offered for the Kharijite's behavior because none was thought necessary. He was, after all, a Kharijite, a member of an extremist movement known for rebelling with sword in hand. Second, we have the reaction of those around al-Hadi. Their fear and revulsion are symbolic of the response of the masses to the threat of the Kharijites. Symbolic, too, is their inability to defend themselves or Islam effectively without the leadership of the caliph. Their only saving quality is that they feared al-Hadi more than the Kharijite, as they should given the caliph's demonstration of power. But the underlying message for the masses is clear: people who live with such fears need the constant guidance and strong hand of the caliph. Finally, we have the hero of the tale, al-Hadi, whose calm and certitude won out over the Kharijite rebel. Unlike the Kharijite, who relied on uncontrolled violence to achieve his goal, al-Hadi employed his wisdom and guile. Of course, the caliph also resorted to violence to dispatch his attacker, but his use of force is presented as controlled and in self-defense. Thus the character of al-Hadi as embodied in the story serves as a model for caliphs. Like al-Hadi, caliphs may find it necessary to be hard-hearted and vicious when dealing with rebels like the Kharijites, but they must also be generous and liberal with those who, though feckless, are loyal. Moreover, all rulers could learn from al-Hadi the importance of a strong defense, for "from that day, he ... always carried his sword." From this encounter with one Kharijite, then, any caliph could take away a formula for dealing with all Kharijites, all rebels: wisdom and strength can overcome violent opposition.

Al-Hadi's confrontation with a Kharijite rebel was recounted in early Islamic sources for the benefit of other Muslims, particularly Muslim leaders. That Kharijism could be a cross-cultural morality tale is evident in the writing of the North African rabbi Sa'adiah (d. 942), the tenth-century Jewish scholar who served as the Gaon or dean of the Babylonian academy. Conversant in several Semitic languages, Sa'adiah Gaon translated the Bible and halakhic works into Arabic. He was one of the first rabbis to adopt a secular science approach to biblical exegesis (*peshat*), one that promoted historical, linguistic, and literary analysis of the text.[78] It was this same method that Sa'adiah brought to bear on the so-called Karaite Jewish heresy that had arisen in the mid-eighth century under the leadership of Anan ben David. Karaism split with rabbinic Judaism over its rejection of the oral tradition, allowing only the authority of the written Torah, hence the common reference to Karaites as scripturalists.[79] Sa'adiah Gaon addressed the errors of Karaism by attacking what was widely perceived as their naive literalism. In his role as defender of rabbinic Judaism, he sought to portray Karaites as enemies of the orthodox Jewish faith, which brings us to the Kharijite connection. In one of his works, he accuses Anan of being a Kharijite; and in another, he adopts the names Kharijites and *ahl al-jama'a*, the Sunni phrase meaning community, to juxtapose, polemically, Karaism and rabbinic Judaism.[80] Here the concept of Kharijism, in its Sunni formulation as the epitome of sectarian heterodoxy, has been brought into a Jewish debate to lend support to the religious establishment by symbolically anathematizing the Karaite opposition. So fixed in the Islamic tradition had the antagonism between Kharijism and Sunni orthodoxy become that its meaning could influence the interpretive maneuvers of a medieval Jewish scholar familiar with the religious language of Islam.

That Kharijites were a driving force in the early development of Islam, and in medieval Muslim representations of that period, is evident from the materials presented thus far. But their dominant impact on early Muslim life and thought did not continue throughout the course of Islamic history. By the mid-to-late tenth century, Kharijite uprisings had waned, although the eastern provinces still experienced isolated episodes. By this time, too, Ibadi communities in Oman and North Africa had established themselves as viable political and military entities, examples of self-sustaining minority religious communities that existed throughout the empire. Their Kharijite loyalty, however, was expressed in historical and ideological terms, not active challenges to the Abbasid Caliphate in Baghdad. For the ruling authorities, the more pressing threat, replacing the Kharijites, was the Rafidites, an extremist Shi'i sect. Their violent tactics, like those of the Kharijites before them, were regarded by most Muslims, Shi'a and Sunni alike, as dangerous to the integrity of the Muslim community and, therefore, un-Islamic. Whether it was due to the fact that the Kharijites had disappeared or that they had lost their dissident appeal, later scholars did not view them in the same obsessive way that earlier Muslim thinkers had.

The famous historian and social thinker Ibn Khaldun (d. 1403), for example, had comparatively little to say about the Kharijites. They were, for him, a historical movement that had a limited impact on the larger issue with which he concerned himself in his classic work the *Muqaddimah*. Ibn Khaldun's real interest was the factors contributing to the ebb and flow of civilizations, particularly Islam. A successful civilization, according to Ibn Khaldun, required two forces: *'asabiyya* or a kind of group solidarity based on either blood, alliance, or clientship; and religion, which unites everyone under the same belief and, thereby, serves to enhance the ties of group solidarity.[81] The decline and fall of a civilization, he maintained, is heralded by signs of weakness, such as division and infighting. The ebb of the Islamic civilization did not occur till the Abbasid period, which explains why Ibn Khaldun could be so dismissive of the Kharijites. They had emerged much earlier, when Islam was at its strongest phase of development, when it was bent on conquest and institution building. Assessing the political situation at the time of the Umayyads, he writes,

> no dissension made itself felt over the whole period of (the Arab Muslim dynasty), except for the disturbances of the Kharijites, who were willing to die for their heresy. That (however) had nothing to do with royal authority and (political) leadership, and they were not successful, because they were up against a strong group feeling ['asabiyya].[82]

Written in the late-fourteenth century, the *Muqaddimah* reflects an intellectual and political climate in which the Kharijites no longer had relevancy. More important, unlike previous Muslim writers, Ibn Khaldun had the historical advantage of knowing that the Kharijites had indeed faded from the forefront of Islamic civilization, surviving in historical memory.

The place of the Kharijites in the Islamic tradition was fixed by the conscious efforts of medieval Muslim scholars who established and passed on what came to be orthodox Sunni Islam, an orthodoxy that cast the Kharijites in the role of heterodox rebels. The introduction of this traditional image of the Kharijites into the political and religious discourse of modern Egypt required a similar conscious effort on the part of thinkers who found the image relevant to the Egyptian condition. What was this condition? Beginning in the 1940s and continuing into the 1990s, Egypt experienced numerous episodic outbursts of religiously justified violence. The goal of this violence, according to the radicalized Islamists who perpetrated it, was to destabilize, if not overthrow, the political system in Egypt, which moderate and radical Islamists alike regarded as corrupt and un-Islamic. The choice of victims reflected the political nature of Islamist militancy; the dead and injured were for the most part government officials and state employees, individuals who in one capacity or another represented the public face of the ruling regime.

In later phases of Islamist violence, Egyptian civilians and foreign tourists were also attacked and killed, but militants continued to see these operations as attempts to undermine the domestic and international reputation of Egypt and hence the legitimacy of the modern state. The Egyptian government adopted a two-pronged approach to these attacks: first, it attempted to destroy the infrastructure of militant Islamist groups through mass arrests and selective executions. Second, it embarked on an official propaganda campaign designed to condemn these groups in the public eye. In official pronouncements and the popular media, the militants were variously described as criminals, terrorists, and social deviants, but the characterization that proved most controversial and divisive was Kharijites. It is to the political culture in which the Kharijite image was first evoked in Egypt that we now turn.

If Ibn Khaldun could survey the modern Islamic scene in Egypt, it would no doubt surprise him to learn that the reverberations of Kharijism echo into the twentieth century, that modern Muslim activists are often accused of being neo-Kharijites. It might also surprise him to learn that his writing receives more attention from non-Muslim thinkers than from Muslim thinkers. In an odd way, these two phenomena converge in the debate over modern Islam in Egypt. Sometimes referred to as the Weber of Islam, Ibn Khaldun wrote from the perspective of an early modern social scientist, not a theologian or establishment ideologue. This has made his insights of special value for modern Western scholars who like to think that his work reflects an unvarnished, insider's view of Islam. By contrast, Islamists largely ignore him, preferring instead those works that transmit the kind of idealized version of Islam that Ibn Khaldun shunned. Whereas Ibn Khaldun sought to extract useful patterns from a comparative study of history, Islamists hold up as a model a particular Islamic period, that of the Prophet Muhammad and the first four caliphs. It is the patterns established by Muhammad that they wish to recreate and follow—spiritually, socially and politically—in their modern lives.

Most Islamists do not naively live in the past, as critics often argue, but they do speak to the times in which they live through the language and ideas of an idealized past. The general trend among Islamists to go forward by looking back creates a rhetorical mode that is foreign to secularists and many modernist Muslims, not to mention Western observers. But it is quite familiar to traditionalists or conservatives who tend to see the modern world through eyes trained in the classics of medieval Islamic learning. Despite their many differences, traditionalists and Islamists share important common ground in the Islamic culture of Egypt. They both imbue the past with an authority that is absolute and that serves their own interests. For they claim to be the modern inheritors of that authority, the ones who decide how the past, and which aspects of the past, is to be interpreted in the modern world. The Kharijites are one aspect of the past that was given new life, at least initially, by establishment-oriented traditionalists. The specific factors that led to this revived interest in the Kharijites will be traced out in the following chapters.

In the brief lines remaining, more must be said about the traditional image of the Kharijites and the way that image was tapped by modern thinkers.

We began this chapter by citing the *al-Ahram* opinion column that spoke out against resorting to the label Kharijite when describing Muslim youth. At first glance, it might seem that this opinion was intended to defend Islamism and its proponents against unjust accusations. Sympathy for Islamist beliefs and goals, however, is not the impetus behind it. The real concern is to prevent the indiscriminate use and manipulation of the foundational stage of Islam, a time that, so the author believes, is so exceptional in Islamic history that it is inappropriate and disrespectful to take its "sacred stories" and apply them in other historical contexts. In effect, the author wants to cordon off this sacred historical ground in order to save Muslims from judging one another according to unobtainable ideals. His agenda, then, if realized, would disarm both the 'ulama', who often wield the label "Kharijite," and the Muslim youth, who stand accused of Kharijism and who wield rhetorical weapons of their own.

Given the importance of Muhammad and his early followers in the religious life of modern Muslims, the opinions expressed in the article were not likely to change many minds. Egyptian Muslims may not always approve of the manner in which the debate about the role of Islam in Egypt takes place. But to give up the terms of the debate simply because they are highly charged would require sacrificing much of the tradition. After all, these early sacred stories do little good for modern Muslims if they cannot be made relevant to their lives. Indeed, it is the circulation and use of these stories across generations of Muslims, both to inspire and criticize one another, that keep the tradition alive. Although perhaps well intentioned, the article's concern about interpretive abuse of the sacred past glosses several fundamental points about the nature of tradition that should guide our analysis. First, the past never arrives in the present unmediated. Modern Egyptian thinkers could only evoke the Kharijites as a ready-made negative symbol to employ against Islamists because of the efforts of medieval scholars, as we have learned. Second, sacred stories, symbols, and ideals are subject to continuous regeneration and reinterpretation. Once awakened, Kharijism could be used to further not only traditional but also nontraditional, nonestablishment ideas, as we shall see.

2

Islamism, State, and Ideology

By focusing on the intentional evocation of the Kharijite image, this study hopes to avoid the pitfall of essentialism. Neither this chapter nor those that follow will argue for a continuous Islamic essence linking twentieth-century Islamists with their putative seventh-century Kharijite brethren. The Kharijites, in other words, are not treated here as a persistent Muslim mentality, destined to reemerge throughout the course of Islamic history. Instead, they will be approached as a sectarian movement that, having been imbued with certain essentialist notions during the formative period, came to have symbolic significance for modern Muslims. While the contemporary Egyptian thinkers under review in this study may see historical and therefore (im-) moral continuity between Kharijites past and present, the more salient analytic point is symbolic and polemical continuity. In short, Muslims in different historical and political circumstances have engaged in rhetorical accusations of Kharijism. The early rhetorical context is considerably obscured by the shadow of the orthodox tradition; the modern context stands more clearly in view.

In Egypt, the accusation of Kharijism first emerged in the confrontation between Nasser's government and the Society of Muslim Brothers. And its purpose was, and is, to persuade the Egyptian audience about the nature of this confrontation, to shape Egyptian perceptions about Islamist violence and politics. Thus, to characterize the accusation of Kharijism as rhetoric is not to deny the reality of a militant strain among Islamists but rather to focus on the role the accusation plays in the debate about the meaning of religiously justified violence. Put simply, the charge of Kharijism attempts to dominate the debate and reject Islamist explanations for the legitimate resort to violence. Indeed, as the traditional image suggests, real debate is unnecessary with Kharijites, since their uncompromising zealotry places them beyond rational discourse. For Egyptian authorities, political and religious, responding to radicalized Islamists with the evocation of Kharijism is a way of not dignifying the challenge of Islamist ideology, of glossing over the troubling issue of political opposition and political violence. The accusation of Kharijism, then, can be said to follow a general pattern within the language of politics: "rather than demonstrating discourse, rhetoric provides a public impression of discourse when in fact there may be none."[1] This chapter examines the rise of anti-extremist rhetoric by getting behind it, by analyzing the nature of the confrontation between Islamists and the Egyptian government that the rhetoric often conceals.

The confrontation between Islamists and government officials in Egypt is the result of two major trends: the formation of the modern nation-state and the political and cultural debate over its ideological direction. These trends are not new to students of modern Egypt (or other developing countries). The search for a modern political identity has consumed Egyptians for the past century; the failure to build a consensus about what that identity might be has prevented them from forming a viable and productive polity. The problem has not been a lack of political convictions or interest in political ideas. There has in fact been an overabundance of both. When nationalism swept through the Middle East in the twentieth century, igniting firestorms of resistance against colonialist rule, nowhere did the fire burn brighter than in Egypt. And when a variety of political and economic ideologies were introduced to the Middle East through contact with Europe, nowhere were they embraced with more conviction than in Egypt. Some ideologies put down deeper roots than others, enabling them to maintain their hold on certain segments of Egyptian society, but over the years most have lost their attraction and all have come under attack for promoting false consciousness. Scholars have already begun to chronicle the passing of the age of ideology in the Arab world and to offer predictions about the eventual collapse of Islamism, which is sometimes regarded as the final impediment to an era of post-ideological realpolitik.[2] We will return to these postmortems at the end of the book. For now, however, our concern lies not with the end of ideology in the 1990s but with its zenith under Nasser's revolutionary government in the 1950s and the '60s.

The process of modernization in Egypt and the beginnings of the state system are commonly dated to the reign of Muhammad 'Ali (1805–48), when industrialization was first introduced and military and agricultural reforms were undertaken.[3] Dating the formation of the modern Egyptian nation-state, however, is more debatable. The obvious choice is the 1952 revolution, which marked Egypt's transition from monarchy to republic. But the revolution did not establish a nation-state, either in the political or cultural sense, as much as it laid the foundation on which one could be built. Like many subversive movements of national liberation in the colonized world, the Free Officers, who led the 1952 revolution, initially had limited goals. They were committed to ending the ancien régime and imperialism. What Egypt would become after independence was less clear. The popularity of the revolution was a reflection of the shared frustrations of the Egyptian people and their desire for change. The impulse toward change had grown since the late nineteenth century, when Egyptians began to engage in public discussions about modernization, patriotism, and independence—ideas that shaped the hearts and minds of several generations prior to 1952. Religion factored into these discussions at various levels; and Islam, not surprisingly, was said to be compatible with, if not instrumental to, all these ideas.

The Free Officers thus came to power on a wave of nationalist sentiment that was not of their own making. They had capitalized on it to foment the revolution, and afterward, they tried to harness its energy to implement their program of reform. Not everyone was won over to their program, however, particularly the Muslim Brothers who had a program of their own that they wished to institute for the country. In the end, the revolution did not fulfill the promises of the Free Officers or the hopes of the people. More important for this study, because the revolution remained "unfinished," even in the subsequent regimes of Sadat and Mubarak, so, too, did the project of creating a modern nation-state. The accusation of Kharijism, it will be argued, is at once a manifestation of this political project and an indicator of the unsettled nature of Egypt's modern system of government. As a traditional religious symbol adapted to modern political ends, it provided a common language through which to debate the form and content of the Egyptian nation. Its persistence demonstrates the importance of the Islamic idiom in Egyptian political life and raises questions about the relationship between religion and politics in modern Egypt.

One of the features of the confrontation between Muslim Brothers and Nasser's government is that each blurred the distinction between religion and politics, and each accused the other of incursions into its sphere of influence. Who really incurred on the other's sphere? Whose motives are religious and whose political? Answers to these questions are often highly charged because they bear on the debate about the type of political order under which Muslims can live and the role of Islam in such an order. In other words, the answers are caught up in the contest over power and authority. For example, according to one of the axioms of Muslim self-understanding, Islam comprises both religion and state, and Muslim society naturally blends these two spheres. The fact that Nasser's government was directly involved with religious institutions and benefited from religious symbols might seem to confirm this point, as might Islamist incursions into the realm of politics. But the explanation for the blending of religion and politics in postrevolutionary Egypt does not lie in this supposed Islamic truism. Indeed, what pass as Islamic axioms in Egypt, and the greater Muslim world, are not neutral observations about Islam and Muslims, but ostensible traditional insights used to sanction Islamist claims or, at least, a more overtly religious conception of modern society.

To avoid confusion and taking sides in the political contestation, it is important to adopt the right analytic language. In a book aptly titled *Muslim Politics*, Dale F. Eickelman and James Piscatori have tried to overcome some of these concerns by pressing a functional understanding of the confluence of religion and politics in Muslim societies. All politics, they argue, are a competition for people's imagination, and all such competitions are culturally determined by local values, customs, and symbols. In Muslim societies, a pattern of "Muslim politics" has emerged, which involves the competition and contest over both the interpretation of symbols and control of the institutions, formal and informal, that produce and sustain them.[4]

"Muslim" modifies "politics" here because the symbols and institutions, though religious, are used to control state authority and define the social order. Islam provides the symbolic language through which the control is effected. This approach has the advantage of leveling the competitors and avoiding judgments regarding their religious or political bona fides.[5]

Our exploration of the rhetorical use of the image of the Kharijites fits neatly into this conceptual framework. Kharijite is a highly charged symbol whose meaning is contested; and the outcome of this contest affects attitudes toward, if not the reality of, the political and social order of Egypt. Yet, while useful for our larger project, Muslim politics needs to be refined to address the historical context of hypernationalism in which the accusation of Kharijism first emerged. Just as there is a difference between normal politics and ideology, so, too, there can be a difference between normal Muslim politics and ideology. It is important to remember that Nasser and the Muslim Brothers went beyond the typical invocation of language and symbols to support their respective visions of Egypt. They were not prepared to recognize, and unwilling to operate within, the limits of a competitive process during which collaboration and bargaining were required. Instead of politics as usual, they were totalistic and highly systematized in the way they viewed society; they rejected distinctions between supposedly autonomous spheres; they demanded an integration of public and private life; they were intolerant of other competing visions of society (and the world); their politics were based on, and organized around, an incontestable authority. In other words, they turned their ideas into ideologies.[6] The result was an ideological conflict over the direction of the Egyptian nation, over who had the legitimate authority to determine that direction.

From Revolution to Nasserism

Whether nineteenth-century social and political developments in Egypt warrant serious consideration in studies of twentieth-century events is a debatable point among historians.[7] Without passing judgment on this question, it can certainly be agreed that the process of political and economic modernization begun by the Ottoman governor Muhammad 'Ali has relevance to understanding the revolution. It was this process after all that led to contact with Europe, contact that started with advising, turned to economic dependence, and ended in British occupation in 1882. The state building initiated by Muhammad 'Ali also created among Egyptians a sense of common identity, one based on local relations and concerns, not affiliation with the Ottoman Empire. In the twentieth century, these two developments—foreign influence and Egyptian identity—reached their apogee in the nationalist movement and drive for independence. The centralized planning and authoritarian style of Nasser's regime has been compared to that of Muhammad 'Ali. The major difference, however, is that Muhammad 'Ali ruled in the nineteenth century when authoritarianism was the norm, while Nasser came to power in the 1950s after Egypt had experienced a period of political openness and constitutional government.

The period, which has been referred to as "the liberal experiment," began in 1922 with the British declaration of Egyptian independence and ended, formally, with the revolution of 1952.[8] In truth, the experiment fell apart well before the revolution, and contributed to the revolution, due to the conditions established by the British and the political inexperience of Egyptian leaders with a liberal, constitutional framework. After the declaration, the British maintained their military control over Egypt, particularly in the Canal Zone, and continued to interfere in economic and government affairs. Although Egyptians became more involved with the running of the country, their decisions were always subject to British approval. As foreigners with the ultimate power of arbitration, the British created an atmosphere of suspicion and distrust, playing off the king against the political party in power or vice versa, as the situation dictated. The heavy-handed and often-insulting behavior of a series of British High Commissioners left a lasting imprint on the Egyptian psyche. Whatever the sins of the British, Egyptian politicians played their own role in the system's failure. In their struggle for power, the king and the various political parties showed a disdain for the rule of law established by the constitution. Conflicts that were to be resolved in parliamentary debate eventually degenerated into mob demonstrations and violence. Economic and social issues also remained unresolved. By the 1930s a pattern of radical politics had taken hold and was only partially checked by the outbreak of World War II.

It was during this liberal period that Hasan al-Banna founded the Society of Muslim Brothers (1928), the prototypical Islamist movement. The Brothers contributed their share to the radical politics of the 1930s and '40s. And al-Banna himself was a victim of it; he was murdered in 1949 in retaliation for the assassination of Nuqrashi Pasha, the Prime Minister, by a lone Muslim Brother gunman. The violence that swept through Egypt at the time was political in nature, caused by a volatile political system and fractured political culture. Yet, despite their involvement in this system and culture, the Brothers tended to see themselves in nonpolitical terms. That is, though they were in the secular politics of the day, they didn't think of themselves as being of it. Indeed, their participation in politics was predicated on dramatically re-forming it, which is no doubt one of the reasons the Free Officers thought to include the Brothers in their plot. Unlike the Free Officers, however, the Brothers had a firm idea about the kind of Egypt they wanted. Theirs was primarily a moral-religious ideal of Egyptian life, one whose basic outline they had been working out in words for several decades prior to the revolution. They lent their assistance to the revolution, limited as it was, in the hope of transforming this ideal into reality. The supportive comments of some Brothers immediately after the revolution, calling it "the blessed movement" and praising its leaders,[9] demonstrated the general mood of cooperation and goodwill that existed, and gave no hint of the disappointment that was to come.

Why did the Brothers grow disaffected with the new government? Ulti-mately, it was a matter of realizing that the government did not intend to live up to the religious image it had promoted. The realization was gradual, coming over the course of two years, 1952–54, when the relationship between the government and the Brothers was at its peak; and it was based on reading bureaucratic and political signs, not clear-cut policy statements. The Brothers were drawn into the government by the Free Officers, offered cabinet posts, and given special consultative status. Though a level of suspicion existed among the Brothers, certain government decisions seemed in line with the Islamist agenda. The law banning political parties is a case in point. For the Brothers, the logic of such a law was based on the supremacy and incontestability of God's law. Since it was unthinkable for Islam to have to compete for Muslim support every election cycle, only one party needed to represent the people—the one that instituted Islamic rule. The Free Officers, however, saw the law as a means of eliminating the opposition and maintaining their own authority. From the outset, their public embrace of the Brothers was part of this same strategy. At no time were the Brothers put in a position of real power. Their voices were always diluted by that of the Free Officers, who were more interested in showcasing the Brothers than soliciting their opinions.

It was the social status and organizational apparatus (i.e., political base) of the Brothers that proved most attractive to the Free Officers, along with the religious legitimacy they might lend. Most of the military officers who fomented the revolution were largely unknown to the Egyptian populace, which is why General Neguib, a man famous for his actions in the Palestine war, was chosen to serve as the figurehead of the Free Officers. Overall, the military enjoyed a positive public image, mainly because it had refrained from participating in the political intrigues that tainted the monarchy and other political parties. Its public reserve, however, kept it from developing a broad base of support. By contrast, the Brothers had been politicking in the streets and back rooms for several decades. They had also established an impressive social services network that extended their popularity well beyond membership rolls. And Brotherhood membership was significant in the early 1950s; although lacking precision, one estimate put the number at 200,000 to 300,000, not including supporters. This was a decline from 1948 when membership had reached a high of 300,000 to 600,000.[10]

A series of disagreements and confrontations eventually soured the relationship for both the Brothers and the Free Officers. The Supreme Guide of the Brothers, Hasan al-Hudaybi, tried to avert a severe clash, but to no avail. In 1954, a Brother attempted to assassinate Nasser during an open-air speech in Alexandria. From the government's perspective, this event was probably not completely unexpected, or even in some sense undesired. Indeed, it became a convenient pretext to clamp down on the Brothers. A show trial of the assassin(s) and the Society put an end to the brief period of tense cooperation between the Free Officers and the Brothers. In a pattern to be repeated throughout the next decades, Brothers were sentenced to death in judicial processes that they neither respected nor recognized as truly legal. Six were hanged in December of 1954; Hasan al-Hudaybi's death sentence was commuted to life in prison.

As a display of power and authority, the hangings bring to mind Max Weber's observation about the modern state, namely that it is "a human community that (successfully) claims the *monopoly of the legitimate use of physical force* within a given territory."[11] Yet despite the obvious military advantage enjoyed by the Free Officers, and their power to handpick the People's Tribunal that judged the case, the new government was far from successful in its claims because its legitimacy had yet to be established. The military could intimidate the populace, but it could not create the political legitimacy that the government required for successful development—and Egyptians were desperate to develop. Thus, if the country was to move forward beyond independence, toward modernization and industrialization, Nasser and his associates had to formulate a political philosophy with which individuals could identify; and if the military leaders did not intend to open the country to the kind of elections that would confer legitimacy on the government, and that clearly was the case, then a philosophy of a self-legitimating nature was needed. What is often called Nasserism evolved into such a philosophy, and it did so, following David Apter's distinction, by using "political religion" and "religion politically."[12] These two notions provide a useful framework for understanding the place of the Kharijite image and the religious dynamic within Nasser's system of rule.

By political religion is meant a particular kind of ideological system, one in which "the state and the regime take on sacred characteristics."[13] Religion here is understood functionally, not theologically or institutionally. A political religion regime, for example, is not concerned with God's existence or qualities, but it may endow its leader with God-like charisma. Similarly, a political religion regime is not as multifaceted as a given religious tradition, but it may adopt common trappings of religion such as ceremony, doctrine, and myth. Most important is the functional parallel in transcendent meaning conferred by both religion and political religion. Though a secular system of rule, focusing on this-worldly issues and ends, political religion endows its activities and citizens with extraordinary significance. This is accomplished by breaking down distinctions between public and private, state and individual. The state becomes a total system of meaning that dominates and informs all levels and spheres of society. Like religion, political religion lends participants a degree of meaning and importance unparalleled in normal political circumstances. That importance is derived from faith in the state's myth of origin and greatness; and from submersion in, and submission to, its greater purpose. The individual and the state are thus joined in a mystical union of sorts, sharing the same mission in this life and destiny in the historical hereafter. This union, it is important to note, is manufactured and enforced by the ruling regime.

According to Apter, political religion is a feature of mobilization systems, those new nations attempting to rationalize and organize their societies and economies at a rapid pace without the requisite social system. For any nation, modernization brings change, innovation, and dislocation, all of which place stress on individuals, families, and other traditional social institutions. Mobilization systems attempt to offset this stress by politicizing all spheres of life and by drawing citizens into a cult of the state. They avert, at least temporarily, the bane of modernizing societies—a crisis of identity—through the organizational and coercive powers of the central authority. Meaning and identity, then, are products of the state, imposed through a combination of strategies: authoritarian policies, political rituals, propaganda and, if necessary, the police. Given the fusion of state, regime, and individual, loyalty and obedience are essential qualities of the citizen; and challenges to the leadership are considered treasonous.

In Egypt, we can see that the transformation of political life to political religion had a slow start. After 1954, with many of the Brothers in jail and the rest underground, the new government was free to set its own political course. It was Nasser who, after outmaneuvering Neguib, provided the compass for the nation. That Nasser understood the importance of articulating objectives and acting on them is clear from his *The Philosophy of the Revolution*, a panegyrical account of the revolution and his heroic role in it, published in 1955. It is equally clear from this work that, beyond the actions of the military, Nasser had not put much thought into how Egypt would progress through the political and social revolution that he believed was necessary.[14] His philosophy was actually more of a vision, a way of imagining Egypt's place in the modern world; and his by-now-famous three circles were the tentative foundation for this vision. Egypt's future, Nasser wrote, was situated within, and conditioned by, three geographically determined spheres of (cultural and political) influence: Arab, African, and Islamic. The Arab circle was for Nasser the most important, though there is no indication at this time of the Arab nationalism and socialism that would come to define Nasserism in the 1960s. Above all, these circles were a schema for framing Egypt's experience in broader revolutionary and historical terms. The Arab world, Africa and the Muslim world were all regions where foreign intervention and domination had prevented local peoples from achieving political independence and social and economic justice.[15]

As foreign policy, Nasser's circles lacked depth of analysis and direction, but they demonstrated the international stage on which he hoped to cast

Egypt and himself. Several events cemented Nasser's domestic reputation as a master of international politics. The first was the arms deal he cut with Czechoslovakia in 1955. At the time, an alliance promoted by the United States and Britain to oppose Soviet influence in the region (the Baghdad Pact) would have prevented such a move. However, by turning to the East for weapons, Nasser sealed the fate of the alliance, undermined Western preeminence in the region, and proved Egypt's independence. Inspiration for this political tack no doubt stemmed in part from his participation in the Conference of Non-aligned Nations held in Bandung earlier in the year. There an inexperienced Nasser found himself in the company of famous world leaders—Tito of Yugoslavia, Nehru of India, Sukarno of Indonesia, and Chou En Lai of China—whose survival and success were based on manipulating, and maneuvering between, the two great powers. At home, Egyptians cheered his entrance onto the world political scene.

The Suez Canal crisis of 1956 was perhaps Nasser's greatest coup. Angered over the refusal of U.S. aid for the High Dam project, Nasser nationalized the Suez Canal, declaring he would use the revenue to finance the dam. The French, who owned and managed the Suez Canal Company, and the British, whose canal base Nasser occupied and whose economy benefited so greatly from the waterway, were incensed. Britain, France, and the United States froze Egyptian assets in their countries and tried to engage Nasser in negotiations. Nasser, however, refused to reconsider the nationalization or to work out a new deal. His actions had struck a nationalist cord among Egyptians who had long resented the concessions enjoyed by European powers. Buoyed by his support at home, Nasser stayed away from an international meeting convened to resolve the matter. Determined to recoup their loses and teach Nasser a lesson, Britain and France decided to act militarily. With grievances of her own against Nasser, Israel entered into the plan, forming what became known in the Arab Middle East as "the tripartite aggression." The threat of war, especially from Israel, increased Nasser's intransigence and rallied Egyptians around the government. The war that broke out was short lived. The Israelis advanced across the Sinai, while the British and French attacked and, after encountering stern resistance, captured Port Said. The United States and the Soviet Union intervened swiftly to end the fighting, and the aggressors were forced to withdraw. Military losses notwithstanding, Nasser emerged victorious in the war of images. He had stood up to the two major colonialist powers of Europe and, in the Arab mind, a regional colonialist proxy. Thus a war that Egypt would surely have lost turned Nasser into a national hero and a Third World symbol of pride and defiance.

Nasser's anti-imperialist stance was codified in the constitution he drafted for the republic in January of 1956. One of the first indications of the regime's political direction, the constitution laid out six principles or goals: the end of imperialism, feudalism, and capitalist dominance over government; and the establishment of a strong army, social justice, and a democratic society.[16] In true revolutionary fashion, the regime entrusted "the people" to bring about these goals. But in keeping with its authoritarian style, the regime also never conferred the power necessary to effect real change. The instrument created to facilitate the six principles was the National Union, a political party formed in 1957 in preparation for elections to the National Assembly. Intended to replace the Revolutionary Command Council, the National Union, as the only legal political party, was in theory open to all citizens. Its organizational structure reached to the village level to bring peasants into the system. In practice, it functioned more like a filtering device, preventing the participation of undesirable elements, such as the Muslim Brothers, communists, and members of the previous government. And once elected, members of the National Assembly became little more than rubber stamps for Nasser's policies.

The collapse of the Egypt-Syria union in 1961 focused Nasser's attention on the weakness of the National Union. Polemical claims of the Union notwithstanding, the masses had not been truly mobilized, and their social and economic condition had not been significantly altered.[17] Nasser's solution was to create a new vehicle for implementing the policies of the regime, and he accomplished this by forming a new government from the top down. After naming a National Congress, Nasser placed before it a Charter for National Action in 1962, which it dutifully approved. The Charter differed markedly from previous government directives in that it provided a theoretical basis for national reform. Political, social, and economic life in Egypt was hereafter to be organized around two programmatic ideas: scientific socialism and Arab nationalism. The Arab Socialist Union (ASU), the replacement of the National Union, provided the political structure for promoting and carrying out these ideas. Two years later, a new National Assembly was elected, much as the previous one had been; and a new constitution was passed, one that gave the President, Nasser, unlimited power.

And what were the results of these changes? Though more elaborate and well-funded than its predecessor, the ASU proved just as incapable of serving Nasser's needs. The fundamental problem was that Nasser had contradictory needs. On the one hand, he wanted to see Egypt evolve into a democracy, as the six principles indicate, and he saw himself as a democratic leader. On the other hand, he was not willing to give up the power that the military had brought him. Single party rule was supposed to mobilize and politicize the masses so that they could recognize and then serve their own best interests, as identified by Nasser. A well-organized party would eventually give Nasser the popular legitimacy that military rule could not, or so he thought. The ASU, then, was Nasser's hope for weakening the military's role in political decision-making and transitioning to politics as usual. The political institutions he gave rise to, however, were structured to discourage rather than encourage meaningful democratic participation. The ASU and the National Assembly were only empowered to act on the orders of the President; they had no true advisory or supervisory role. The fear of losing control of the system overrode his desire for a more politically engaged and enlightened citizenry. In the end, the military and military style of rule won out in Nasser's political calculus.[18]

The infusion of socialist and pan-Arabist ideas into the body politic might have raised the level of intellectual debate, but it did not provide the longed-for moral glue. Viewed one way, the content of Nasser's ideology is moot. For no matter how compelling the ideology, it could not hold together an Egyptian polity that nondemocratic institutions and an overly controlling bureaucracy effectively suppressed. But there is also a question of whether socialism and pan-Arabism adequately addressed the particular concerns of Egypt at the time. In 1962, when the Charter was published, socialism and pan-Arabism had already shaped a number of nationalist movements. They were in fact the ideological blend of choice for those Arab countries opposing Western capitalist powers. Independence, however, diminished the appeal of pan-Arabism. Once unity had served its immediate purpose, Arab differences, which had always existed, came to the fore. Certainly the Syrian union debacle showed the limits of Arabism, and the Palestinian issue would serve as a continuous reminder. The political merger forged between Syria and Egypt in January 1958—a melding of Nasser's charismatic leadership and the power of the Syrian Baath party—was thought to herald the eventual unification of all Arab states. By 1961, however, the Syrians dissolved the United Arab Republic (though the name was retained by Egypt), having grown disaffected with the domineering attitude of their Arab Egyptian partners.

Pan-Arabism and socialism were international rallying cries; and because Nasser imagined himself an international figure, he promoted an ideology that suited his agenda, not that of his country. Nasser's long-awaited ideology, then, did not speak to the economic and social concerns of Egyptians as Egyptians. The political and intellectual elite were drawn to these ideas, but Egyptians on the street had their minds on more immediate problems.[19] In the end, Nasser's political reorganization had little impact on the existing system of rule in Egypt, and for good reason: behind the institutional reforms and ideological gloss, the real source of power remained the same—Nasser's state or, more accurately, Nasser as the state.

In his memoir, Sadat called into question the very purpose of the Charter, dismissing it as a means of distracting Egyptians from the failed Syrian union. Given Sadat's anti-Nasserist agenda after taking over the presidency, his comments might be seen as somewhat self-serving (like much of his autobiography). But even if the Charter is not a part of Nasser's "usual tactic of diverting people's attention to something else,"[20] its practical results are indicative of Nasser's will to power and the subordination of the Egyptian polity in the course of realizing that power. The real constant throughout Nasser's rule was Nasser himself: his image, his authority, and his identification with Egypt. "Personal loyalty to Nasser," one scholar observes, "became the key to obtaining and retaining power. The army provided the 'legitimization' of the regime—Nasser was its personification."[21] The military-bureaucracy of post-revolutionary Egypt channeled political life in this authoritarian direction. But the adulation enjoyed by Nasser could not be completely manufactured.

For a mystical union of the kind entailed in a political religion to take place, some degree of willing participation on the part of citizens is required. They have to see themselves, collectively, embodied in the regime and in the state. That such a fusing of individual and group purpose transpired under Nasser is confirmed in the Egyptian playwright Tawfiq al-Hakim's introspective account of the Nasser era. Describing Nasser's hold over Egyptians, he writes:

> he had inundated us with magic and dreams in such a way that we
> didn't know how he had inundated us. Perhaps as they said it was his
> personal magic when he spoke to the masses, or perhaps it was
> the dream in which we had begun to live because of those hopes and
> promises. Whatever the fact, those glowing images of the accom-
> plishments of the revolution made out of us instruments of the broad
> propaganda apparatus with its drums, its horns, its odes, its songs
> and its films. We saw ourselves as a major industrial state, a leader of
> the developing world in agricultural reform, and the strongest strik-
> ing force in the Middle East. The face of the idolized leader, which
> filled the television screen loomed at us from the podia of the pa-
> vilions and of auditoria, related these tales to us for long hours and
> explained to us how we had been before and what we had now be-
> come. We could not help but believe, and burn our hands with
> applause.[22]

Of all the insights into Nasser's charismatic appeal, al-Hakim's uniquely captures the overwhelming awe (and later cynicism) that Egyptians felt toward their leader. Here Nasser is portrayed in all his mystagogic splendor, transfixing people with his oratory and initiating them into the mysteries of the modern industrial state. Here political religion is the operative mode of political discourse.

At the same time that Nasser was creating a cult of the state, he was also subverting or assimilating other spheres of authority that might affect the hegemony of his regime. Islam, in its popular and official expressions, was one such sphere. The goal of the postrevolutionary government was to tap into the Islamic authority enjoyed by its recognized bearers and to use this authority to legitimize the regime and its various policies and programs. The Muslim Brothers were not amenable to this master-client arrangement, which, their militancy aside, made them a threat. Al-Azhar and its affiliate institutions, the embodiment of official Islam, proved more cooperative and useful to Nasser. That Nasser viewed Islam as something to exploit for political effect is evident in his reflections on the pilgrimage found in *The Philosophy of the Revolution*. While discussing the Islamic circle, he mentions his state visit to Saudi Arabia, where he found himself standing in front of the Ka'ba and thinking:

> that our view of the Pilgrimage must change. It should not be regarded as only a ticket of admission into Paradise after a long life, or a means of buying forgiveness after a merry one. It should become an institution of great political power and significance. Journalists of the world should hasten to cover the Pilgrimage, not because it is a traditional ritual affording interesting reports for the reading public, but because of its function as a periodic political conference in which envoys of the Islamic states, their leaders of thought, their leaders of thought, their men learned in every branch of knowledge, their writers, their captains of industry, their merchants and their youth can meet, in order to lay down in this Islamic-world parliament the broad outlines of their national policies and their pledges of mutual cooperation from one year to the next.[23]

These were the reflections of a revolutionary, but a political revolutionary, not a religious one. Nasser was not calling for pan-Islamism, for a universal Islamic awakening that would militate against a separate Egyptian nation and thus his own sovereignty. He wanted an Islam that stayed within the limits fixed by national governments, and Muslims whose "cooperation [would not go] beyond the bounds of their natural loyalty to their own countries."[24] For

Nasser, then, Islam could and should be politicized, as long as it remained subordinate to the state's political purpose. The politicization of Islam began as a function of Nasser's activism, of his willingness to use all national resources available to bring about change. His activism shaded off into ideology, however, as these resources, cultural and otherwise, became one with the state.

Even as the Free Officers were courting the Muslim Brothers in the early years of the revolution, they also reached out to the old religious guard at al-Azhar. Free Officers commonly attended Friday prayer at al-Azhar or at another of the great mosques of Cairo, making a public display of the regime's piety and respect for traditional Islamic learning. Government policies directed at al-Azhar and the official religious leadership, however, tell a different story. Although reform of religious institutions had preceded the revolution, with social functions of religious authorities coming increasingly under government control, the Free Officers embarked on a "more coordinated and intensive policy, with ideological overtones."[25] The policy had two main thrusts that sent mixed messages about the secular versus religious nature of the regime: weaken existing religious institutions that hindered reform, and create new religious institutions that subverted traditional authority and empowered voices of reform.

An example of the latter strategy was the Islamic Congress, formed in 1954, with Sadat named as Secretary General. Located in Cairo and staffed by supporters of the regime, the Congress was international in its scope and membership. Little important emerged from the Congress, whose meetings were more likely to dwell on anti-imperialist polemic rather than Islamic principles.[26] Its value to the Nasser regime was largely symbolic. The mere existence of the Congress allowed the message of the revolution to be taken abroad under an acceptable guise, while at home religious leaders were forced to operate within an Islamic organization run by the government. Sadat, who had been the point man of the Free Officers on matters religious, was quite open about the fact that the Congress was intended to supplant the guidance of traditional religious bodies.[27]

The Ministry of Waqfs (endowments) drew the attention of reformers under the monarchy and the Free Officers. In 1952, the new government abolished private or family waqfs as part of its land reform measures. The Ministry's power would experience continuous erosion over the next decade, with perhaps the most devastating blow seeming to come from within. In 1960, the regime founded the Supreme Council of Islamic Affairs inside the Ministry proper. The task of the Council, as Morroe Berger has pointed out, was identical to that of the Director General of the Ministry: the spread of

Islamic culture, Qur'an publication, and oversight of mosques.[28] In effect, the regime created a parallel institution, one that could officially carry out the same functions as the Ministry but that answered to a regime-appointed supervisor, not to the existing Director General. Indeed, the operational brief of the Supreme Council exceeded that of the Ministry and painted the Ministry as hamstrung: "The noble objective of the Supreme Council of Islamic Affairs requires that it be completely free of the restraints of routine, so that it may proceed to its goal free of shackles."[29] Obviously, no vehicle of the regime was to be slowed down by bureaucratic procedures or functionaries.

The consolidation of state power also affected other branches of the official Islamic establishment. In 1956, the shari'a courts were closed and their caseload transferred to the state court system. The pretext for this move was to eliminate corruption, but the loss of power and the threat to the job prospects of present and future sheikhs did not go unnoticed.[30] The most dramatic religious reform came in 1961, with the announced reorganization of al-Azhar. Once the details of this government-initiated plan were revealed, it became evident that al-Azhar's semi-autonomous status had come to an end. Despite its threat to institutional independence, the reorganization had support among the sheikhly caste. Disquiet over the pace of modernization, over organizational and intellectual stagnation, had split al-Azhar into progressive and conservative camps. The Free Officers had taken advantage of this division, wooing progressive sheiks into prized positions and isolating conservatives. So frustrated did the progressives eventually become with the lack of change from within al-Azhar that they were willing to tolerate, and even invite, assistance from the government.[31]

Under the reorganization, al-Azhar was transformed into a public university, administered by the state system of education. Its faculty and staff became employees of the government, subject to the oversight and wishes of government ministries. The curriculum was expanded beyond Islamic sciences to offer degrees in the secular arts and sciences. Al-Azhar, then, gained depth and breadth in its academic program but lost its unique character as an Islamic institution dedicated solely to Islamic learning. There was no question about how the regime had fared from these reforms. Through a complete restructuring of al-Azhar's internal administration and bureaucracy, the heretofore de facto government control became de jure. It was in this reshuffling that the Supreme Council of Islamic Affairs emerged as the dominant force, entrusted with the overall operation of al-Azhar.

For the regime, the benefits of the reorganization became apparent when the Charter for National Action was issued a year later (1962). Though a political policy initiative, the Charter was treated at al-Azhar with the seriousness reserved for Islamic principles; and not surprising, it received glowing reviews. The newly discovered ideological foundation of the revolution engendered even more interest. Legal opinions of jurists confirmed the compatibility, if not the unity, of Islam and Arab socialism; and representatives of official Islam took up the cause of Arab socialism as if it were their own. Material on the subject poured out of the publishing arm of al-Azhar, especially *Minbar al-Islam*.[32] That Nasser would readily equate socialism with Islam in many of his speeches was to be expected. That al-Azhar would embrace it with the same fervor could not have been predicted a decade earlier and speaks volumes about the degree to which the institution had accommodated itself to Nasser's leadership. Of course, opposition to Arab socialism and the reorganization could still be heard at al-Azhar. But the voices were weak, and the drum beat of support from the Supreme Council of Islamic Affairs, the government-controlled media, and other compromised institutions all but drowned them out.

The importance of the Supreme Council of Islamic Affairs cannot be overstated in a study of the rhetorical uses of the accusation of Kharijism. As its power grew in the 1960s, the Supreme Council was charged with publishing *Minbar al-Islam*, the journal in which Sayyid Qutb's *Signposts Along the Road* was reviewed and linked with Kharijite ideas. It was the Supreme Council of Islamic Affairs that also issued a collection of anti–Muslim Brother essays (to be taken up in the next chapter), entitled *The Opinion of Religion Concerning the Brothers of Satan*, that captured the prominence and type of anti-extremist rhetoric deployed at the time of Sayyid Qutb's arrest and trial, 1965–66.[33] Given the expansion of government influence over religious institutions such as the Supreme Council in the early 1960s, however, the line between religious opinion and that of the government was hazy at best. By absorbing official Islamic institutions into the state bureaucracy, the regime extended its control over the voice of official Islam, or at least over some of its constitutive voices. Nasser's nationalization of resources made the opinion of religion tantamount to the opinion of the regime; and by extension, it brought the charge of Kharijism into the orbit of government policy. Thus, although the anti-model of the Kharijites had traditionally been supportive of established authority in a general way, it was transformed in modern Egypt into state propaganda— propaganda in support of a reputedly, modern secular nation-state.

The regime's reliance on the image of the Kharijites presents something of a challenge to the notion of nation-state–building in Egypt. The revolution was to be the turning point in Egyptian history, when the forces of political and social liberalism won out over foreign domination and native conservatism. A decade after the revolution, however, democracy still had not been tried or tested. And political legitimacy was still being coerced rather than earned. The accusation of Kharijism, a product of government-controlled religious institutions, reflects this coercion. It also highlights the connection between religious legitimacy, secularization, and Egypt's experiment with political modernization. As long as Nasser depended on religion to maintain rule, secularization in any meaningful sense was out of the question; and as long as secularization could not be implemented, the hold of traditional beliefs and customs on the masses could not be broken, making political modernization illusory. The social transformation that Nasser advocated, then, was impeded by his regime's attachment to traditional values.

The use of political religion and religion politically were Nasser's means of mobilizing the masses for modernization. The former was a wholly secular project, while the latter, though reminiscent of traditionalism's manipulation of religion, had a secular political goal. Both gave way to the retrenchment of traditionalism when Nasser's use of religion politically turned into dependence on it.[34] The authoritarian nature of the regime remained, but it was weakened by its failure to secure a new basis of political authority. With such a basis, there would have been no need to resort to the accusation of Kharijism to defend against Islamist opposition. The continued dependence of Egyptian leaders on religion for political legitimacy is testimony to the persistent weakness of the Egyptian state.

From Muslim Reform to Islamism

For the Muslim Brothers, Nasser was a secularist par excellence. He borrowed Western political and economic ideas to underwrite his regime, and he sought to control Islam for his own benefit instead of instituting God's law. Under the subsequent governments of Sadat and Mubarak, the complaint was much the same: modern Egypt had forfeited its Islamic roots in the hope of achieving parity with the West, which itself was in a state of moral decline due its godless, secular culture. Muslim Brother opposition to Egyptian leaders, and the state they created, was based on the understanding, whether accurate or not, that Egyptian society had in fact become Western or secular in style and content. And the supposed intractability of this situation, along with the government's manipulation of religious rhetoric and institutions, is what drove some to militant action, hence provoking the charge of Kharijism. Behind this antagonism toward secularism lay a commitment to an alternative course of modernization in Egypt and other Muslim countries, which came to be known as Islamism.

Islamism is a designation used to capture a certain "type" of Muslim response to modernity, one that can be found throughout the Muslim world and one that is defined by its "tendency to view Islam as an ideology."[35] Those who fit this type, such as Hasan al-Banna, Sayyid Qutb, Maulana Mawdudi, and the Ayatollah Khomeini, emphasize Islam as a vehicle for social and political change; the spiritual and ritual aspects of the tradition are not denied as much as they are subordinated to that of action and the improved condition of Muslims. Islamists portray Islam as a universal, comprehensive system of belief and behavior that necessarily blends religious, social, political, and economic spheres. They embrace the scientific and technological achievements of modernity, but they reject modern "cultural forms" of political and economic development, such as capitalism, communism, nationalism, and secularism.

Put simply, Islamism is a counter ideology that posits an authentic, Islamic model of political, social, and economic development, in opposition to those models emanating from the West. It is important, however, to distinguish between Islamism as a type and specific Islamist movements, such as the Society of the Muslim Brothers in Egypt and Jamaat-i-Islami in Pakistan. Confusing the two often allows Islamist axiomatic claims about the nature of Islam to go unchallenged and, thereby, prevents a clear understanding of the particular circumstances out of which Islamist movements arose.

In the case of Egypt, the ideology and programs of the Society emerged in a period of nationalist ferment and should be viewed as an attempt to shape Egypt's political and social order according to indigenous Islamic values—in short, a kind of religious nationalism. Nationalism, as theorists have noted, is first and foremost about identity: how the identity of a given people is constructed (i.e., style) and the basis of that identity (i.e., content).[36] The formation of a national identity, to borrow Benedict Anderson's terminology, is a process of imagining a political community, of drawing on land, language, ethnicity, history, myth, and religion to create a sense of collective self.[37] In Egypt and the larger Middle East, three types of nationalist thinking have dominated since the nineteenth century: ethnic or linguistic, territorial, and religious.[38] These have not been exclusive ways of imagining the Egyptian nation. Political movements in Egypt have blended elements from each type. Nasser, for example, drew on all three in his three circles (Arab world, African world, and Muslim world), although his emphasis was clearly on Arabism. The Society, too, recognized the existence and appeal of different national identities, but its ideological core was religion.

The unique character of Egyptian Islamism is best seen in comparison and contrast with its religious antecedent, the Muslim reform movement of the late nineteenth and early twentieth centuries. Muslim reformers, most notably Jamal al-Din al-Afghani (1839–97) and Muhammad 'Abduh (1849–1905), set the stage for a Muslim response to the military, scientific, and cultural challenge of the West. Their anger over imperialist intervention and frustration with Muslim impotence led to a two-pronged approach: a rigorous defense of Muslim sovereignty in their own lands and an equally rigorous call for the reform of native attitudes and institutions that had allowed Muslims and Muslim society to decline from a once-glorious past.

Al-Afghani's answer to the backward state of Muslim learning was to draw attention to the contributions and splendor that Islamic civilization had achieved and could achieve once again. He had developed an appreciation of the connection between civilization and human progress after reading the work of the European thinker Guizot. People imbued with a sense of their common identity and greater purpose, it was thought, could hone their intellectual and moral capacities and work toward the good of the entire society. For al-Afghani, membership in the *umma*, the Muslim community, provided the proper social context in which Muslims could understand their place in history and begin to address their present condition. The strength of Muslim society might ebb and flow, but Islamic civilization was strong and eternal. Only armed with such an enlightened perspective, al-Afghani believed, could Muslims encounter and learn from the clearly superior Western powers without loosing their cultural identity.

Based on these ideas, al-Afghani became of proponent of pan-Islamism. In his travels throughout the Muslim world, and in his scattered writings, he promoted the political organization of Muslim peoples around their common Islamic heritage. The European model of separate nations was not suitable in the Muslim world, according to al-Afghani, despite the inroads it had already made. In place of it, he called for Muslim solidarity, which also served his vision of Islamic civilization. For he feared that, without political unity across borders, the cohesion of the Muslim umma would falter. Al-Afghani promoted, along with pan-Islamism, science and rationalist thinking. Both were in accord with Islam, he maintained, both had roots in Islam, and both were essential for the development of Muslim society. His student and publishing partner, Muhammad 'Abduh, shared this view of science, but he was doubtful that political organization could free Muslims from their historical morass. The problems of Muslim society were too thoroughgoing, in 'Abduh's opinion, to allow for an easy fix. All areas of Muslim society—science, education, law, philosophy, Muslim institution—needed to have fresh air breathed into them; and this kind of fundamental restructuring of society required time.

'Abduh's greatest contribution came in the reform of law and education. In his role as mufti of al-Azhar, a post he assumed in 1899, he set about to modernize and systematize Islamic law. He advocated legal principles that would streamline the process and allow more freedom of interpretation to scholars. His goal was to update the legal system and make it a viable institution for accommodating change in an Islamic manner. 'Abduh also attempted to bring changes to the daily operation and teaching at al-Azhar. Though certainly not as far reaching as the reorganization in 1962, his suggestions were viewed as dramatic at the time and met with significant opposition from his fellow 'ulama'. His wider views of education, which limited training and exposure to knowledge based on profession, were never implemented.

Overall, al-Afghani and 'Abduh, along with their more conservative intellectual heir, Rashid Rida (1865–1935), transformed the way Muslims, particularly intellectuals, perceived Islam. They freed Islam from the traditional preserve of conservative legists and scholars and imbued it with a sense of political and social dynamism. This in turn was to make modernity and its accompanying challenges less daunting to Muslims and Muslim society. The success of their efforts is a matter of some dispute among scholars. Some fault the reformers for trying to go forward by returning to the time of Muhammad.[39] Others see this strategy as more in keeping with progressive developments in Muslim society.[40] However one judges their intellectual rigor, the reformers did leave a legacy of Muslim activism. They founded no movements or political parties, but they did pass on the very nontraditional idea that Muslims could determine their own fate and that Islam was instrumental in this process. But it was not Islam traditionally understood that played this new role. Instead, a new image of Islam began to emerge, one that was less religiously or faith-oriented and more like a self-consciously deployed trope denoting a modern, reinvigorated identity.[41]

This legacy of activism and self-conscious Islamic identity was passed on to the Society, although Muslim Brothers had their own opinions about their connection to the reformers. On the one hand, they clearly saw themselves as heirs of the reformers. Pictures of al-Afghani, 'Abduh, and Rida often appeared in Society publications alongside those of Hasan al-Banna and other Muslim Brother notables. On the other hand, the Brothers regarded the Society as unique in the history of Muslim activism, at least the modern history. Their point of distinction was that, while reformers preached and agitated, the Brothers actually constructed and organized. In contrast to the theorizing attributed to the reformers, al-Banna was cast as the "builder of a renaissance, the leader of a generation, and the founder of a nation."[42] Given the extensive social and political activities of the Society, the Muslim Brothers had every right to feel that they were members of an unprecedented movement. After all, what had been an informal association of like-minded thinkers and writers during the time of the reformers was transformed under the Brothers into an organized movement, with creedal/ideological consistency, elaborate economic programs, and a sophisticated administrative structure. What had taken the form of isolated publishing ventures and episodic political commentary became a systematic outreach effort, encompassing every variation of the print media and aimed at all sectors of society.

The range of Society activities and ventures was broad and impressive. In keeping with its teaching and preaching mission, the Society was quick to move into publishing. Through its own press, it published over the years numerous books, magazines, newspapers, and newsletters. Public lectures and mass meetings were also organized to spread the Society's message. Propaganda was at the center of Muslim Brother activity, although it was sometimes symbolically communicated. The founding of mosques and primary schools were explicit efforts to change the way Egyptians thought and behaved. Running technical schools, small businesses, factories, hospitals, and clinics directly improved the lives of Egyptians, not just of Society members, and demonstrated the commitment and effectiveness of the Society. The Brothers also provided welfare and social services for the poor, funding for which was supplemented by government assistance. Before its dissolution in 1954, the Society had an active political life. Even after al-Banna's unsuccessful bid for office in the 1942 national elections, the Brothers continued to pursue their agenda in the halls of various governments. And to deal with potential threats, a security unit known as the Secret Apparatus was formed.

Some of the Society's affairs fell under the rubric of Muslim social welfare, a fulfilling of traditional Islamic moral obligations; others made the organization seem like a political party, for which it received formal recognition in 1952; and still other placed it in direct conflict and competition with the Egyptian government. The extent of these activities led one Egyptian magazine to observe, shortly before al-Banna's murder in 1949, that the Society "was not just a party but rather resembled a state with its armies, hospitals, schools, factories, and companies."[43] The point was well taken. With its own finances, administration, security, and values, the Society had in effect become a state within a state. And the same ideological mix of religion and politics that motivated the Society to take on the appearance of a mini-state put it on a collision course with the constituted power structure of Egypt. The full impact did not occur until the Nasser period, when it became impossible for any subgroup, religious or political, to survive beyond the control of the government.

Whereas Nasser's government was an authoritarian military regime in search of a legitimating ideology, the Society was an ideologically and socially developed political movement in search of power. Its claim to power seemed to flow naturally out of its interpretation of Islam, as the writings of the two principal Muslim Brother thinkers, Hasan al-Banna and Sayyid Qutb, confirm. The ideology of the Society and of Islamism in general was constructed around and expressed through three interrelated religious axioms: that Islam was comprehensive or totalistic, that it was universal or transnational, and that it was true and consistent throughout time or transhistorical. For al-Banna and Qutb, these truths were self-evident from the teachings of the Qur'an and the model established by the Prophet Muhammad, making them unchallengeable and relevant for Muslims in all times and places. Separately or together, explicitly stated or implied, these axioms were used to justify every argument made and action taken by the Society; and this in turn allowed the Society to portray itself and all its activities as logical outgrowths of being Muslim, as realizations of eternal, unalterable Islamic principles. Rather than confirm or challenge these axioms, the task here is to show how they played into the context of modern Egyptian politics and furthered the Society's religious nationalist agenda. It is important to bear in mind that it was the Society's attempts to implement these axioms that led to the adoption of political violence and the accusation of Kharijism.

Perhaps al-Banna and Qutb tell this story best, for theirs, like that of the reformers before them, was a self-conscious recovery of Islam. Thus their point of departure was the modern Muslim condition, which they hoped to change. Modern Muslims, according to their Islamist vision, were faced with dire choices. The world was divided into power blocs, East and West, and Muslims resided in that region—the East—where material development had been stagnant and where foreign intervention had led to moral and economic degradation. Muslims needed to decide whether they would seek independence and development by adopting the ideologies of the foreign oppressors or whether they would take another path. The best option was that of Islam, but it was not commonly viewed among Muslims as being a serious path toward economic and political progress. Al-Banna asked Muslims to return to their spiritual roots and to understand Islam the way the Society did:

> The Muslim Brotherhood believe that God, when He revealed the Qur'an and commanded His worshippers to follow Muhammad, and when He wished to grant them Islam as a religion, endowed this true religion with all the fundamentals essential for the life of nations, their progress, and their good fortune.... If you carefully study

the teachings of Islam, you will find that it establishes the soundest
principles, the most suitable methods, and the most detailed laws
for the life of the individual, man or woman; for the life of the family in its formation and dissolution; and for the life of nations in
their growth, power and weakness. It sanctions ideas that give reformers and national leaders pause.[44]

In short, al-Banna claimed that Islam held the key to national progress,
and he did so by operating like many other advocates for religious change or
change through religion. First, he evoked the transhistorical truth and relevancy of Islam: as Islam was at its founding so it is today—a view to which
most Muslims would readily assent. Then he read into the mythic period of
early Islam the outcome that he wished to bring about. Of course, Muslim
reformers engaged in the same interpretive process. In his famous work on the
unity of Islam, Muhammad 'Abduh emphasized the long-standing tendency
toward reason, natural theology, and liberalism in the Islamic tradition—
trends that he wished to see embodied among modern Muslims.[45] Muslim
Brother thinkers, however, differed significantly from reformers in the depth
and extent of their back-reading and in their uncompromising hold on the
Islamic legacy. Rather than a deferential nod to the past, al-Banna and Qutb
equated the entire spectrum of Society activity and ideas with Muhammad and
his mission, particularly its aspirations to establish and oversee an Islamic
system of rule. And their defense of this spectrum took the form of a defense of
Islam. The Society's continuous fixation on the comprehensive nature of Islam
must be seen against this backdrop.

According to Society teachings, nothing fell outside the purview of Islam,
so there was no need to divide the world into neat categories such as politics,
religion, and society; or rather, the distinctions could be made, but they actually merged into the all-inclusive notion of Islam. Al-Banna's oft-quoted
words from the fifth conference of the Society are emblematic of this view:

We believe that the principles and teachings of Islam are comprehensive, regulating human affairs in this world and the next. Those
who think that these teachings deal only with the spiritual side of life
and nothing else are mistaken. For Islam is ideology and worship,
homeland and nationality, religion and state, spirituality and activity,
Qur'an and sword.[46]

Here the comprehensiveness of Islam is asserted over the objections of those
who would limit it to spiritual affairs. But the description of what Islam
comprehends is precisely the complex religious, political, and social agenda

that the Society set for itself. Again, context is everything. No other political movement prior to the Society had expanded into so many sectors of Egyptian society, nor had any movement so overtly relied on religion to explain and legitimize its raison d'être. As a result, the Society came under criticism for projecting religion into affairs for which secular ideologies were well known but for which Islam as a religion traditionally understood and lived was not. The response coming from inside the movement was an exposition on the true nature of Islam—pious, progressive, activist, politicized, and nationalist—that served to rationalize Society activities by identifying the Society as the embodiment of that nature.

Islam's comprehensiveness was also used in the discourse of the Society to highlight the unique character of Islam in comparison with the ideological competition and, in an interesting twist, to coop the strengths and renown of these same ideologies. For example, in two of his early works, during his premilitant phase, Qutb discussed the comparative advantages and disadvantages of communism, capitalism, and Islam. He conceded that communism and capitalism appeal to certain constituencies and address important material needs. He was especially sympathetic to communism, no doubt in part because of the popularity that socialist ideas enjoyed at the time. For Qutb, however, Islam was the perfect system of human organization because of its comprehensiveness, which was a function of the divine plan. Secular systems were by definition incomplete because they had a limited vision of humanity.

> Communism views man only on the basis of his material needs. In fact, it views humanity, even the entire universe, on the basis of material substance alone. Islam, on the other hand, views man as a unity—one that neither separates his spiritual desires from his sensory inclinations nor divides his spiritual from his material needs. It sees the universe and life holistically, without (inappropriate) differentiation and division.[47]

The rhetoric of Islam's comprehensiveness suggests that Islam has what secular ideologies lack and could never attain. But the equally important point is that Islam also has the ability to address practical social, economic, and political matters in a manner similar to that of the secular ideologies. Among Egyptians, it wasn't Islam that was known for fomenting social, economic, and political change. Capitalism, communism, and nationalism, by contrast, had cachet based on their historical contributions to the development of other lands. Qutb and al-Banna exploited this cachet, even while declaring these ideologies failed, and Islam's comprehensiveness provided the interpretive strategy. Qutb, for example, sought to depict Islam as open to outside influences as long as these influences were situated within an Islamic framework. His use of the idea of Islam as a system (*nizam*), which was first developed by Mawdudi, helped in this regard.[48] The Islamic system, he maintained, is unlike any human or secular system and owes nothing to them; it arose independent of other systems and never borrowed from them in the course of its development.[49] At the same time, Qutb allowed a degree of flexibility within this system for the inclusion of non-Islamic contributions:

> The Islamic system can accommodate dozens of forms, which are consistent with the natural progress of society and with the new needs of the age, as long as the comprehensive concept of Islam rules over these forms in its wide external scope.[50]

In a similar vein, juxtaposing the Islamic mission (da'wa) of the Society with that of other secular missions, al-Banna wrote:

> Our position regarding the different missions, which have inundated this age, dividing people's hearts and confusing their thoughts, is to weigh them in the balance of our mission. Whatever is in agreement with it is welcomed, but whatever diverges from it, we disavow. We believe that our mission is universal and comprehensive, but it does not turn away from the benefits of any mission without being familiar with them and calling attention to them.[51]

At work in these passages, and throughout Society literature, is an attempt to organize and critique modern politics and society according to Islamic standards. The standards are largely historical and conceptual, but the goal of the analytic process is quite practical: to demonstrate that Islam could provide the social and political glue to form a modern national identity and could govern a modern nation-state. Nationalism presented perhaps the greatest obstacle for Society ideologues. A Western political concept, nationalism was perceived, rightly, as secular and limiting to Islam's universal claims. But it was also recognized as a vital way to create unity and solidarity among Egyptians for their drive toward independence, a way that Egyptians themselves had embraced. This explains why ambivalence reigned in al-Banna's treatment of nationalism, why he was in effect an antinationalist nationalist. His distaste for nationalism was itself based on pro-nationalist principles. In al-Banna's estimation, Western society had achieved complete dominance over the Muslim East. This dominance was felt in all areas of life, in their military weakness, in their political and economic subservience, and, most notably, in their dependent patterns of thought. Eastern peoples, according to al-Banna, had been so beguiled by the imperialist occupiers that they even sought their freedom in a Western manner:

> People are sometimes seduced by the appeal to patriotism and at other times by that of nationalism, especially in the East, where Eastern peoples are aware of the abuses of the West toward them, abuses that have injured their honor, dignity and independence, and also that seized their wealth and cost their blood.... But then they try to free themselves... with whatever possible strength, resistance, effort and endurance they can muster: the tongues of their leaders are given free rein, a stream of newspapers flows, their authors write books, their orators make speeches, and voices shout out—all in the name of patriotism and the glory of nationalism.
>
> This is well and good. But it is neither well nor good that when you try to convince Eastern peoples—they being Muslim—that what Islam possesses is more complete, more pure, more sublime, and more noble than anything coming from the mouths of Westerners and the books of Europeans, they deny it and persist in blindly imitating them, claiming that Islam belongs to one sphere and this idea to another. Some of them believe that [including Islam in the same sphere as patriotism and nationalism] is what divides the unity of the nation and weakens the solidarity of the young.[52]

Like many Islamist assessments of Western ideologies, al-Banna's message regarding nationalism and patriotism was mixed and subversive. First, these ideas were cast as negative because they were associated with the West, the West that conquered Muslim peoples militarily and continued to subjugate them culturally and ideologically. Then, these same ideas were tacitly promoted in as much as they were attributed to Islam, albeit in more perfect form. And that form was distinctively modern. Though the emphasis was on "Islamic," and references to Muhammad's style of rule extensive, al-Banna's political ideas and values were conditioned by the needs and expectations of the modern nation state; and he was careful to communicate that Islam did in fact meet those needs and expectations. Indeed, he tried to harness Islam, or more accurately Islamic resurgence, to the star of national resurgence. In a letter to King Faruq and other leaders of Muslim countries, written in 1947, he touted Islam as the only complete and effective solution to their national predicament. But to do so, he had to trace Islam through a range of characteristics that reveal the modern nation-state to be the standard of measurement. Thus, he pointed out, Islam provides hope for the nation and a sense of national pride; Islam fosters a strong national military, public health, and commitment to science; Islam also addresses the need for morality, an economic system, and social institutions; and finally, in a clear attempt to rescue Islam's image, Islam is said to respect the rights of minorities and foreigners, along with being open to relations with the West.[53]

Essentially, al-Banna aligned Islam to follow the protocols of the modern nation-state, all the while claiming that Islam was unlike its ideological counterparts in Europe. It differed, he claimed, because European forms of nationalism are self-limiting according to language, ethnicity, and land, while Islam is universal in its vision and goal. The universalism espoused by al-Banna and the Society, however, was an outgrowth of seeing Islam as an ideological response to the penetration of international ideas and powers in Egypt and the Muslim world. Islam's universalism put Islamism on a par with communism, socialism, and capitalism: all were ideologies international in scope, but particular in their application; all were forces of universal liberation with the capacity to improve the conditions of oppressed or underdeveloped peoples. As a native counter ideology, Islamism highlighted "Islam" or "Islamic" as the distinguishing character of Muslim societies over and against foreign, Western invaders. Islam functioned, then, like an ethnic or racial marker, which Muslims naturally have and outsiders do not. This interpretive trend was common in religious nationalisms, in which "religion is likely to be the most important distinction, sometimes the only one, differentiating a self-conscious group from others in its vicinity."[54]

What is notable about al-Banna's religious nationalism is its promotion of strict Muslim values and ritual performance. The religious aspect of many nations that adopt a religious nationalist outlook, such as Northern Ireland, Bosnia, and Serbia, is superficial, intended primarily to draw mundane, political boundaries around different "religious" communities. By contrast, Islamism as a type of religious nationalism takes religion seriously and factors religion into all decisions, policies, and explanations. But here, too, despite the pious rhetoric, the boundaries should be seen as predominantly political. The line that is being drawn, however, is within Muslim society, between Muslims who view their national identity differently.[55] In Egypt, where international politics played out on the domestic stage, the self-conscious assertion of true faith marked Islamists off from other Muslim Egyptians who enthusiastically embraced foreign ideologies. For al-Banna and other Islamists, then, Islam ideologically deployed divided the true Muslim wheat from the Western-tainted Muslim chaff. In short, it became a wedge issue that opened up a domestic political niche for the Society.

Islamism resonated on the supranational and national levels because international and national politics overlapped and blurred the distinctions between outsider and insider and between "outside other" and "inside other."[56] This phenomenon of turning the anti-imperialist critique inward on variously defined native enemies, which is a common experience in the political discourse of the colonized world, was rampant in Egypt. When the Society's religion-based critique of the West was turned inward, it reduced domestic political differences to religious ones and called into question the faith of fellow Egyptians. This point was nicely captured in al-Banna's religious assessment of nonmembers of the Society:

> The difference between us and our people . . . is that their faith is
> anesthetized, asleep in their souls; they have no desire to submit to it
> or act in accordance with it. The Muslim Brothers, on the other hand,
> have a faith burning in intensity, one that is vigilant in their souls.[57]

The advantage lent to the Society in the above statement is clear. With religion the measure of all things, the political competition is dismissed as short on faith and, therefore, unable to lead effectively; only the Society had the right religious stuff.

As the above quote suggests, al-Banna did not merely participate in Egypt's "Muslim politics"; he tried to dominate it by arrogating to the Society the sole right to speak on behalf of Islam and to rule Egyptian Muslim society. How would the Society under al-Banna's leadership have ruled Egypt? What kind of nation-state would have emerged? To respond that it would have been an Islamic system of rule and an Islamic nation provides little, if any, clarification. In the religious nationalism promoted by al-Banna, Islam often served as little more than a cultural marker, something to differentiate the authentic native from the sham foreign. This is evident in calls for the implementation of Islamic law, the supposed cornerstone of an Islamic government. Serious shortcomings of the shari'a—how it could be updated and expanded, how it would be implemented and enforced—were deemed irrelevant in comparison to the fact that it represented a uniquely Muslim system of governance.

Visions about the exact makeup of an Islamist government in Egypt were mixed and confusing because the Society never had the opportunity to test its ideas in practice. The confusion was compounded by al-Banna's ideological writings, and those of the early Qutb, which projected a rejectionist front toward modern political forms, but tempered this with practical concessions. Hence the trademark rhetoric of the Society outlined above: a denial of foreign ideologies, even while absorbing them; a denial of the modern nation-state, even while demonstrating compatibility with it; a denial of political parties, even while behaving like one; a denial of the (secular) political process itself, even while engaging in it. Indeed, al-Banna made a virtue of the politics of rejection. It allowed him to cast the Society as possessing the moral high ground, above the secular political fray, and from this moral perch, he preached a unique kind of Egyptian politics.

One characteristic of al-Banna's take on the Islamic nation seems certain. He conceived of it as a unitary, not a composite entity. That is, the Islamic nation was in some sense regarded as a "collective individual" with rights that superseded those of its member citizens, instead of an "association of individuals" whose collective (democratic) voice defined it.[58] Such an understanding of the modern nation was common in Egypt and the Middle East and had no necessary links to Muhammad's early rule.[59] Nasser's was a collectivist conception of the nation, although the precise basis of the collective remained vague. As examples of collectivist nations, the theoretical one posited by al-Banna and the actual one that later took shape under Nasser shared a common theme—authoritarianism and inequality between ruler and ruled. A collectivist nation requires that its collective individual will be divined and expressed by a select segment of society: "the elite, in such cases, represents the nation to the people, rather than representing the people."[60] And by virtue of its direct insight into the nation's will, this same elite enjoys a privileged status vis-à-vis other members of the society.

Al-Banna certainly endowed the Society with this kind of insight, based on the Brothers' superior faith and commitment to Islamic activism. Ideally, the message and the organizational breadth of the Society were to transform, fundamentally, the way Muslims thought about and acted in modern society; and this transformation of individual Muslims was to lead to a transformation of society and the nation. The Society's agenda, however, ran afoul of Nasser's regime, in part because of its militant aspect but primarily because it was ideological and Nasser did not tolerate ideological opposition. The ensuing confrontation led to significant shifts in the Society's attitude toward the modern nation-state and its possible transformation. Banned from legal activities, with many of its members in prison, the Society saw a more militant approach to social and political change evolve within its ranks. Qutb was the recognized leader of the militant trend, but it is important to note that the potential for violence was with the Society from the start.

Al-Banna made provisions for the use of force in keeping with the needs of the Islamic nation measured in modern political terms, and he authorized the Society as the microcosm of any future government to maintain its own defense force. *Jihad*, for al-Banna, was the Islamic cultural rubric under which the use of force was legitimated against the foreign enemies of the developing Muslim nation.[61] After the crackdown on the Society by Nasser's government,

Qutb effaced the distinction between outside and inside enemies and brought jihad into what had been the domestic political calculus. In Qutb's radicalized writings, the only true location of anything Islamic was the vanguard of Society activists. Fellow Egyptian Muslims, who al-Banna said possessed "an anesthetized faith," were classified as unbelievers by Qutb. Egyptian society, which al-Banna regarded as basically Islamic, was labeled *jahiliyya,* or pre-Islamic paganism by Qutb. Indeed, everything outside the Society became jahiliyya and therefore subject to jihad. And from the perspective of an underground and imprisoned religious nationalist movement, there was some logic to this judgment. Egypt had gained its independence and become a modern nation, at least in name. But this new nation, under Nasser, proved to be even more hostile to Islam (ism) than the pre-independence, imperialist enemy had been.

Thus Qutb constricted his interpretive language to match the social and political restrictions placed on Muslim activism. The early rhetoric of rejection balanced by concession, which characterized the writings of both al-Banna and Qutb, turned to pure rejection and removed any possibility of tolerating anything besides the Islamist ideal.[62] One example is the way Qutb eliminated ambiguity about the axiom of Islam's universalism. Al-Banna's ideal Islamic nation was transnational in scope, but he also qualified this ideal by advocating a staged process of realizing it: first a Muslim Egyptian nation would arise, then a pan-Arab nation, and finally a pan-Islamic one. Qutb came to disallow a gradualist approach to the modern situation or any limitation on the Islamist ideal, as he came to disallow interpreting Islam through modern political ideas and ideologies. On the subject of solidarity, he made it clear (in the judicial inquiry leading up to his trial) that patriotism and nationalism were only to be understood by Muslims in terms of faith (*'aqida*), not land or ethnicity, and that Islamic nationalism superseded all other political formations.[63] On the subject of world politics and ideologies, Qutb also turned to a more faith-oriented view. Instead of portraying the world as divided into political power blocs of capitalism, communism, and Islam, as he had in the past,[64] he came to use the simplistic and highly volatile medieval distinction of *dar al-harb* and *dar al-Islam,* the abode of war and the abode of Islam.[65]

In essence, Qutb narrowed the understanding of religious nationalism. In response to the absolutist, secular nation that won out in Egypt, he constricted the boundaries to the point that the Islamic nation was symbolically identified with the Society, with the movement of ideologically committed Muslims. Qutb continued to advocate the formation of an Islamic nation, but it now shared little in common with the modern nation-state. It was exclusively, uncompromisingly Islamic, just as the vanguard of Muslims had become the exclusive, uncompromising remnant of the Muslim community. Moreover, Qutb's depiction of the Society as a ship afloat on an ocean of jahiliyya meant that the would-be Islamic nation could only come about through war.[66] Again, Qutb was not the first to legitimize the use of violence, and it would be naive to claim that Islamist radicalism could have been averted if Nasser had established an open, civil society, in which the Society was able to preach and politic freely. It would be equally mistaken, however, to overlook the extent to which Qutb's militant Islamism directly responded to the fate of the Society under Nasser's authoritarian rule. Unlike al-Banna's Islamism, that of the later Qutb made confrontation and martyrdom seem more inevitable, more necessary to the modern Muslim condition; and this outlook was clearly shaped by Nasser's prisons, in which Qutb and thousands of Brothers spent years contemplating and debating the fate of the Society and the Islamic revival.

The negative impact of this experience can be seen most vividly in the final chapter of *Signposts*, in which Qutb draws on a story from the Qur'an to depict the life of Muslim Brothers in Nasser's Egypt.[67] Taken from the Sura of The Constellations (85:1–16), it relates the experience of believers who were persecuted and tortured in a pit of fire merely because of their faith in God. The moral of the story, according to the Qur'an, is that those who persecute believers will be punished in hell for their actions, while the faithful will be rewarded in heaven. As is typical of his style of qur'anic interpretation, Qutb sees this story not as a parable but rather as a dramatization of real life events, an acting out of human nature.[68] In effect, the persecuted and tortured life of Muslim activists in Egypt is a representative unfolding of the archetypal story in the Qur'an. And Qutb's advice to Muslims in this situation was commensurately bleak. Muslim activists, he wrote, should expect a physical life of frustration and pain, but they can overcome it by adopting a long-range perspective that distances them from the immediate social reality in which they live; instead of their bleak physical existence, they must concentrate on the larger spiritual battle of good and evil that links this life and the next. And if the struggle results in physical death, in martyrdom, the rewards have been clearly laid out in the Qur'an.[69]

Living life at a spiritual remove, focusing on the world to come, accepting a constant state of jahiliyya and jihad, being resigned to persecution, torture, and death—all reflected an apocalyptic prison mentality, not the Islamism of al-Banna or the sectarianism of the Kharijites. Qutb's radicalized Islamism was an adaptation of religious nationalism to the political spirit of the times, to a time when the playing field of Egyptian politics was dominated by the machinery of Nasser's government and the Society's survival seemed uncertain.

It was a form of political violence directed against an authoritarian, oppressive, and unstable regime that had acquired and maintained power through the military. The situation was not unique to Egypt. Military regimes emerged in other Middle Eastern countries after the fight for independence from colonialist rule, and these regimes also came into conflict with Muslim activists who espoused an Islamist international agenda with local political impact.[70] In fact, in the post-war, post-colonial period, the Third World was dominated by military-controlled nations. Like the Free Officers in Egypt, many of the revolutionary forces that came to power in Africa and Asia had initially advocated political reforms but then proved unwilling or unable to share power and address the economic needs of their people. As a result, they fell into a pattern of authoritarian rule, and their countries were often fractured by militant political opposition and successive military coups. Throughout the Third World, political illegitimacy and government instability have gone hand in hand.[71]

The confrontation between the Muslim Brothers and Nasser's regime was an outgrowth of the search for political legitimacy and stability in Egypt—a search that ended in failure. Analyzing this confrontation through the prism of the accusation of Kharijism draws attention to the underlying causes of Islamist rhetoric and thus to the way the rhetoric masks these causes. It also helps explain how the rhetoric was connected to the violence that it was supposed to counter. As deployed by government-controlled religious institutions and the media, the accusation of Kharijism was an aspect of state propaganda and an example of using religion politically. However, Nasser's use of religion politically exceeded the boundaries of ordinary political competition over Islamic institutions and symbols—what has been called "Muslim politics." Indeed, he eliminated the competition by dominating Muslim politics, as he dominated all spheres of potential political influence in Egypt. Moreover, the restrictions that he imposed on political participation and the operation of civil society, especially as enforced by the secret police, provoked Muslim Brothers to sharpen their critique of the modern state and turn to violence. Thus, to the extent that the accusation of Kharijism allowed Nasser's regime to demonize Muslim Brother opposition and legitimize authoritarian measures, it contributed to the emergence of Islamist violence.

Because of Nasser's domination of political life, it is tempting to conclude that his vision of Egypt won out. After all, he remained in power for some eighteen years and died a national hero, while the Muslim Brothers languished in prison and underground. A more accurate assessment of the confrontation between Nasser and the Society of Muslim Brothers, however, would be that an ideologically driven Muslim politics won out and the process of nation-state–building foundered. It is important to remember that Nasser resorted to the manipulation of religious institutions and symbols more out of ideological weakness rather than out of a stated desire to lead politically through the cultural idiom of Islam. He was, by political nature, a secularist, but his authoritarian policies—the use of religion politically and political religion—prevented the establishment of a decidedly secular political framework. The Muslim politics that emerged, then, were as much the result of a failed political process as they were a cultural appeal to the Muslim imagination.

3

The Muslim Brothers and the
Neo-Kharijite Challenge

Given the legacy of the Kharijites within the tradition, it is not surprising to find the name evoked. At first glance, there might seem much to warrant such a comparison. Both the original Kharijites and their putative modern descendants thought of themselves as the moral conscience of the Islamic community, and they acted on their convictions by waging war against anyone who opposed their agenda, particularly those in positions of authority. Another point suggestive of comparison was their seemingly shared zeal to live an uncompromised Muslim life or to die trying. Even many Western scholars came to draw parallels with the Kharijites when analyzing radical Islamist activities; some, behaving more like Muslim insiders, started to label militant Islamists as Kharijites.[1] Few remained as circumspect as Richard Mitchell, who observed that though such "comparisons are worth while . . . the historical periods in question are too disparate to bear extensive comparison. And historical analogies are always potentially misleading, always potentially destructive of the uniqueness which inheres in each historical event."[2] Mitchell was, of course, correct, but his respect for the particularity of historical events was not shared by Egyptian Muslim commentators (and some Western academics) who saw the image of the Kharijites as a useful means of analysis and an ethical-historical policing mechanism.

The existence of a traditional countermodel of rebellion might strike some critics as an unassailable good, something to be promoted about the tradition, not called into question. The problem, however, is the extent to which the polemical content of the name skews historical understanding, whether of the classical or modern period. As previously shown, knowledge of the original Kharijites has been dramatically affected by the shaping hand of Sunni orthodoxy. It is no accident that "Kharijite" in the tradition denotes illegitimate rebellion and thus legitimates a forceful counterresponse by Muslim leaders. For this reason, comparing someone in the modern period with the Kharijites is not a neutral, descriptive assessment; it is normatively and politically weighted against rebellion and in favor of the ruling authorities. The violence perpetrated by someone who is a Kharijite is by definition extremist, unlawful, and intolerable. There is no moral flexibility in the designation, unlike the term *mujahidun*, fighters or warriors (from the Arabic word jihad), which traditionally has generated debate about whether a cause is just or conditions are right for making war. Whereas mujahidun may be fighting in the way of God, Kharijites never are, because they are fighting against God's legitimate representative rulers on earth. This explains why militant Islamist thinkers have commonly proposed a theory of jihad to fit their critique of Egyptian society: they recognized the need to justify their recourse to violence in acceptable Islamic terms, to portray themselves as righteous Muslim warriors.[3]

In theory, when the polemical content of the name "Kharijite" is directed against Islamist opponents of the ruling regime, the aim is to delimit options for violent confrontation by prejudging them as Islamically unjustified, or to undermine the defense of those charged with acts of violence. The accusation of Kharijism, if convincing, militates against Islamists receiving widespread public support for acts of rebellion, let alone an Islamic revolution. No matter how authoritarian and corrupt the Egyptian government might be, militant Islamist ideology will never be mistaken for a kind of liberation theology if pro-state propaganda succeeds in characterizing it as Kharijite. Thus the spectre of Kharijism, in its retroclassical formulation, enters the political fray of modern Egypt firmly on the side of the Egyptian state, which explains why caution is required when discussing so-called modern Kharijites. For, in place of a critical examination of the causes of political revolt in Egypt, the accusation of Kharijism offers an ad hominem attack on militant Islamists, one based on a kind of Islamic essentialism, which takes as its motto "as the religion once was, so it shall ever be." The charge of Kharijism, in effect, glosses over the particular historical events that give rise to Islamist opposition, explaining a complex sociopolitical phenomenon with a loaded religious epithet.

Like many of the religious trends that have emerged in modern Egypt, the evocation of Kharijism first occurred in connection with the activities and ideas of the Society of Muslim Brothers. On at least two separate occasions, in 1948 and 1954, during periods of tense confrontation with the government, the Muslim Brothers were accused of being Kharijite. In each instance, the accusation was flatly denied, and the matter seems to have gone no further.[4] These isolated episodes are not part of the full-scale debate over Kharijism that would take hold in Egypt, starting in the 1960s and continuing into the 1990s. They do, however, adumbrate the trend toward the accusation of Kharijism that came to inform a range of political and religious rival groups in Egypt—government, official al-Azhar, conservative, Islamist, and secular. This chapter examines the first wave of accusations of Kharijism as they were applied in general to the Society of Muslim Brothers and in particular to the writing and figure of Sayyid Qutb, a one-time literary critic who became the voice of Islamist militancy.

Although the spectre of Kharijism has an inherent establishment orientation, it has the potential to be interpreted and applied differently. Like all symbolic language, the content of the Kharijites is never completely fixed, for its meaning derives in part from the context in which it is spoken. Put differently, when, how, why, and by whom the Kharijites are evoked will affect the specific transformative power of the epithet. The various meanings ascribed to the Kharijites by rival religious and political factions in Egypt will be explored in the following chapters. That competing groups make use of the same Islamic idiom, bending it to their respective agendas, does not render the idiom vacuous and unworthy of study. As the sociologist Sami Zubaida points out, "It is important for us to listen to the discourses of these different groups and to understand their social and political constructions."[5] One of the fundamental arguments of this work is that the Islamic idiom, of which Kharijism is a part, cannot simply be viewed as an epiphenomenon hovering above real life social and political processes, a way of talking that is unrelated to action and social reality. What people do matters, but how people think and talk about what they do matters also. And in modern Egypt where political and economic modernization have stalled, where civil society is severely limited and controlled, the stakes involved in how people think and talk are high, for the secularizing forces in power, the Islamists who wish to supplant them, and the masses caught in the middle.

Sayyid Qutb and the Plot Against Jahiliyya Society

Kharijism emerged as a major motif in the public discourse of Egypt in 1965, after the secret police uncovered a Muslim Brother plot to overthrow the government of President Gamal Abdul Nasser. In its physical details, the plot appeared like many others that have shocked the Egyptian public. There was the usual band of conspirators paraded before the cameras, the discovery of a secret cache of weapons, the show trial and the denouement on the scaffold. What made this case singular was the forceful ideological challenge posed to state authorities by one of the conspirators. According to media reports, the radicals who were arrested had in their possession a book that argued that the Egyptian government and society at large were un-Islamic and that the only way to change these corrupt institutions was through force. The author of this revolutionary primer and the supposed mastermind behind the conspiracy was Sayyid Qutb, the man who emerged as the intellectual and moral leadership of the Society of Muslim Brothers in the years following the death of Hasan al-Banna.

Born in the village of Qaha in Asyut Province in 1906, Qutb went on to receive his higher education at Cairo's Dar al-'Ulum, where he studied Arabic language and literature. Upon graduation, he worked as an inspector for the Ministry of Education, but eventually left the post to dedicate himself full-time to writing. He was a prolific writer, publishing works of fiction, poetry, and literary criticism—works which in retrospect, are conspicuous for their lack of religious ideas and themes. His religious consciousness began to change in the late 1940s. A two-year stay in the United States on an educational mission, 1948–50, appears to have been a seminal experience leading to his conversion to a life of religious activism. He joined the Muslim Brothers on his return to Egypt in 1951.[6] Though initially on good terms with the Free Officers, he split with them over their rejection of Islam as the foundation and measure of Egyptian citizenship. After an attempt on Nasser's life in 1954, the government cracked down on the Muslim Brothers imprisoning hundreds. Qutb was given a fifteen year sentence, but he was released at the end of 1964 after the President of Iraq interceded on his behalf. Within a few months, he was implicated in the 1965 plot and rearrested, and following a well-publicized trial, he was executed in August 1966 along with two fellow Muslim Brothers.[7]

While in prison Qutb continued his passion for writing, completing two major works that would become modern classics among Islamists around the world: Ma'alim fi'l-tariq, or Signposts along the Way, the revolutionary primer which reputedly inspired the participants in the 1965 plot;[8] and Fi zilal al-Qur'an, or In the Shade of the Qur'an, a Qur'an commentary which broke new ground in the genre.[9] Of the two works, Signposts has received the most critical attention from both Muslim and Western scholars, despite the fact that four of its chapters were adapted from the Qur'an commentary. In both works, the twin concepts of jahiliyya, or ignorance, and *hakimiyya*, or sovereignty, provide the basis for reinterpreting and reviving Islam in the modern world. Both works also exhibit an aggressive, uncompromising stance toward the sins of Muslims, often juxtaposing those possessing true faith in Islam over against those with false. But whereas the commentary is interspersed with anecdotes, stories and lessons unrelated to the corrupt condition of modern Islamic society, *Signposts* is a relentless, vitriolic attack on it. Indeed, in *Signposts*, Qutb does not allow his readers to ignore or to misunderstand what he characterizes as "the ocean of jahiliyya inundating the entire world."[10] He confronts them with it and tries to incite "true" Muslims to act against it.

Qutb justifies the need for action, and the direction in which Muslims must act, through a systematic unfolding of the idea and social reality of modern jahiliyya. Traditionally, jahiliyya refers to the era prior to the advent of Islam, when Arabs were living in a state of ignorance, unaware of God's power over them and of their obligations toward God. It often appears in the literature as a historical and theological counterpoint to Islam, a way of differentiating what once was from what the Islamic message finally and irrevocably brought about. Qutb, however, borrowing from the writings of the Indian Muslim activist Abu 'Ala Mawdudi, regards jahiliyya as a perpetual condition, something into which people fall during any historical period when they turn away from God. For Qutb, jahiliyya in its pre-Islamic and modern manifestations is rooted in the sinful human tendency to supplant God's sovereignty (hakimiyya) over the earth with that of man. The early Muslim community under the direction of Muhammad, Qutb claims, gradually defeated the jahiliyya forces, which surrounded them, but once again this ungodly current has taken hold, threatening the future of Islam. This time, however, jahiliyya is more evil because it permeates all aspects of Islamic life:

> Everything around us is jahiliyya. People's ideas and beliefs, their customs and culture, their arts and manners, their law and principles. Even much that we consider as Islamic culture—like Islamic sources, Islamic philosophy, and Islamic thought—is a product of jahiliyya. For this reason, Islamic values never properly enter our hearts, nor Islamic ideas our minds, and among us no people emerges who are of the same stature possessed by those who arose during the first generation of Muslims.[11]

Thus the pervasive influence of jahiliyya is so great, in Qutb's estimation, that Muslims can no longer think and act like Muslims. In fact, in *Signposts*, Qutb denies the existence of any Muslim societies in the modern world, maintaining that those alleging to be so are actually jahiliyya societies.[12] This is the case, he argues, because in none of them does God's authority hold sway, in none of them is God's law enforced; instead, these societies adopt other legal and cultural systems which do not allow the worship of God alone. Despite this bleak assessment, Qutb offers his readers a ray of hope. Islam can be revived, and hence jahiliyya opposed, he believes, if another pure community of believers arises as it did among the followers of Muhammad. Once formed, this vanguard (tali'a), as Qutb refers to it, will lead the Islamic revival, but it must remain alert to the dangers facing it, hence the purpose of writing Signposts.[13] In general, Qutb sees the vanguard carrying out two main tasks: first, bringing the Islamic message anew to so-called Muslims living in so-called Muslim societies; and second, systematically challenging jahiliyya institutions and leadership.

That Qutb was doubtful of the Islamic bona fides of most Muslims is evident in the instructions he gives for calling people to Islam (da'wa). "Those who call people to Islam," he writes, "must first have them accept Islam's basic article of faith [i.e., the shahada], even if these people call themselves Muslims and their birth certificates attest to their being Muslims."[14] Qutb, then, exempts no one from the demand to acknowledge the truth of Islam, but he also emphasizes that a believing community was an insufficient sign of Islam's revival. Islamic societies are obliged to act on the belief of their Muslim citizenry, creating social institutions sympathetic to Islamic teachings and enforcing Islamic law. This is only natural for the religion of Islam, which, according to Qutb, differs from other religions in that it has always been an actual movement (haraka), a divine method (manhaj rabbani) established to aid people in not only thinking about the meaning of life but actually structuring the way they live it on a daily basis. The problem, Qutb asserts, is that jahiliyya places impediments in the path of those Muslims seeking to make Islam an active social and political movement, just as it did at the time of Muhammad. For example, Muslim nay-sayers, who are actually voicing jahiliyya views, raise doubts about the feasibility of implementing an Islamic system before all the details are worked out, before the system is fully functional. This type of thinking, in Qutb's opinion, runs counter to the true divine method and hinders Islam's "passing from the stage of belief to a tangible movement."[15]

A related obstacle, for Qutb, is the false notion, fostered by orientalists and Muslim defeatists, that jihad, force or physical struggle, is incompatible with Islam. Jihad, he believes, is an integral part of the divine method taught in the Qur'an and exhibited in the life of Muhammad. It is also quite realistic (waqi'i) and practical ('amali). Like the divine method itself, it is designed to address the full range of human and social conditions. For this reason, the Islamic movement makes use of both forms of jihad, spiritual struggle and martial struggle (i.e., holy war), depending on the existing circumstances. In its confrontation with jahiliyya, Qutb writes, the movement struggles against false beliefs and ideas with preaching and teaching, but it opposes organizational systems and political authorities with physical force.[16] The resort to force or jihad with the sword is only logical, Qutb maintains, when jahiliyya is so deeply ingrained in the sociopolitical system. Mere preaching can neither dislodge jahiliyya from its seat of power, nor defend the Islamic movement and therefore Islam from the oppressive arm of jahiliyya governments.[17] And it is clear that the governments in question, the ones Qutb wishes to unseat through jihad, are those that now rule over Muslim societies, such as the government of Egypt. Thus the elaborate argument constructed by Qutb about the nature and extent of jahiliyya influence is meant to explain or justify why it is necessary to wage war against fellow Muslims.

It is necessary, according to Qutb, because the majority of Muslims but especially Muslim leadership no longer adheres to the Islam that captured the hearts and minds, and emboldened the swords, of the first generation of Muslims. In short, modern Muslims are not true Muslims, which is why they need to be brought back into the faith by the vanguard. Qutb places responsibility for this dilemma mainly on so-called Muslim leaders who have imposed foreign systems of rule on the Muslim masses, leading them astray. Instead of seeking guidance for living in the modern world in the divine system of Islam, these leaders look to secularism, nationalism, capitalism, communism, Western science, and foreign legal systems to organize and rule their societies; and in so doing, Qutb claims, they become unbelievers, or *kafirs*, for as the Qur'an (5:48) states "Whoso judges not according to what God sent down, they are the unbelievers."[18] Although Qutb only quotes this qur'anic passage verbatim once in *Signposts*, it underscores much of his criticism of contemporary Muslim society and leadership as jahiliyya. In fact, his general characterization of jahiliyya, as the tendency to supplant God's sovereignty with that of man's, has unmistakable interpretive parallels to this verse.[19] As a result, everything Qutb labels as jahiliyya—all societies, all leaders, the West, the majority of Muslims—becomes tainted by the associative quality of unbelief (*kufr*). This metonymic transference elicited by Qutb's rhetoric has grave implications, since it is unbelief and unbelievers that the Qur'an, along with the tradition, commands Muslims to fight. Qutb's vanguard, then, is not simply permitted, but obliged, to take up the sword against their fellow Muslims who are, in truth, unbelievers posing as believers.

Another association made by Qutb draws the noose of jihad even more tightly around the neck of so-called Muslim society. In a discussion of the true Muslim nation, Qutb introduces the idea of *dar al-Islam* and *dar al-harb*, or the abode of Islam and the abode of war, the binary ethical-political categories into which classical Muslim scholars divided the world. Traditionally, *dar al-Islam* is the geographic area where Islam ruled and peace prevailed, and *dar al-harb* is where the enemies of Islam ruled and war obtained. Qutb glosses *dar al-Islam* as the place "where the Muslim state is established, where God's law is enforced."[20] For him, all else is the abode of war. It follows that in Qutb's militant Islamist schema modern Muslim societies must be included in the abode of war, because in none of them, as he points out, is God's law enforced. Thus war is the dominant mode for the Muslim vanguard living in jahiliyya society.

The interpretive ease with which Qutb shifts between, and equates, jahiliyya, unbelief and the abode of war is consistent with a type of militant preaching in Egypt, which Patrick Gaffney identifies as mujahid or warrior rhetoric.[21] The mujahid rhetor addresses his audience from a perspective of unmediated insight, one in which "a logic of association dominates which does not specify an intervening interpretive phase or any distinction standing between the divine will and the human imperative."[22] Committed to practical problem solving and action, the mujahid applies the Islamic message directly to the real world, with little regard for traditional forms and classes of religious knowledge. Indeed, his knowledge stems not from sacred sources per se but "from the self-validating capacity to effectively control or manipulate the natural and social world."[23] Free-floating associations, semiotic inversions and transpositions of identity are all part of the mujahid's metonymic style which, despite its confusions and distortions, provides the necessary interpretive leeway to address an ever changing sociopolitical context. Islamist literature dealing with the greatest enemy of Islam is a good example of this style in action. Communists, Jews, Zionists, the West, Crusaders, Mongols and jahiliyya have all been named as the prime enemy, but they have also been variously grouped together or subsumed under one rubric, depending on the issue at hand and the concerns of any given Islamist thinker. These same shifts and reversals can be seen in Qutb's writings over the span of his Islamist career.[24]

Of course, Qutb's critics did not take issue with the style as much as the content of *Signposts*. But it was one of his stylistic competitors, the official religious scholar, who first raised the spectre of Kharijism in connection with the ideas expressed in Qutb's work. According to Gaffney's analysis, this type of rhetorician addresses his audience from the perspective of traditional religious learning. He is someone steeped in the literary sources and tied to a socially and often politically recognized body of scholars. His authority rests on intellectual abilities demonstrated within, and sanctioned by, established institutions of learning. Unlike the warrior's public voice, the voice with which the scholar speaks is always mediated—through the tradition, through the sources, through religious institutions and, more often than not in Egypt, through the political establishment which supports and controls religious institutions. This mediating tendency is also reflected in the operational style of the official scholar whose model of discourse is the metaphor, in contrast to the metonymic style adopted by the warrior. The metaphoric style is exercised through the traditional tools of the scholar ("principles of rational exegesis, appeal to precedent, analogy, and implicit comparison"[25]), which order the otherwise incoherent world according to the principles of traditional Islamic knowledge, and which thereby safeguard and promote the elitist profession to which the scholar is attached. The projection of Kharijism onto the ideas expressed by Qutb in *Signposts* and the agenda of the Muslim Brothers is an example of the metaphoric style in action.

The Response of Official Islam

As expected, initial reactions to the conspiracy were decidedly negative, especially in the government-controlled media, which, like the traditional religious scholar, has official and semi-official capacities. Reactions were also an interesting mix of political and religious commentary, reflecting the degree to which the interests of the state and official or institutional Islam had merged in Nasser's Egypt. Rhetorical references to Kharijism in modern Egypt emerged out of and expressed this convergence of interests, even though over time its appeal spread to a wider religious audience. Despite the prominence of the Kharijites in the tradition, the image of these prototypical rebels did not dominate the first accounts of the 1965 Muslim Brother plot against Nasser. Only gradually did Kharijism evolve as a critical rejoinder to the ideas and actions of Qutb and other Islamists. Indeed, the accusation of Kharijism was a learned response to militant Islamists; and those who instructed the wider Egyptian public about the appropriateness of the Kharijite comparison were the official religious scholars, the bearers of traditional learning. Official religious scholars had at their disposal a number of forums for communicating their disapproval of the Muslim Brother conspirators. We will examine three such forums, selected because they represent different levels and modes of official religious discourse. Our intent here is to draw attention to the content of the criticism and the context in which it was made. Both are essential for understanding the way the accusation of Kharijism was transmitted and received in Egyptian culture.

Popular Media and Popular Images

The first example is taken from the popular media and consists of several articles appearing in 1965 in two consecutive issues of *Akhir Sa'a*, or *Final Hour*, a weekly news and entertainment magazine.[26] In one of these articles, the Sheikh of al-Azhar, Hasan Ma'mun, the leading voice of official Islam in Egypt, offers his opinion of the Brothers and tries to correct some of what he claims is the false information they spread about Islam. This series of articles in *Akhir Sa'a* is not in any way unique to what was appearing at the time in other publications, although the pieces are no doubt less thorough than accounts in the popular daily *al-Ahram*. The Kharijites were never mentioned in the magazine's coverage of the plot, either by the staff writers or most notably Sheikh Ma'mun. This, too, was typical of early reports. The fact that the Kharijite connection was not well-developed at this stage of the public debate over the Brothers is important for two reasons. First, it emphasizes that, in the mid-1960s, the charge of Kharijism as a polemic against radical Islamists was not an automatic, unthinking response on the part of Egyptian Muslims, even those well-trained in Islamic learning. In contrast, by the 1970s, Kharijism was to become a mainstay of both religious commentaries and press reports on the radicals. Second, it forces a comparison between Kharijism and other rhetorical tools that were used to deal with the accused plotters.

The concern expressed in the popular media centered primarily on the danger posed by the Muslim Brothers to the good order of society and the Egyptian way of life, with a heavy emphasis on the Brothers' secret activities and tendency toward violence. In keeping with the popular appeal of mass circulation dailies and weeklies, the stories were pitched at a level accessible to a diverse public, and photographs accompanied, if not dominated, written accounts of the plot. Readers pressed for time, or even the illiterate, could follow the narrative and the nature of the threat by viewing scenes of the plotters, raided apartments, weapons and religious literature. In many instances, news was secondary to a vigorous denunciation of those who had yet to go on trial for a crime, let alone be found guilty. The articles in September 15th issue of *Akhir Sa'a* are a case in point. No doubt assuming more complete coverage in daily newspapers, the first piece relates details of the plot in a captioned photo montage, while the magazine's editor opines on the asocial, immoral behavior of the Brotherhood. In a blatant play on his readers' sensibilities, the editor juxtaposes his own editorial assignment at the time when the plot was discovered, that is, reporting on "smiling children," with the deadly activities of the Muslim Brothers. A series of dramatic comparisons between the life and love of children and the destruction and hatred of the Brothers clearly indicates that those who care about the lives and future of children reject the Brothers. Credit for the defeat of the Brothers is given to the Egyptian people (al-sha'b) and the revolution (al-thawra), a collective force that effectively leveled "a shout in the face of the conspirators: Don't kill our children!" The stated intention of the editor is "to repeat the same shout."[27]

This emotionally laden commentary is followed by an equally one-sided sketch of the ideas and history of the Brothers since 1954, a time referred to as "the new beginning of the terrorist organization (al-tanzim al-irhabi)." And a time, not coincidentally, which marked Nasser's emergence as the real power behind the revolution. Here, not one positive image of the Muslim Brothers is allowed to emerge. The Brothers are portrayed as a monolithic movement, with no divergence of opinion or disagreement over ideas and tactics among the membership. They are all, according to this sketch, murderers bent on destroying Egypt and Egyptians. The basis for the Brothers' discontent is largely ignored. The only unfiltered Muslim Brother opinion presented is an extract from Qutb's Signposts, a book cast as a tangible demonstration of their "terrorist orientation." The brief quote speaks of the pervasive reality of jahiliyya throughout the world, that all societies are jahiliyya.[28] In other words, it is Qutb's dramatic judgment about Egyptian society, not the reason for the judgment, that serves to explain why the Brothers took up arms, why they sundered the Qur'an. Although the piece never directly denies the Muslim identity of the Brothers, it does question their adherence to basic Islamic teachings: "Their principal maxim is no longer 'In the name of God, the Merciful and Compassionate.' Rather, they begin [by saying] 'Murder, immediately!' "

In addition to their underscoring misguided religious views, the magazine also presents a more familiar and, given the political climate of Egypt, more plausible explanation for the Brothers' actions. It introduces the idea that imperialist forces are behind the conspiracy. This connection is made through the figure of Sa'id Ramadan, a Muslim Brother whom the Egyptian government had charged with treason in 1954 prior to the assassination attempt on Nasser. Living abroad at the time, Ramadan supposedly solicited donations from foreign powers and used the money to foment criminal deeds in Egypt.[29] The article accuses the Brothers of having never ended their "alliances" with these outside powers, making their then-current activities liable to the same charge of treason. No actual proof is offered for the various accusations made against the Brothers, and none is probably expected by the magazine's readers. Much of what passed for public political discourse in Egypt at the time occurred in coded language understandable to Egyptians and other Arab nationals. It consisted of innuendo and name calling, polemical associations intended to identify and impugn enemies of the nation. The enemies were, for the most part, foreign powers and ideologies, but, as in any good conspiracy theory, agents supposedly operated on the inside. In the 1954 incident, the press had trotted out a list of these names to condemn the Brothers:

> 'Evidence', sometimes old, sometimes new, was produced to show
> that the Brothers were the agents and lackeys of the monarchy, the
> old ruling classes, the British, the French, the Zionists, Western
> Imperialism, communism, and capitalism.[30]

As indicated previously, many of the names on this list had been used by the Brothers in their various polemical writings. Thus, for a period, the enemies of Islam named by the Brothers and the enemies of the state named by Nasser's propaganda machine overlapped. There was also considerable overlap between the methods of discourse adopted by the Brothers and those of the state. The Revolutionary Command Council, the institutional base of the Free Officers, was trying to break with the ancien régime and set a new course for Egypt. So, much like the warrior style adopted by the Brothers, it did not concern itself with consistency of thought. Action and results were the more pressing concerns.

The willingness of *Akhir Sa'a* and the Egyptian press to defend the revolution that brought Nasser to power and attack its reputed opponents stemmed from both the popularity and power of the revolutionary government. The Egyptian army enjoyed a level of institutional trust far exceeding that of the palace, although it was not known for its nationalist fervor. The Free Officers drew on that trust, naming as their leader General Muhammad Neguib, an older and more experienced officer and hero of the Palestine conflict. Nasser eventually emerged as the real power behind the coup, and he went on to earn a reputation as primus inter pares among Arab nationalist leaders and defender of the Third World against imperialist aggression, roles which brought him the respect of Egyptian intellectuals and the adoration of the masses. Even after his fall from grace following the 1967 war with Israel, he maintained his grip on the hearts, if not the minds, of Egyptians, as witnessed by the unprecedented outpouring of emotion at his death. The Free Officers, however, were not prepared to rely solely on the good will of the press. Rather, they wished to ensure it. From the outset of the revolution, the media, both public and private, came under the direct supervision of the regime. Party presses were shut down, and those publications that remained open were heavily censored. *Akhir Sa'a* was a private publication, owned and operated by 'Ali and Mustafa Amin. The Amin brothers had welcomed the revolution and cooperated with the regime. Over the years Mustafa Amin developed a personal relationship with Nasser and continued to support him despite press nationalization measures in 1960.[31]

Under Nasser, then, state interests overrode concerns about balanced reporting and journalistic integrity. In fact, the media in general often blatantly functioned as an outlet for state propaganda. *Akhir Sa'a*'s interview with the Sheikh of al-Azhar must be seen against this backdrop: his opinions are given weight and attention because they support the government line on the Muslim Brother plot. Ostensibly, Hasan al-Ma'mun appears in the magazine because he holds the highest office of any Muslim religious authority in Egypt, perhaps the Islamic world. The interviewer goes to great lengths to mention the Sheikh's various titles and professional positions. In the context of *Akhir Sa'a*'s overall coverage, however, it is clear that his Islamic authority and learning are being paraded for public consumption. That is, the image rather than the substance of Islam has priority here. Once again, the visuals reveal the subtext. Sheikh al-Ma'mun's face dominates the first page, with the words "the Grand Imam speaks" to one side. A few pages later a caricature of a bearded Islamist holding a Qur'an and prayer beads is shown. A disembodied hand lifts his *galabiyya* to reveal feet made of missiles, legs of rifles and buttocks in the shape of bombs. The brief caption reads "the concealer." The religious message conveyed by the magazine, such as it is, lies in the very contrast between these images, between established religious authority and religious impostors bent on violence. Established authority wins out, but it owes its victory to the filtered media environment in which it appears, an environment which is itself controlled by the government.

Given in response to a series of questions posed by the interviewer, the Sheikh's remarks are terse and in many ways theologically generic. The rhetorical framework established by the interviewer is that the Sheikh is putting to rest rumors or false information spread by the Brothers. The responses elicited from the Sheikh are intended to juxtapose the goals and methods of the Brothers, whom the interviewer constantly refers to as terrorists and criminals, with those of true Islam. Once completed, the article lays out the following complex of contrasting views: whereas the Brothers believe that true Muslims must be members of their organization, and that Islam is not to be found apart from the Brothers, Islam in truth does not divide Muslim against Muslim with such exclusive organizations; instead it promotes equality and good relations among all Muslims. Whereas the Brothers seek to compel others to submit to their ideas, Islam advocates freedom of the individual and rejects the use of force. Whereas the Brothers deny the legitimacy of human rulers, Islam recognizes the need for Muslims to subject themselves to fellow humans as long as they rule according to God's commands. Whereas the Brothers set high standards for judging whether someone can be considered a Muslim, Islam is more reasonable, demanding only that one adhere to the five pillars of Islam.

Throughout his interview, Sheikh al-Ma'mun never mentions the Brothers by name. Nor does he indicate that he has read Qutb's Islamist manifesto, *Signposts*. This lends his remarks a rather timeless quality, as if they would be relevant for Muslims in similar circumstances in any age, which is the aura that often surrounds traditional religious truths. But the eternal verities of Islam are not in and of themselves what the magazine seems interested in communicating to its audience. For when the magazine deploys Sheikh al-Ma'mun to counter the errors of the Brothers, the impact is not to promote the moral and social importance of Islam as much as it is to dismiss it from the political scene. By challenging the Brothers' claims and undercutting their religious justification for opposition, the Sheikh proves that Islam does not support the conspiracy. In addition, based on his acknowledgment that Muslims need to submit to rulers as long as they are obedient to God's command, he indicates that Nasser's regime is Islamically sound and therefore owed the loyalty and obedience of Egyptians. Thus the functional relevancy of his remarks lies in their affirmation that Islam does not interfere in politics, except to the extent that Islam verifies this fact or contributes to the regime's authority. What remains of the Brothers' agenda once their religious justification has been removed is unfounded violence. The magazine, then, introduces a representative of official Islam into its coverage to clarify that the real conflict is not religious but political. It is not a debate between the Sheikh of al-Azhar and the Muslim Brothers but rather between the revolutionary government of the Egyptian state and its subversive opponents. And the incessant focus on terrorism by *Akhir Sa'a*, and the rest of the media, is intended to skew the outcome of this debate.

Throughout these articles, the Brothers are tagged with the label "terrorist." The Brothers who foment social divisions are called "philosophers of the terrorist organization," an organization that Sayyid Qutb and his brother Muhammad are accused of leading; relatives of Hasan Hudaybi, Supreme Guide of the Muslim Brothers after the death of al-Banna, are linked to the financing of "terrorist activities"; and Sayyid Qutb is said to be "president of

the terrorist brotherhood organization." Sheikh al-Ma'mun does not introduce the term in his interview, but elsewhere he spoke of the Brothers as
"medieval terrorists."[32] In the political climate of Nasser's Egypt, the charge
of terrorism carried no overt religious significance. Instead, it denoted any
number of activities that could be viewed as threatening to the political and
social order of Egypt. State authorities were constantly unearthing terrorist
plots against the regime, usually fomented by foreign powers; and the media
was all too eager to play up these threats and the government's prowess at
thwarting them.[33] The responsibility for preventing such deeds or punishing
those who commit them fell to the state, which is why terrorism has an
inherent political valence. Terrorism or the accusation of it also has benefits
for the state. As one student of political violence has observed:

> The resonance of the word *terrorist* makes it an often valuable tool in
> political conflict. If the tactics and organizational entity of rival po-
> litical forces can be described as terrorist and that label can be made
> to stick, two consequences follow: no pressure for concessions on
> political grievances and acceptability of the use of ruthless means and
> suspension of normal constitutional limitations to inflict pain and
> death.[34]

The name Kharijite came to have much the same resonance in Egyptian
discourse.

In a sense, all terrorism is political and directed at the state since state
authority and interests are subverted by it. The terrorist acts attributed to the
Muslim Brothers were obviously understood to be religiously motivated,
which is why the Sheikh of al-Azhar's opinion was solicited. The Society of
Muslim Brothers was founded on religious principles and it was engaged in
health and social welfare activities based on these principles. Nasser's regime,
however, neither respected nor tolerated any rationalization for political action
that challenged its hold on power, whether it resulted in violence or not.
Sheikh al-Ma'mun's comments, along with those of other religious figures,
were meant to deny the ideological right of Islam to challenge the political
status quo. And without an Islamic legitimacy that might trump state authority, the Brothers' conspiracy was reduced to just another politically inspired act of terrorism to which the strong arm of the state needed to respond.
Thus the Sheikh's scholarly opinion became an extension of state propaganda,
solidifying the power and authority of the modern Egyptian nation-state.

Through its control of the media, then, the state used the authority of
official Islam to restrict Islam's place in Egypt's civil society. Although the
Sheikh of al-Azhar may have been representing traditional Islamic views in

his condemnation of the Brothers, the practical outcome of his pronouncements was modern and secular. The positive image of Islam perpetuated in
the popular media was an Islam subservient to the state, one that rejects the
use of violence, remains obedient to state authority, emphasizes faith and
social welfare over political involvement, and defends the gains of the revolution. The filter of the media promoted this variant of Islam and deplored
others that exceeded the ad hoc participatory civil limits established by the
government.

The Official Review of Signposts Along the Road

The institution that represents official Islam in Egypt did not depend solely
on the popular media to communicate its views. It had its own publication out-
lets that catered to a more religiously conscious clientele. It was in one such
outlet that the first authoritative statement linking Qutb with the Kharijites
appeared. Some four months after news of the conspiracy broke, a lengthy
review of Sayyid Qutb's work Signposts Along the Road was printed in Minbar
al-Islam, a monthly religious journal published by the Supreme Council of
Islamic Affairs. The reviewer was Sheikh 'Abd al-Latif Sibki, who was then
head of the fatwa commission. As in other assessments of this work, the ideas
and views expressed in it were ascribed to all Muslim Brothers, not just a
militant faction of the movement. The subtitle of the review in Minbar al-
Islam makes this clear when it describes the book as "the constitution of the
depraved brothers."[35] Despite its more scholarly facade, the journal, like the
popular media, was not immune to relying on crude visuals to communicate
its views. The heading of the review contains a rough graphic depicting a book
consumed by flames; a devilish figure with horns and a trident adorns its
cover. The demonization of Islamists was a common counterresponse of the
religious and political establishment in Egypt, which saw itself being demo-
nized by Islamists.

At the outset, Sibki cautions readers, particularly the young and ingenu-
ous, not to be taken in by the book. It may seem to advocate Islam, he maintains, but it has an "inflammatory style." Citing extensively from throughout
Signposts, Sibki's stated goal is to provide readers with "a conception of
(Qutb's) depraved attitudes." He focuses his critique on the twin concepts that
drove Qutb's work—jahiliyya and hakimiyya—and the activist means by which
Qutb proposed to overcome the crisis of Islam—the vanguard and jihad. Although Sibki does not get into a discussion about whether jahiliyya is a specific
period or a condition, his dismissive attitude indicates that for him, unlike

Qutb, the former is the case. He disdainfully points out that, according to the book, all things Islamic seem to have been part of jahiliyya until Sayyid Qutb entered the scene to set them right. No doubt believing that readers will reject the notion that jahiliyya surrounds them and dominates their lives, Sibki, eschews any detailed analysis. For the most part, he is content to cite without comment several extracted passages dealing with the accusation. Qutb's views on hakimiyya, or sovereignty, by contrast, draw a number of responses from Sibki, the most notable being the charge of Kharijism.

Sibki introduces the idea of the Kharijites when analyzing a passage from the chapter entitled "The Nature of the Qur'anic Method," in which Qutb laid out the content and purpose of the qur'anic message during the Meccan period. The immediate context is a section of the chapter in which Qutb discusses why God had chosen not to induce Muhammad to resort to Arab nationalism (*qawmiyya 'arabiyya*) as a means of appealing to and organizing Arab tribes. In the book, Qutb claims that such an appeal would have been successful because Arabs were exhausted from tribal warfare; that Arab nationalism would have allowed the Arabs to defeat the Romans and Persians sooner, thereby regaining Arab lands. But, Qutb continues, God chose not to let this happen because (following Sibki's quote of Qutb):

> The way [of God] was not to free the earth from Roman or Persian tyranny in order to establish Arab tyranny. All tyranny is oppressive! The earth belongs to God.... The way was not for man to be liberated from one tyranny only to become subject to another.... Man is the servant of God alone.... There is no sovereignty but God's, no law except that from God, no authority of one man over another.... This is the way.[36]

Arab nationalism, then, according to Qutb, was just another oppressive system of social organization, one that was contrary to God's design. Islam did propose a type of nationality (*jinsiyya*), Qutb concedes in *Signposts*, but it was based on faith, not on race and color. Despite references to Persia and Rome, Qutb is clearly writing about Muslim societies in the twentieth century, particularly Egypt, not seventh-century Arabia. He projects a nineteenth-century concept of nationalism back into the first century of Islam to condemn the modern division of Muslim peoples into isolated nation-states. He employs the same tactic against socialism when a few paragraphs later he states that the message of Islam delivered by Muhammad was not an appeal to the equal distribution of wealth, to a type of class consciousness.[37] For Qutb, the time of the Prophet provides the moral vantage point to criticize aspects of Nasser's secular political ideology. To achieve vastly different ends, Sibki, too, speaks through the images of the past when he invokes the Kharijites. Repeating Qutb's phrase that there is no sovereignty but that of God's, Sibki states that these are "words spoken by the Kharijites of old."[38] By this, he no doubt means to suggest a parallel between the notion of sovereignty found in Qutb's phrase and the notion of judgment contained in the famous Kharijite watchword "There is no judgment but God's." "Sovereignty" (hakimiyya) and "judgment" (hukm) are cognates deriving from the same Arabic root (ha-ka-ma). The overlap in meaning is similar enough to allow Sibki to equate the contents of the two phrases and imply that the same fundamental claim is at stake. And to further burden Qutb and the Muslim Brothers with the Kharijite label, Sibki recalls the response of the caliph 'Ali to the "no judgment" shibboleth of the Kharijites: "These are words of truth intended to deceive."[39] This phrase, then, is made to apply to the modern manifestation of Kharijism just as it did the Kharijites of old.

In addition to the explicit comments indicated above, Sibki hints at other parallels between Qutb and the Kharijites. Most obvious is the tendency to provoke *fitna* or civil discord. As discussed in the chapter 1, the original Kharijites had emerged out of, and contributed to, the first internal crisis of the Islamic polity, which is commonly referred to as the first civil war. It was, Sibki maintains, the phrase uttered by the Kharijites that caused "a split within Islamic society and division among the ranks"—the same phrase now supposedly uttered by Qutb. Sibki associates Qutb with the same destructive tendency of fitna, saying that, although Islam rejects it absolutely, Qutb wants to bring it about on a grand scale. In Sibki's analysis, fitna seems to be the inevitable consequence of Qutb's confused and idealistic view of sovereignty. Relegating sovereignty only to God is problematic because it undermines the practical necessity of human rule, which, according to Sibki, Islam readily acknowledges. The Qur'an, he states, clearly recognizes the validity of Muslim rulership, and it places obligations on both the ruler and the ruled: sovereigns must treat their subjects fairly and subjects must obey their leaders. Contrary to Qutb's unrealistic expectations, Islam does not require Muslim rulers to be infallible. They do and will make mistakes, Sibki concedes, but with the aid of the Qur'an, the sunna, and learned Muslims, leaders will stay on the straight path. Moreover, Sibki adds, real-life situations demand that rulers use both religious law and secular law (*qanun*) to govern human affairs. Thus Sibki is willing to admit that Islamic law, the shari'a, has its limitations, an admission that Islamists have largely been unwilling to concede, perhaps more for polemical than religiolegal reasons.

Sibki upholds here what has come to be the standard Sunni line on sovereignty and authority within the economy of the Islamic system of rule.

On a personal, spiritual level, God may indeed be the only sovereign, as Qutb and the Kharijites seem to maintain, but in the everyday life of the Islamic community, Muslims must submit to their political leaders, despite their sometimes-disturbing behavior. To avoid civil unrest, obedience to one's rulers and communal unity must take priority over individual claims to religious truth. Or looked at another way, Islam places limits on religious and political dissent, on the means one can use to change the religious and political status quo. In his review of *Signposts*, Sibki condemns a particularly egregious violation of these limits. In a series of articles that appear in *Minbar al-Islam* for several months following the review, he takes up the etiquette of religious propaganda (da'wa) in more general terms.[40] His suggested means of propaganda, not surprising, avoid direct challenges to the state. Sibki also wishes to avoid confrontations with other (religious) peoples and other countries, which is why he finds Qutb's linkage between propaganda and jihad so troublesome.

For Qutb, as mentioned previously, jihad is a necessary outgrowth of da'wa. It is required to confront those people and places that remain resistant to Islam. More specifically, Qutb believes that jihad applies wherever jahiliyya society dominates, which turns out to be Muslim and non-Muslim societies alike. Sibki either overlooks or is unaware of this aspect of Qutb's argument. He expresses more interest in the implications of Qutb's thinking for relations with foreign powers. The issue arises in a passage in which, in Sibki's estimation, Qutb relates jihad and da'wa in such a way that can only lead to war, in a way that would force the Islamic homeland into war even when it is clearly in a state of peace.[41] Here again, Sibki points out that the Qur'an, sunna, and general Islamic teachings do not call for such a violent outcome. Islam only demands war under certain circumstances, for example, to suppress fitna or to defend the propagation of Islam. On the one hand, Islam's primary goal, according to Sibki, is that of peace: it advocates peace, and it attempts to make peace with other peacemakers, regardless of their religious affiliation. Supporters of *Signposts*, on the other hand, do not have the same vision of Islam. For them, Sibki writes, "Islam is a religion that assaults every religious faction, in every country at any time."[42]

The tactic adopted by Sibki throughout the review is to contrast two types of Islam. There is the Islam represented by Qutb and those who adhere to his analysis in *Signposts*, an Islam that foments violence, pits Muslim against Muslim, and contradicts traditional Islamic teachings. Then there is the Islam represented by Sibki, an Islam that embodies peace, cooperation, and the true essence of the sacred sources. The goal of this rhetoric is not to affirm the point often made by Western scholars that there are several Islams, that religious traditions are never monolithic. Rather, it is to argue that Qutb's is an Islam in name only. In fact, Sibki accuses Qutb several times of having confiscated or usurped Islam, which turns out to be the "crime" in which official Islam is most interested. For from the perspective of official religious functionaries, Islam in its public or civil expression is their area of responsibility. They are the authorized teachers of Islam and thus the arbitrators of Islamic discourse. When Qutb and the Brothers spoke and acted publicly in the name of Islam, they challenged that authority and preempted the discourse for their own ends. Sibki's review, then, should be viewed as having a dual purpose: first, to re-affirm the Islamic ethos that the Brothers had breached in their conspiracy; and second, to defend the role and status of the maintainers and transmitters of that ethos. Both purposes are in accord with the scholar's style outlined earlier and are furthered by the metaphoric reference to the Kharijites.

The official scholar uses the metaphor to mediate between the collective tradition, of which he is the recognized master, and the everyday life of Is-lamic society. His task is to make the community of Muslims attentive to the teachings of the tradition by making the tradition relevant to the issues confronting the community. Sibki accomplished this task, in part, by calling up the example of the Kharijites. The rebellious and uncompromising ten-dencies of the Kharijites seemed to fit precisely with the path adopted by the Muslim Brothers, at least when historical particulars are reduced to sketchy, impressionistic generalities. The story of 'Ali also provided an apt historical anecdote demonstrating that past leaders had to face challenges identical or similar to what the leaders of Egypt were now facing. The Kharijite metaphor allowed Sibki to take control of the situation, rhetorically; and he did so by mediating the past and, at the same time, demonstrating his importance and standing in the community. Simple as this may sound, it was not destined to be so. Sibki could have selected a different metaphor. If, as Kenneth Burke has written, "metaphor is a device for seeing something *in terms of* something else,"[43] then surely Sibki could have chosen to see the Brothers through a more benign or socially acceptable metaphor. It makes a great deal of dif-ference, after all, whether one calls those who engage in violence "confused youth" instead of "Kharijites"; just as it makes a great deal of difference whether one describes one's society as Muslim instead of jahiliyya, or one's leaders as rightful Muslims instead of tyrants. The metaphor one decides upon—and it is clearly a decision—is important because of its normative im-pact. It interprets and judges situations, and these judgments can in turn lead to a prescribed set of actions. Or as one group of concerned social scientists studying American culture has put it, "finding the right metaphor . . . [is] critical to the outcome."[44]

Although the content of the metaphor "Kharijite" was culturally encoded in the early history of Islam's intellectual development, Sibki's motivation to invoke the Kharijites unquestionably arose in the modern context of Egypt. He selected the metaphor, in other words, because he thought it apt and hoped it would bring about the outcome that he desired—one that includes but also goes beyond the discrediting and isolation of radicalized Islamist elements. In his review, Sibki only mentioned the deviant thinking of Qutb and its dangerous consequences as motives for introducing the Kharijites. Yet his decision-making process cannot be separated from the office he held as official religious scholar. For him, ethical judgments were professional judgments, and vice versa. Moreover, since the state under Nasser came to have such a strong hand in all professional organizations, normative Islamic judgments were potentially highly politicized. Based on its formulation during the classical period, the relationship between rulers and representatives of the religious establishment was to be one of respectful distance. The religious elite would show due deference to rulers in political matters, and rulers would avoid interfering in religious affairs. On occasion this relationship broke down, but in large part it held because both parties understood the advantage of avoiding conflict and thereby maintaining their respective fields of authority. Under Nasser, the traditional rules of engagement were rewritten. The extent to which the state came to dominate Egyptian society, ideologically and otherwise, and how this affected relations between religion and state, was taken up in the last chapter. The remainder of this chapter further documents the emergence of accusations of Kharijism in the official religious response to Qutb and the Brothers, and the convergence of this rhetoric with state interests.

Though present, this convergence was only hinted at in Sibki's review. In his critique of the Brothers, Sibki followed the traditional protocol of an official religious scholar; he advocated obedience to rulers and nonviolence but did not champion particular leaders or their policies. His summary remarks diverged from this policy, however. There he asserted that the revolution had achieved glorious results "in all areas of life." In contrast, the Brothers' message led to the destruction of the revolution; it also undermined the nation, "reducing it to disparity and exposing it to adversities that cause the heart of humanity to bleed."[45] Such unqualified support for the revolution and defense of the nation—the modern Egyptian nation, not the Muslim nation—went hand in hand with official Islam's condemnation of the Brothers. It reached a crescendo in 1966, the same year Qutb and the other accused conspirators came to trial, with the publication of a collection of essays entitled *Ra'y al-din fi ikhwan al-shaytan* or *The Opinion of Religion Concerning the Brothers of Satan*.[46]

Kharijites, Citizens, and the Modern Egyptian State

Like the journal in which Sibki's review appeared, *The Opinion of Religion* was published by the Supreme Council of Islamic Affairs. The work is divided into two parts. The first is composed of twenty-five essays (previously published in other venues), written by both sheikhs and lay commentators, concerning the dangerous implications of the Brothers' ideas and actions. The second part is a report (*bayan*) from the Supreme Council that presents a detailed accounting of the outreach efforts made by Egypt to spread the message of Islam at home and abroad. The report contains lists of the religious institutions founded and the journals and magazines published, along with information about the countries and languages in which these efforts were carried out. Its particulars are not directly relevant to the focus of this study, but the religious legitimacy that the report lends Nasser's regime hints at the political line that underlay the official "opinion of religion" in the essays. The introduction to the report reads in part: The Council is pleased to present to Muslims some of the results produced by the revolution of 23 July 1952 in the service of Islam and Muslims at home and abroad.[47] According to the Supreme Council, the Egyptian state deserves a great deal of credit for putting itself in the service of Islam. Viewed critically, however, the essays paint a different picture of the relationship between Islam and the Egyptian state than the one depicted in the report. Taken as a whole, they suggest that the revolution didn't serve Islam as much as Islam was made to serve the revolution.

The point here is to glean from the work as a whole how, under the authority of official Islam, the image of the Kharijites was initially deployed against the Brothers and to what end. Based on the traditional image of the Kharijites, the issue might seem to warrant little discussion. As an anti-model of rebellious sectarianism, the Kharijites serve simply as a counter to Muslim zealots who rise up against lawful Muslim political authorities. In essence, "Kharijite" is an Islamic category of thought that carries a religious judgment. Those so designated are heterodox, or heteroprax, Muslims whose status in the community is in jeopardy because of their judgment and action against fellow Muslims, especially against rulers. The image of the Kharijites, then, speaks to the issue of who is a Muslim, who meets the criteria for membership in the Islamic community. The Kharijites epitomize those who demand maximalist conditions and an exclusivist community of true believers, a position in stark contrast to the mainstream Sunni tradition that advances minimalist conditions and a more inclusive society. Although the essayists who introduce the Kharijites into their anti-Brotherhood discourse are clearly drawing on these ideas, an intellectual strain emerges in their rhetorical reference to the Kharijites when this traditional religious metaphor is adapted to the political life of modern Egypt.

It is primarily the sheikhs, the representatives of official Islam, who evoke the Kharijites in their comments. It is also the sheikhs who are most reluctant to enter directly into the political fray. Instead, they often back into the subject after first expounding on some of the relevant truths of Islam. The essay of Sheikh 'Abdallah al-Mashad, for example, begins by discussing two of the most important blessings of Islam—peace and security.[48] God provided these blessings through the religion of Islam, according to Sheikh 'Abdallah, and they are available to the Muslim community for its obedience to God's commands. Anyone who brings discord to the community, who interferes with its peace and security, is "following in the footsteps of Satan." In the past, Sheikh 'Abdallah points out, the Muslim community has witnessed such discord. It was caused by criminal elements such as Ibn Sabah, the Jewish convert to Islam who is associated with the rise of Shi'ism, and the Kharijites. After elaborating on the historic dangers of such criminals and terrorists and the divine injunction to deal with them harshly, Sheikh 'Abdallah turns his attention to "our Islamic, Arab country." In the current circumstances, which the Sheikh characterizes as "warlike conditions," Egypt must be unified in its outlook and in its support of its leaders. Egypt must also be ready to defend itself, exercising its martial capabilities and drawing on the power of religion. The linkage between Sheikh 'Abdallah's traditional teachings and his observations on the contemporary situation is more implied than stated. Readers make the logical leap dictated by the context. The historical examples proposed by an official interpreter of the tradition, by definition, apply. Egypt must defend itself against the warlike conditions created by Kharijite-like rebels who spread dissension and discord.

The opening essay, written by the Sheikh of al-Azhar, Hasan Ma'mun, takes a similar approach to linking the Muslim Brother conspirators to the Kharijites. True to his official role, the Sheikh speaks of the need for al-Azhar to fulfill its historic teaching obligations, to inform the Muslim community of what is and is not valid in Islam. His main concern is the inexperienced Muslims, those who may be deceived by those calling for war in the name of Islam. Egyptian youth, he maintains, must be protected from the influence of the criminal element that assaults Islam. To this end, he offers a mini catechismal lesson intended to address the various errors at issue. He goes on to explain the fundamentals of Islam, the requirements for membership in the Muslim community, quoting the famous hadith that portrays Muhammad being instructed by the Angel Gabriel about the five pillars of Islam, faith (iman), and right action (*ihsan*). For Sheikh Ma'mun, these basic beliefs and rituals are the historic obligations established by the example of the Prophet Muhammad, and they are the only ones that al-Azhar is prepared to uphold and enforce. The conspirators, by contrast, make stipulations, such as rebellion, that exceed the limits of Islam. They also take action against other Muslims based on these stipulations that are unwarranted and un-Islamic; shedding blood, terrorism, and assassination are all rejected by the Sheikh as legitimate examples of Muslim behavior.[49] Such religious insights are in line with his earlier interview in the magazine *Akhir Sa'a*, in which he maintained a refined distance from the events in question by sermonizing on established Islamic views of rulership, tolerance, and rebellion. Toward the end of the essay, however, he moves beyond the abstract world of Islamic doctrine and ethics to address the impact of imperialism on modern Egyptian society, a problem that he correlates with the Muslim Brothers and the Kharijites.

In the recent past, the Sheikh writes, imperialism dominated the affairs of Egypt, consuming its resources, destroying its profits, and hindering its progress. And this threat still looms, he warns, for if Egyptians fail to recognize the schemes hatched against them, they will revert back to the prerevolutionary ways of "dependency, feudalism and capitalism."[50] Out of gratitude to God for saving Egypt from this fate, the Sheikh advises his fellow Egyptians "to appoint judges over every sinful traitor," a suggestive reference to the means by which the authorities should deal with those involved in the conspiracy, that is, the Muslim Brothers. For the Sheikh, the conspirators are not imperialists per se, but imperialism provides the modern political backdrop against which their activities must be understood. Hence any threat to the unity of the nation and the harmony of society evokes the recent experience of foreign domination and plays into the hands of would-be oppressors. If not imperialists, who are the conspirators, in the Sheikh's estimation? The notion of appointing judges gives us a hint. At the battle of Siffin in 656 c.e., it will be remembered, the Kharijites emerged out of 'Ali's camp after judges or arbiters were appointed to resolve the conflict. Calling for judges to be placed over sinful traitors, then, might be seen as a subtle allusion to Kharijite origins. The allusion is confirmed when, without citing 'Ali by name, the Sheikh paraphrases his warning about the famous Kharijite watchword. "Beware, Muslims," he writes, "you are taken in by words of truth intended to deceive."[51] Thus, although not mentioning the Kharijites, the Sheikh manages to link the Muslim Brothers, and other like-minded sinful traitors, with the early rebellious sect.

For representatives of official Islam such as sheikhs 'Abdallah and Ma'mun, the past is a natural starting point for any kind of reasoning. Even though the object of this reasoning is to isolate, if not eliminate, the Muslim Brothers, a modern movement, the path to this goal proceeds through the founding model and sources of Islamic authority. A cursory glance at the essays demonstrates, however, that the Muslim Brothers are only part of the problem as envisioned by these thinkers. That is, the authority of the past is marshaled not merely to condemn the Brothers but also to vilify a number of political forces and ideologies that have shaped the modern history of Egypt and the Middle East. And in many cases these other forces and ideologies are correlated or identified with the Kharijites. Sheikh Ma'mun, for example, confronts his readers with a highly charged, though largely unsubstantiated, triangulation of identities. Imperialists, Muslim Brothers, and Kharijites are all conflated into the same immoral universe. Another sheikh, writing under the heading "What does the Qur'an Command Regarding Evil Doers," claims that the Brothers are friends of the imperialists and Israel, while they model their behavior on the Barmakids (one of the regional families that rose to power in the Abbasid period) and the Kharijites. Like the Barmakids, the Brothers relied on daring to gain power; and like the Kharijites, they adopted horrible methods to achieve their ends. Of all the influences, it is the Kharijites, for this commentator, who stand out because the Qur'an (5:36) prescribed a clear way to deal with them:

> This is the recompense of those who fight against God and His
> Messenger, and hasten about the earth, to do corruption there: they
> shall be slaughtered, or crucified, or their hands and feet shall al-
> ternately be struck off, or they shall be banished from the land.[52]

By accusing the Muslim Brothers in the subtitle of the piece of "spreading corruption in the land," the author makes his argument quite apparent: God commanded the fate of the Kharijites in the above quoted verse; and since the Muslim Brothers are like the Kharijites, they, too, should suffer this fate.

The charge of Kharijism, in theory, is an expression of the operational style of official religious scholars, whose task it is to order the otherwise incoherent world according to the principles of Islamic knowledge: militant Islamists create disorder in the Muslim community, and order is restored by categorizing this behavior as Kharijite and acting on this categorization. In *The Opinion of Religion*, however, official scholars employ the accusation of Kharijism for purposes other than the condemnation of Islamist militancy and according to principles unrelated to Islamic knowledge. This is evident in the tension that emerges, in and throughout the essays, between the traditional Islamic idiom and the modern political idiom of Arab nationalism. The traditional Islamic idiom is the language of faith and religious knowledge, rooted in the Qur'an, sunna, and Islamic sciences. It is native to the religious scholars, but in rudimentary ways it is spoken and understood by all Muslims. The political idiom of Arab nationalism, by contrast, is a modern secular language, rooted in the confrontation with, and eventual overthrow of, foreign/Western domination. It is a regional dialect, spoken and understood by Arabs throughout the Middle East, regardless of their religious affiliation. These idioms, then, represent distinct communal identities, one religious and one political, although they are often thought to overlap.

In the essays, the Islamic idiom includes overviews of the faith and references to the Kharijites, along with other names from Islamic history, such as Ibn Sabah (= the Shi'ites) and the Barmakids. The political idiom of Arab nationalism is composed of appeals to Arab unity and solidarity and references to Israel, Jews, Zionism, imperialism, and the English—references that, individually or as a group, are used to embody the negative experience and condition of modern Arabs. The writers wield these idioms simultaneously, blending them together as if they were one. Thus the Kharijites are placed side by side with Israel, Jews, Zionism, imperialism, and the English to provide a negative basis of comparison with the Brothers. The authority of official Islam attempts to tie these disparate political and religious identities together, arguing implicitly that, in various ways and at various times, they have threatened Muslim rulers, the Egyptian nation, or both. They are all cut, in other words, from the same rebellious cloth, a cloth that was woven at the beginning of Islam with the Kharijites. The Islamic past here seems to provide a framework for understanding the Arab Egyptian present. However, while the accusation of Kharijism might suggest this interpretive direction, especially given the official religious auspices under which the book was published, it is actually the politics of modern Egypt that drives the rhetoric and informs the Islamic idiom.

At this stage of the rhetoric's development in the modern period, the Kharijites are equated only with the Muslim Brothers. The Kharijites and the Brothers share similarities with Jews, Zionists, and imperialists in that they are all part of the history of opposition, but the reasons for their opposition differ. Kharijites and Muslim Brothers are internal or native sources of opposition, while Zionists and imperialists are external or foreign sources. This distinction is important because it is the foreign sources that generate the most concern and command the most attention. They are clearly viewed as the greater and more pressing threat, which accounts for the need to explain the internal opposition of Muslim Brothers in terms of foreign powers. As in the essay cited above, Muslim Brother opposition is portrayed as wrong because it aids and abets the activities of imperialists. Of course, internal opposition is wrong in and of itself, but the danger it poses is most grave when outsiders are waiting to take advantage of internal discord. Those like the Muslim Brothers and the Kharijites who cause such discord play into the hands of foreign oppressors and are considered traitors (*khawana*), an accusation leveled by several critics. One writer entitled his essay "Between Imperialism and Traitors," thereby highlighting the dilemma in which Egyptians find themselves.[53] He maintains that Egypt and other Arab nations have great promise and potential, if they can free themselves from the dual threats of foreign imperialists and terrorist factions within the Muslim Brothers. His sense of the priority of these threats, the order of importance that they have for modern Egyptians, leans decidedly toward the political challenge of imperialism. For him, Egypt's hard-won battle to gain political independence and freedom, the successes of the revolution, will be thwarted if imperialists regain control. From a practical perspective, then, Egypt's survival demands that local religious revolt (fitna) be seen against the modern backdrop of international Middle East politics, not the traditional backdrop of sectarian infighting and caliphal authority. Or put differently, the traditional Islamic idiom is subsumed under the political idiom of Arab nationalism.

This view is captured in both the words of the writer and a cartoon caricature that accompanies the article. A Western-looking man wearing a plaid jacket is depicted; his top hat has the British Union Jack emblazoned on it, with a Star of David drawn in the interstices of the lines. Leaping out of his jacket pocket is a puppet-like, bearded Islamist wielding a dagger. The scale and interaction of the figures indicate that militant Islamist opposition is minor in comparison to the imperialist conspiracy fomented by Britain and Israel, and that Islamist rebels are doing the bidding of (in the pocket of, as it were) foreign powers, hence the charge of treason.

The notion of treason as applied to the Muslim Brothers and, by association, the Kharijites needs to be explored further, for it clarifies the way the modern political idiom shaped references to the Kharijites. In modern usage, to be treasonous or a traitor commonly means to betray or to be disloyal to one's people or country. The offense is directed against the state or its representative authorities. The trust that is betrayed is a trust of citizenship, of a polity of like-minded individuals. This modern understanding of traitor can apply to the Muslim Brothers since they were citizens of the Arab Republic of Egypt when they rebelled. But it does not fit the traditional profile of the Kharijites. Though the original Kharijites revolted against the lawful authorities, this revolt, this act of political betrayal was categorized as a religious act. The classical tradition rationalized all factions in early Islam, regardless of their motives, in terms of sin and faith. As an Islamic sect, the offense of the

Kharijites was a sin against God's law, against the divinely guided community established for Muslim believers. It was punishable by Muslim authorities who were entrusted to carry out God's will, but the act itself was ultimately viewed as an episode in the cosmic drama of good and evil. By evoking the Kharijites, the essayists hoped to tap into this religious drama and bring down divine judgment on the Muslim Brothers. Although the charge of Kharijism conveyed this divine judgment, it did not bring about divine ends. For equating the Kharijites and the Muslims Brothers meant that Nasser could be cast in the role of 'Ali, which he in fact was. And this, in turn, conferred Islamic authority on all of Nasser's political projects (i.e., the revolution, Arab nationalism, Arab socialism, and so on). In short, by symbolic association, the modern Egyptian nation-state received the blessings of religious legitimacy without adopting the burdens of religious life.

That the accusation of Kharijism had the effect of calling on the sacred past to promote a secularized political present can be seen in the definition of a Muslim offered by one of the essayists. It will be remembered that, in the tradition, the Kharijites played a seminal role in raising and answering the question "who is a good Muslim?"

> The first thing to make clear is that a Muslim is in compliance with his religion and nationality unless he rebels against the community, or he cooperates with the enemies of Islam and the homeland, or he commits crimes against anyone whether Muslim or not.[54]

Here the requirements of Islam are minimal and political; traditional emphasis on the practice, belief, and intention of Muslims has given way to the pragmatism of forging a nation-state. A good Muslim is nothing more than a good citizen of the state, someone who obeys the laws and remains loyal. Kharijite and traitor to the modern state have become one in this definition, but only because religion has deferred to the state.[55]

It was this deferential attitude that angered many Islamists and motivated them to adopt violent methods. Islamists had their own vision of the modern state, one that competed with Nasser's on the level of ideology and total domination. Indeed, rhetorical references to the Kharijites in modern Egypt were a response to the political aspirations of the Islamist movement, particularly the Muslim Brothers. This chapter has outlined the initial ways in which the Kharijite image was deployed as a form of state propaganda. The next will explore how Muslim politics and accusations of Kharijism evolved under Sadat and Mubarak.

4

The Era of Sadat

Continuity and Change in Anti-Extremist Rhetoric

In Egypt of the 1950s and '60s, the image of the Kharijites was part of a one-sided discourse that lent total support to the state and un-equivocal condemnation of radical, and often moderate, Islamists. This was to change by the 1970s, and further in the '80s and '90s, when Anwar Sadat and Hosni Mubarak began to ease some of Nas-ser's more restrictive policies on the media and opposition groups. As openings were achieved in Egyptian civil society, participation in the political culture expanded and so, too, did the instrumental use of culture for political and social advantage. In short, Muslim politics became more complex and competitive, which parallels developments in understandings of Kharijism. This chapter traces out these devel-opments, examining several cases of Islamist violence and the religio-political debates that accompanied them. The analytic focus is the changing role of the image of the Kharijites in Egyptian political dis-course. Whereas the image of the Kharijites under Nasser had been a hegemonic tool of the regime, it evolved under Sadat and Mubarak into a symbolic setting for negotiating the boundaries of Islamist opposition and the nature of the Egyptian polity. That the idea of Kharjism went on to play such a mediating role is testimony to the adaptability and importance of Islamic symbols in Egyptian society. It also serves as commentary on the limits of the modern Egyptian state's domination of religious culture.

As the previous chapters have shown, filiation between the me-dieval Kharijites and the Muslim Brothers was established in a political context in which religion was made to serve the state. Nasser's policies toward official Islamic institutions and the Muslim Brothers were intended to eliminate Islam as a potential counterrevolutionary force. Reflecting his authoritarian corporatist model of rule, Nasser tried to bring these expressions of Islam into the sphere of state authority and harmonize their agendas with that of his regime. Official Islam proved susceptible to these efforts, while the Muslim Brothers did not. Representatives of official Islam became propagandists for the regime, while the Brothers became its ideological enemies. In the end, however, the Egyptian state even managed to benefit from militant opposition, for Islamist violence "allows the state to hold up before the society an image of the chaos that would threaten everyone if the state were to falter. Authority is vindicated because the alternative is depicted to be a reign of 'virtue and terror' that has few, if any, takers."[1]

Yet it was not simply the Muslim Brothers that were held up by the state; it was the Muslim Brothers cast in the mythic image of Kharijite chaos. Moreover, it was the state's emasculation of official Islam and other institutions that ensured the legitimacy of this image and facilitated its public presentation. Nasser successfully transformed rebellious Muslim Brothers into a progovernment propaganda coup because he had assumed preemptive authority over religion and public life in general. With the instrumental use of culture firmly in the hands of the regime, the Kharijites appeared to be the sole symbolic property of the Nasserist state and its supporters. Symbols, however, are polyvalent expressions, capable of sustaining various, even conflicting, moral views within a given culture, which accounts in part for what has been called the "Janus-faced" nature of culture.[2] Thus, though traditionally a counter model of rebellion, and hence naturally supportive of the state, the image of the Kharijites in fact had the capacity to promote other propagandistic ends. In Egyptian society in which the history and symbols of Islam held sway, educated citizens might reasonably compare and contrast the views and behavior of the Muslim Brothers and other Islamists with the Kharijites. Indeed, an open debate about the ethical-legal accuracy of the appellation "Kharijite" to describe Islamist political violence—including questions about the legitimacy of the regime against which the violence was directed—could pass for public education, a venting of all sides. But such a potentially threatening debate was anathema to Nasser's regime, which preferred to manufacture the moral will of the people rather than solicit it.

State domination of religion in Egypt might seem to confirm Fouad Ajami's observation that in the modern world "civilizations do not control states, states control civilizations."[3] Although there is much to recommend this view, especially as a corrective to those who see a "clash of civilizations" on the international scene,[4] it tends to gloss the ways in which a particular state becomes enmeshed in the very civilization or culture it attempts to control. Put differently, control over culture has consequences. In Egypt, the nationalization of Islam made political leaders subject to one of the laws of the construction and corrosion of authority: "those who wrap themselves in the cloak of religion make themselves vulnerable to the charge that they are insufficiently, inadequately, or improperly religious."[5] By relying on Islamic culture to vindicate its authority, the Egyptian state was drawn into a web of meaning and interpretation that it only partially understood but continuously had to police. Of course, as long as Nasser's popularity lasted and the military regime remained strong, voices of opposition, religious and otherwise, were either silent or silenced. With Egypt's stunning defeat in the June 1967 war, however, the situation changed.

The war sent shock waves through Egypt and the Middle East. The Arab leaders who had pressed the war and the political-economic systems that supported them were called into question. Above all, there was a rethinking of modernization and its meaning for national identity. For a time, Egypt experienced a general breakdown of the political, social, and economic order. Humiliated and weakened, Nasser changed political course, or at least he signaled such a change. Regionally, he scaled back his revolutionary agenda and made peace with those Arab nations whose assistance he now desperately needed, most notably Saudi Arabia. Domestically, he sought refuge in the conservative forces that had watched the revolution set sail without them. Islamic symbols and institutions, which had been so cynically manipulated by the regime, now provided a safe harbor of consolation. In fact, the nation as a whole witnessed a demonstrable rise in religious affiliation and sentiment. Mosque attendance increased, as did that of the church, and regime officials made a point of being seen at services. A sighting of the Virgin Mary above a church in the suburbs of Cairo enthralled the nation and provided consolation for both Christians and Muslims. Popular interest in all things religious raised the public status of Muslim officials and Islamic learning. Economic aid from Saudi Arabia emboldened the Muslim Brothers and strengthened their hand with the regime, which in a concession released a number of Muslim Brother prisoners.[6] Most dramatic of all, however, was Nasser's religious reading of the defeat. In a speech given shortly after the war, he intoned that

> Allah was trying to teach Egypt a lesson, to purify it in order to build a new society. The nation had to accept this testing as its destiny. It had known the Israeli attack was coming but had been unable to prevent defeat.[7]

The sense of political vulnerability here is tangible. With his authority and power in doubt, Nasser surrendered ground to the Muslim politics that he had once so thoroughly dominated.

The war of 1967 left immediate visible scars on the geography and economy of the region. It also loomed large in the Arab Muslim psyche and in cultural debates.[8] Leftists, nationalists, Islamists, and diverse others saw the war as a pivotal "event," one that they drew upon to redefine the history of the region and reshape its political future. As an event that quickly became a trope, 1967 has much in common with the Kharijites. Of crucial comparative importance for this study is the extent to which the impact of political and religious ideas and symbols can be measured. Survey research is notoriously lacking in the Arab world,[9] which has led scholars, for better or for worse, to rely on written records to discern political trends and attitudes within a given political culture.[10] This chapter and the one that follows draw largely on "content analysis" to trace out the rhetorical use of the accusation of Kharijism in Egyptian political and social thought. A technique used in the study of propaganda, content analysis assesses the amount and extent of propaganda, along with a categorization of themes and symbols according to their desired ends.[11] Though clearly not as ubiquitous as the "event of 1967," the threat of Kharijism went on to receive attention from a diversity of audiences, including the Muslim Brothers.

Prison Debate and Divisions among the Muslim Brothers

During the 1950s and '60s, the Muslim Brothers had largely ignored or dismissed the accusations that they were modern Kharijites. Sayyid Qutb, the figure most often linked with Kharijite ideas and actions, never addressed the comparison in his numerous books and articles. He even managed to avoid referring to the Kharijites in his Qur'an commentary when treating verse 5:44—"Whoso judges not according to what God has sent down—they are the unbelievers"—where commentators typically cite the Kharijites as one example of unbelievers, along with Jews and Christians. The reformers Muhammad 'Abduh and Rashid Rida, in their commentary, follow the lead of traditional scholars by referring to the Kharijites. They also adapt the verse to a modern context, questioning whether ruling according to English laws (in India) constitutes unbelief.[12] For his part, Qutb discusses the verse's application to Jews but ignores the problem of the Kharijites. And he, too, offers a modern reading of the verse. Instead of approaching the passage as a divine response to those who try to challenge rightful rulers, Qutb sees it as a lesson on jahiliyya systems of rule and jahiliyya societies. It is under such systems and in such societies, he writes, that God's law is not applied.[13] Thus Qutb reinterpreted the verse to challenge the very Muslim rulers whom the accusation of Kharijism was used to defend. By dismissing the interpretive relevance of the Kharijites, he also dismissed any attempt to identify his views (and Mawdudi's) with those of the Kharijites, an association that had supposedly troubled him.[14]

The first sign of Muslim Brother concern about the charge emerged in the by-now–famous prison debates that split the Muslim Brothers into moderate and radical factions.[15] At the heart of the debate lay the jahiliyya-based critique of Egyptian society, along with its jihad consequences, that Qutb propounded in *Signposts*. The debates took place following the 1965 crackdown, in which Qutb was rearrested. The trial and execution of Qutb brought the views expressed in *Signposts* to the attention of the wider public. It also generated among Muslim Brothers a reassessment of their situation and the militant tactics that supposedly landed them in prison. The man who initially pushed for moderation in the prison debates and came to represent the reformist wing of the Muslim Brothers, Hasan Isma'il al-Hudaybi, was himself a conflicted figure. A wealthy landowner and judge, al-Hudaybi joined the Muslim Brothers in 1947. His public stature led the movement's leadership to appoint him to the post of general guide after al-Banna's death. Though a staunch supporter of al-Banna and critical of the political status quo, al-Hudaybi tried to steer the Brothers away from confrontational politics. He was challenged from within by 'Abd al-Rahman al-Sanadi, the leader of the secret organization. The failure to reign in the militarist wing resulted in the assassination attempt on Nasser in 1954 and the conspiracy to overthrow the regime in 1965. Al-Hudaybi paid a personal price for this failure, receiving prison terms for both incidents.[16] His apologia took the form of a prison polemic that refuted the radical views expressed by Qutb and advocated by others.

Written in 1969, *Propagandists... Not Judges* (*Du'ah..la qudah*) summarizes and systematizes al-Hudaybi's side of the prison debate.[17] Qutb is not mentioned by name in the work; his popularity as martyr to the cause would not permit such blatant disrespect. But Qutb's ideas are clearly under attack, and the Kharijites emerge as one of the prime weapons. As the title suggests, for al-Hudaybi, the responsibility of Muslims and therefore of Muslim Brothers is to call people to Islam, not to judge them. Only God, he believes, can pass judgment on whether someone is truly a Muslim, and God's standard of judgment is established in the confession of faith (shahada). Thus, if someone pronounces the confession, al-Hudaybi maintains, "we consider him a Muslim...and we have no right to examine the extent of the truth-fulness of his confession."[18] Someone who meets this minimum criterion, then, cannot be accused of being an unbeliever (kafir) or a polytheist (mush-rik). Al-Hudaybi attributes the confusion that has arisen among Muslims over this issue to a misunderstanding of Islamic ideas, specifically to the term "jahiliyya"; and he identifies Abu 'Ala Mawdudi, Qutb's Indo-Pakistani mentor, as the source of this misunderstanding. Jahiliyya, according to al-Hudaybi, is not a condition as Mawdudi claims but a specific historical period, a period when the basis of judgment among Arabs was very different from what it became. By introducing this designation into modern discussions of Islam and Muslim society, Mawdudi confused the communal standards of Islam with those of jahiliyya.[19]

This misunderstanding, al- Hudaybi argues, has led some Muslims to become preoccupied with differentiating between major and minor sins, and then judging people accordingly. In so doing, these judgmental Muslims fall victim to the very sinfulness they are trying to uproot. When Muslims judge the sinfulness of others, al-Hudaybi points out, they usurp the authority of God and, as the orthodox tradition makes clear, themselves become un-believers.[20] Moreover, when these usurpers of God's authority extend the ac-cusation of unbelief onto the entire community, they compound their error and adopt the behavior of the Kharijites. With the Kharijites, the danger moves beyond mere theological disputation and personal sinfulness. Because they were men of action, willing to kill those judged to be unbelievers, in-cluding the leader, the issue becomes one of social discord (fitna). Here again, according to al-Hudaybi, the orthodox scholars are united in their response: for their actions, the Kharijites are eternally damned and their lives are forfeit. Leaders seeking to preserve the peace of the Muslim community are justified in eliminating the threat posed by the Kharijites, just as the caliph 'Ali had done in the past.[21]

Al-Hudaybi's willingness to introduce the specter of the Kharijites into the prison debate is testimony to how seriously he viewed the Muslim Brother situation. By acknowledging the reality of the Kharijite threat, it might appear as if his loyalties had shifted. But his rhetorical use of the accusation of Kharijism is quite different from the way it was directed against the Muslim Brothers in the government-controlled media. For official scholars who spoke for the establishment, the Kharijite image served to condemn the Muslim Brothers and support the authority of the state (and their own interpretive authority), whereas, for al-Hudaybi, it served to articulate acceptable methods of outreach for the Islamist opposition and thereby ensure their survival. Rather than silence the voice of the Brothers, as some might have expected, the image of the Kharijites facilitated communication, between Muslim Brothers divided over their future and between the reformist-minded Brothers and the authorities. The polyvalent nature of the symbol allowed those tainted by the Kharijite label to turn it to their advantage.

To his imprisoned compatriots, al-Hudaybi intended the Kharijite image to be a warning. The organization could not hope to continue its mission if some Brothers took the Islamic axiom of "commanding the good and forbidding evil" too far. If they picked up the sword, even for a noble cause, and became like the Kharijites, then death and imprisonment would be their fate. Instead of the sword, al-Hudaybi tells his fellow Brothers, teaching and preaching are the only acceptable means of Islamic outreach. In short, there are limits beyond which the Brothers may not go, even when dealing with an unjust ruler, a tyrant. On the subject of tyranny, al-Hudaybi carefully distinguishes between what is permissible and forbidden. Brothers, he argues, may curse, disavow, repudiate, and disobey a tyrant. They may not, however, pass sentence of unbelief upon him.[22] The former is presumably respectful Muslim dissent, while the latter is taking the path of the Kharijites. Thus, while al-Hudaybi sets limits, he also affirms the need to continue a course of opposition. That opposition, al-Hudaybi believes, must avoid passing mistaken judgments on the tyrant. Some judge the tyrant an unbeliever (i.e., the Kharijites), and others judge the tyrant a Muslim (i.e., representatives of official Islam). The Brothers are advised to refrain from passing judgment on the tyrant altogether. Thus al-Hudaybi uses the image of the Kharijites to anathematize both radical Muslim Brothers and the official religious authorities who pass favorable judgment on the tyrant (=Nasser).[23]

The prison debate was an exchange between Muslim Brothers, but its outcome, especially al-Hudaybi's stylized rendering of it, sent a message to the regime and Egyptian society. That message was one of concession and cautious challenge. When al-Hudaybi charges his fellow Brothers with Kharijism, he admits that the organization had exceeded its religious mandate and that the government crackdown was legitimate. Al-Hudaybi, then, is confessing the errors of the Brothers and, in so doing, laying the basis for their rebirth as chastened and reformed activists. Admitting the accuracy of the charge of Kharijism is something of a symbolic concession, for it affirms the dominant discourse of the authorities. Yet within this discourse, al-Hudaybi finds ways to undermine the ruling authorities. First, at the same time that he directs the charge of Kharijism against radical Brothers, he also draws attention to the corrupt ruler whom the Kharijite-like radicals improperly labeled an unbeliever and tried to overthrow with the sword. The need for social and political stability might protect the tyrant (=Nasser) from radical rebellion, but moderate protest is a moral imperative. Second, by recognizing the reality of the Kharijite-like radicals and dealing with them, al-Hudaybi demonstrates that the (moderate) Brothers pose no threat to the ruler or Egyptian society, thereby putting pressure on the regime to permit them to operate freely.

Given the circumstances in which al-Hudaybi made his case for moderate Islamism, the extent to which his thinking was affected specifically by the Kharijite symbol of chaos is impossible to determine. Government suppression and enlightened self-interest were equally plausible motivators for writing *Preachers... Not Judges*. What is apparent, however, is that al-Hudaybi used the image of the Kharijites to come to terms with the Brothers' weakened situation and to try to change it to their advantage. He adroitly manipulated the symbol of the Brothers' subordination, thus demonstrating that "the dominant discourse is a plastic idiom... capable of carrying an enormous variety of meanings, including those that are subversive of their use as intended by the dominant."[24] Al-Hudaybi was the first Brother insider to take the accusation of Kharijism seriously, but he would not be the last, as Islamist activism and writing in the 1970s illustrate.

Radical Islamism in the Era of Sadat

Upon Nasser's death in 1970, Sadat inherited the office of president and the burden of Nasser's social, political, and economic legacy—a legacy that Sadat would later characterize as "pitiable."[25] By 1971, he had consolidated his power base, eliminating Nasserite loyalists from the government, and embarked on the so-called corrective revolution. The release of unlawfully jailed political prisoners, including the Muslim Brothers, was high on Sadat's list of corrections. He and his advisors seem to have been unaware of the prison debates and the subsequent falling out between moderates and radicals. In his memoir, Sadat portrays the Brothers as victims of Nasser's will to power; he even dismisses the 1965 plot involving Qutb as a fictive creation of corrupt government officials.[26] Although no doubt genuinely sympathetic to the plight of the Brothers under Nasser, Sadat also viewed them as a helpful political counterweight to the remaining Nasserite and leftist forces that objected to his liberalization campaign. But when the jails were emptied, it was not just a weakened Society of Muslim Brothers that returned to the streets. Instead, it was a fragmented Islamist movement whose theoretical differences presaged fundamental organizational and political realignments.

The divide that came to separate al-Hudaybi's neo-Muslim Brothers from the heirs to Qutb's jahiliyya-based critique rested on differing attitudes toward reforming Egyptian society. In their prison debates, both factions agreed that Egypt was in a state of Islamic decline, but they advocated dramatically different responses to this situation: nonviolent activism vs. jihad or holy war. Since the long-range goal of both factions was the establishment of an Islamic order, marked by the implementation of Islamic law, their differences over method might appear tactical rather than strategic.[27] However, these tactical differences hardened into organizational splits once the survival of the Brothers came to depend not just on nonviolence but also on publicly defending their accommodation with the state and censuring their radical Islamist colleagues. Freed from prison and permitted a measure of latitude in their social activism, the neo-Muslim Brothers took up their role as the tolerated Islamist opposition, though their legal status remained in question. They were eventually allowed to republish the long-banned monthly magazine al-Da'wa, which became an important platform for advancing moderate Islamism.

Al-Hudaybi set the interpretive stage for this internal Islamist confrontation. The drama played out during the 1970s, with radicals following through on their threats of violence and the Brothers providing an Islamist counter critique. Caught between the radicals with whom they were ideological allies and the government whom they had to placate, the Brothers found themselves in an awkward position. Condemning radical violence made them in effect defenders of a government that they regarded as corrupt and un-Islamic. To the radicals, the Brothers had sold out to the government, becoming traitors to the Islamist cause. Yet the rejection of violence is what kept the Brothers in the good graces of the wider public, to whom they wanted to appeal, and of the Sadat regime, which, despite its liberal policies, policed participation in civil society. The Brothers' discussions of violence, then, had to walk a fine line, and this became apparent in their interpretation of the charge of Kharijism. At the same time, representatives of official Islam also developed a more nuanced approach to violence and the image of the Kharijites than they had previously exhibited under Nasser.

The two most prominent militant Islamist organizations of the 1970s were the Technical Military Academy group (Jama'at al-Fanniya al-'Askariya) and the Muslim group (Jama'at al-Muslimin), more popularly known as Excommunication and Emigration (al-Takfir wa'l-Hijra). Of these two, the Military Academy group drew the least public and official attention. In fact, the dismissive way in which it was treated would later be cited as one of the many signs of a militant Islamist underground that Sadat's government failed to detect.[28] Led by Salih Sirriya, a Ph.D. in education whose radical views were honed in the Islamic Liberation Party, the group planned to take control of the

Military Academy in Heliopolis and from there stage an attack on Sadat. When put into action in April of 1974, the plan failed early in its execution. Responsibility for the plot was attributed to Libya, and the trial did little to uncover the larger Islamist discontent that lay behind it. The quick resolution of the case, along with the lack of radical written evidence, muted serious analysis of the group. But a document emerged after Sirriya's trial and execution that gives some insight into the concerns that even radicals were beginning to have about the Kharijite label.

In a pamphlet entitled "Treatise on Faith," Sirriya lays out many of the standard positions of the radical trend.[29] Current leadership and society, he writes, are jahiliyya, making them unbelievers and therefore subject to jihad; anyone who supports or defends an infidel regime himself becomes one; anyone who participates in an association or political party that is not Islamic is an unbeliever; anyone who enforces or follows laws not based on the Qur'an is an unbeliever; anyone who shows signs of obedience to the modern nation-state is an unbeliever; it is permissible to subvert the authority of the infidel state and its system of governance in the interest of creating an Islamic government; it is permissible to pronounce the takfir—to label someone an unbeliever or infidel—as long as certain rules are followed; and anyone who denies these rulers is himself an unbeliever. According to Sirriya, the aforementioned judgments and rules are applicable to the modern jahiliyya conditions that bear upon the political life of believers. In the past, he explains, different problems of political unbelief, such as the Shi'ites and Kharijites, pressed upon Muslims, but these are not relevant to the Muslims of today.[30]

Sirriya's brief remarks about the Kharijites (and Shi'ites) preface a much longer criticism of modern jahiliyya circumstances, and they are conspicuous for how little they contribute to his analysis. However, addressing the historical reality of the Kharijites, and dismissing their relevance to current problems, does have rhetorical value for Sirriya. With accusations of Kharijism commonly directed against those who label other Muslims "unbelievers," debunking the legitimacy of the accusation is an astute defensive measure. Ultimately, Sirriya was not successful at deflecting criticism of his ideas and actions, but his decision to address the charge of Kharijism is evidence of its expanding usage.

Perhaps no other Islamist organization has received the kind of unanimous and resounding criticism as *al-Takfir wa'l-Hijra* (hereafter Takfir). They became for many the epitome of modern Kharijism. Even before the group adopted a violent course of action, making it a household word in Egypt, it had been associated with the Kharijites. Indeed, there is some evidence to suggest that the charge of Kharijism may have impelled the group toward violence, instead of dissuading it from such a path. The Takfir group had its origins in the hotbed of Nasser's prisons.[31] Its leader, Ahmed Shukri Mustafa, an agronomy student, was arrested in 1965 for distributing Muslim Brother literature at Asyut University. While in prison, he became associated with a Qutbian faction of Brothers who advocated complete physical and spiritual separation from jahiliyya society. This separation was modeled on Muhammad's hijra from Mecca to Medina, whereby the Prophet removed his band of believers from the dangers and corruption of the unbelievers. For Mustafa, separation was necessary because Egypt had become part of the abode of war (dar al-harb), the lands with which Islam is in a state of war. Members of the group were encouraged to emigrate to the abode of Islam (dar al-Islam), from which they could take up a defensive position and eventually shift to the attack.[32] Holding to a rigorous code of spiritual conduct, members viewed themselves as untainted by the major sinfulness that dominated Egyptian society. People who joined the group ensured their purity and salvation, but those who refused, including the reformed Muslim Brothers, were judged "unbelievers" and thus subject to the group's (=Allah's) retribution.[33]

Released from prison in 1971 as part of Sadat's corrective revolution, Mustafa returned to Asyut to finish his education. His preaching in the area earned him a following among young high achievers from the lower and middle classes.[34] The activities of the group drew the attention of the local authorities, and, in 1973, several members were arrested. The group, then, emigrated to the hills and caves in the Minya region, enacting the pure model community that Mustafa had idealized in prison. The arrested members were released following the October war of 1973, but the group once again came under official scrutiny after the failed takeover of the Military Academy in 1974. A scathing portrait of Mustafa and his followers appeared in the daily Akhbar al-Yaum (May 1975), and al-Azhar soon responded with a booklet intended to undermine the group's ideas and practices.[35] When the group violently confronted several suspected backsliders, the police made a number of arrests. In hiding from the police, Mustafa attempted to address what he considered a growing public misperception of the organization, but to no avail. In a final act of desperation, the group kidnapped Sheikh Muhammad Hussein al-Dhahabi, an ex-government minister, and tried to ransom him for the release of their jailed brethren. The government refused to negotiate, and the group executed its hostage.

Sheikh al-Dhahabi was not an accidental victim. As Minister of Awqaf in 1975, he had written the introduction to an al-Azhar booklet, entitled *Firebrands from the Divine Guidance of Islam*, that excoriated the ideas and behavior of the Takfir group, though the group itself is never mentioned by name.

In addition, a year later he published another book about deviant interpretations of the Qur'an that was widely regarded as a repudiation of Mustafa's understanding of the Qur'an.[36] Thus Sheikh al-Dhahabi emerged as a leading figure in official Islam's refutation of the group's heterodoxy. For Mustafa and his followers, al-Dhahabi symbolized a religious establishment whose loyalty to jahiliyya government took precedence over its obligations to God and the Muslim community, and by attacking this symbol, the group hoped to raise the conscience of the nation.[37] For religious authorities, the Takfir group was best symbolized by the Kharijites.

In the 1975 booklet *Firebrands from the Divine Guidance of Islam*, al-Dhahabi and his colleagues at al-Azhar address several of the interrelated issues of faith, sin, unbelief, and the proper method of propagating Islam—issues that were thought to be in a state of confusion based on the opinions held by some Muslim youth. In brief, they offer the following instructions: (1) the faith of Muslims is determined by their willingness to pronounce the shahada or profession of faith ("There is no God but the God, and Muhammad is his Messenger"), without any testing of someone's sincerity; (2) sin, even major sin, is not identical with unbelief; (3) those who accuse other Muslims of unbelief because of sin are taking the path of the Kharijites; and (4) preaching and teaching are the proper methods of Islamic outreach, and these methods fall under the authority of official religious scholars ('ulama'). Readers are also advised that the punishment for declaring someone an unbeliever because of sin (Kharijite behavior) is severe, for such people themselves become unbelievers.[38]

The goal of this instruction, according to al-Dhahabi's introductory remarks, is to correct the errors of Egyptian youth and set them on the right path. The religious enthusiasm of the young, it seems, has made them vulnerable to a band of extremists who do not care about Egypt's stability. Claiming that Egypt is an infidel society, this evil group has led some youth astray and perverted their understanding of Islam, of what is good. The young, al-Dhahabi writes, are "by nature good-hearted and free from evil," so if given the proper religious advice and direction, they will be able to resist deviant ideas. The task of religious authorities, and other social institutions, is to shape the conscience of the young, which is why the Ministry of Awqaf decided to publish the booklet. And if young believers heed the arguments presented in the booklet by knowledgeable and uncompromised experts, they can reorient their thinking and return to their "natural healthy disposition."[39]

The radical ideas that led to extremist action were thought to lie in misreadings of the Qur'an. The booklet published by the Ministry of Awqaf briefly outlines the correct method of interpretation, emphasizing the kind of knowledge and abilities that only formally trained scholars would have.[40] In another work, *Deviant Trends in the Interpretation of the Qur'an*, al-Dhahabi reviews the interpretive errors made by Muslim sects, such as the Kharijites. Though rooted in history, these errors still pose a danger, according to al-Dhahabi, because they are passed on unknowingly in modern works of interpretation; and as a result, people can be led into un-Islamic groups.[41] All the Kharijite sects, al-Dhahabi points out, agree on two principles, and a third is agreed on by the majority. The first is that the accusation of unbelief must be leveled at 'Uthman, 'Ali, Mu'awiya, the two arbitrators, their companions, and anyone who approved of the arbitration [at Siffin in 657]; the second is that the lawful ruler is to be attacked; and the third, less widely held principle, is that those who commit grave sins should be charged with unbelief. These mistaken principles, al-Dhahabi informs readers, arose mainly from a misunderstanding of Qur'an 5.44: "Whoso judges not according to what God has sent down—they are the unbelievers."[42] More cautious than some of his colleagues, al-Dhahabi acknowledges that he knows of no surviving Kharijites, except for the Ibadis. Nevertheless, he draws attention to the continued impact of their doctrines.

Al-Dhahabi's accusation of Kharijism here is subtle, mediated as it is through the tradition, but it would have been difficult for readers to miss the parallels between the Takfir group and the Kharijites. Certainly, Takfir members were aware of the rhetoric being deployed against them. One ex–Mustafa loyalist wrote in his memoir of trying to raise concerns with Mustafa about the Kharijite comparisons that were being made in order to reign in the group's militant methods.[43] Although the precise readership of these books cannot be calculated, it is clear from their length and content that they were intended for a popular audience. And once Mustafa and his followers abducted and executed al-Dhahabi, the famous victim's anti-extremist writings became part of the news story.[44] By condemning "deviant" ideas and actions, al-Dhahabi and his al-Azhar colleagues were clearly fulfilling their traditional role as representatives of official Islam, but this role was also clearly being exercised in a different political climate—one in which the conditional element of al-Azhar's legitimating authority was no longer being subverted.

As transmitters and defenders of the faith, al-Azharites maintain the integrity of all things Islamic. They are essentially a conservative force, which validates the status quo (variously understood) and is suspicious of change. Thus they view the stability of Muslim society and its related institutions— mosque, family, school, and government—as paramount. When militant Islamists disrupted that stability, threatening what are considered otherwise sound institutions, al-Dhahabi and his colleagues attempted to reestablish social equilibrium by evoking the primal image of sociopolitical disorder in Islam, the Kharijites. This image, ideally, undermined the legitimacy and purpose of the radicals, thereby disabusing the young of their errors and restoring Muslim society to its natural condition. But because the political dynamics changed from the era of Nasser to that of Sadat, so, too, did the meaning of the Kharijite image within the discourse of official Islam. In other words, the reiteration of traditional definitions of the Kharijites in a different political setting impacted the functional meaning of the symbol. Al-Dhahabi's *Deviant Trends in the Interpretation of the Qur'an* offers an interesting example of this transformation of meaning.

Published in 1976, when Egyptians were taking note of the Takfir group, the book was first written in 1966, when Qutb and the Brothers dominated the headlines. Despite the time lag, al-Dhahabi felt no need to rewrite for accuracy. With no mention of specific modern groups or events in the book, his conservative scholarly style suggests the unchanging nature of deviant trends. The chapter on the Kharijites, then, seems to remain relevant for understanding the errors of the seventh century, 1966 or 1976. However, these supposed transhistorical errors were committed against distinct political systems (= Muslim rulers) whose relationship with religion affected perceptions of what constituted orthodoxy. When the state, under Nasser, reigned supreme over religion and religious authorities, labeling radicals as Kharijites unconditionally supported the revolutionary regime, regardless of its policies. When the state, under Sadat, eased its control over religion and religious authorities, the same label was used to defend a regime that could be taken to task if it ran afoul of Islamic teachings. The public commentary occasioned by al-Dhahabi's murder in 1977 shows that the status quo being reaffirmed by the image of the Kharijites had changed from 1966.

From the outset, media accounts of al-Dhahabi's murder tended to blend factual events and religious commentary. As in the coverage of the 1965 Muslim Brother plot, there was a blurring of civil and religious pronouncements about the Takfir group. Government and religious officials rallied to condemn Mustafa, and their moral characterizations of his group—"criminals," "terrorists," "Kharijites"—appeared to intermingle. In some publications, Kharijism emerged as just another of the "facts" surrounding the case.[45] But the public commentary also reflected a degree of independent religious thinking that had not been seen during the Nasser years.[46] Despite al-Dhahabi's status as an ex–government minister, the state and its laws were not the focus of attention. His killing was widely portrayed as a breach of the Islamic moral order, not a national civic one. And instead of the state compelling religious authorities to do its bidding, state authorities, most notably Sadat himself,

THE ERA OF SADAT 131

spoke on behalf of Islam, Muslim leadership, and the Islamic nature of Egypt.[47] In this changed political setting, radicals accused of being modern Kharijites were portrayed as traitors to Islam and Muslim society, not to the modern state. No longer dominated by the state, official Islamic authorities in the 1970s evoked the Kharijites to restore and affirm an Egypt where Islam held sway, not an authoritarian ruler.

Joining the chorus of opposition to the Takfir group were the Muslim Brothers. Like al-Dhahabi and other al-Azhar officials, the Brothers addressed the perceived threat of the Takfir group before violence had erupted. Early in 1977, the Muslim Brother press Dar al-Ansar published two works directed at extremist tendencies among the young, and both were suffused with references to the Kharijites. The first was appropriately titled *The Kharijites: Historical Roots of the Problem of Excommunication of the Muslim (al-Khawarij: al-usul al-ta'rikhiyya li masalat takfir al-muslim)*, which was to be the first book in a series entitled "Don't Follow this Path."[48] The book, written by Mustafa Hilmi, is a study of the rise of the Kharijites, their errors, and the early criticisms leveled against them in Islamic sources. But the iteration of these historical facts is for a modern end: to prevent the young from adopting improper missionary activity that leads to the reemergence of Kharijite civil discord and, more important, to critique the modern un-Islamic context in which such behavior occurs.

In the introductory remarks to the series, readers are told that a certain anxious type of activist youth has taken up the path of the Kharijites of old. They are sincere Muslims, but their sincerity has overshadowed their rationality. Obsessed with the moral shortcomings and intellectual errors in Muslim society, they have grown frustrated with the pace of change and have turned to extremist methods. The anxiety that drives these young Muslims, according to the series editor, is part of a general problem of decay or corruption (*fasad*) that affects everyone from time to time in the Muslim community. The problem is that Muslims have lost their "cultural identity," immersing themselves in the ways of the West; and as a result, they have become weak and divided. The young have lived through this cultural decay, and they have also witnessed the harsh manner in which Muslim activists have been treated in the recent past. Thus their natural instinct is to change the situation and to seek revenge.[49]

In the body of the work, Hilmi also draws attention to the modern condition in which Kharijite thinking reemerges. But, instead of a psychosocial explanation of Kharijite-like extremism as provided in the series introduction, he points to a historical one that relies on interpreting the underlying cause of seemingly dissimilar events. Modern Muslim youth, writes Hilmi, devolved into Kharijism at a time when colonialist aggression laid ruin to Islamic lands.

Throughout these countries, the native political, legal, and educational systems have been subverted and replaced with foreign ones. According to Hilmi, these dramatic events have the same causal root as the rise of the Kharijite sect—Jewish plotting.[50] The historic connection, Hilmi argues, runs from the Yemeni Jew Ibn Sabah, who is mentioned in some Islamic sources as an instigator of early Kharijites, to the "fifth protocol" of the Protocols of the Elders of Zion,[51] which attests to an ongoing Jewish conspiracy:

> The world alliance of goyim may be able to resist us for a time. But
> we are certain of the final result because the roots of dissension
> among them are so deep that they are difficult to extirpate. We cre-
> ated rancor among the personal and national interests of the goyim
> by awakening religious and racial hatred, nourishing it in their
> hearts for twenty centuries.[52]

For Hilmi, this knowledge about Jewish operations behind the scenes explains both the original Kharijite uprising and all subsequent sectarian divisions, including the Kharijite-like behavior of modern Muslim youth. Among Muslim Brother thinkers in the post-Hudaybi period, this explanation is unique, for it seemingly links causes of and conditions for extremism across time. The typical approach is to explain modern Kharijite-like behavior in modern terms. Such explanations are essential within the Brothers' oppositional discourse because they highlight problems in society and hence the need for change. Unlike representatives of official Islam, the Brothers are not content with the status quo, and this is reflected in their understanding of the Kharijites. Hilmi's work, then, shares common ground with official Islamic discourse on extremism; it acknowledges and refutes Kharijites in their primal and newly constituted forms, and it relies on similar primary sources to do so. Yet in contrast with al-Dhahabi's rhetoric, Hilmi's seeks not to restore but to critique Muslim society and its compromised institutions. A similar pattern appears in *Judgment and the Problem of Muslim Excommunication (al-Hukm wa qadiyya takfir al-muslim)*, another Muslim Brother book published during the public controversy over the Takfir group in 1977 but prior to al-Dhahabi's abduction and murder.[53]

The author, Salim 'Ali al-Bahnasawi, is more forceful in his denunciations of the practice of excommunication than Hilmi, and his adherence to al-Hudaybi's moderate path is more clearly articulated. But like Hilmi, al-Bahnasawi wants people to take young militants more seriously, because their presence is a barometer of other fundamental challenges affecting Egyptian society. Thus he advises readers to move beyond the superficial treatment of the Takfir group found in newspapers.[54] Al-Bahnasawi's book reads much like a historical critical account of extremism among the Brothers. He traces out the history of the Brothers in Egypt, focusing on the trials and tribulations they experienced when spreading the message of Islam. Of primary concern is their mistreatment in prison and the court system. It was in Egyptian prisons, he points out, that the idea of excommunication began, and it then spread from Egypt to other Arab countries. The young, then, according to al-Bahnasawi, resorted to the behavior of the early Kharijites because of local conditions, because they grew angry and frustrated about living in a country where Muslims were prevented from freely preaching and teaching Islam.[55]

Although Brothers like al-Bahnasawi and Hilmi were careful not to valorize the young radicals, their reasoned analysis of extremism stands in stark contrast with the approach of official authorities. For official Islam and the popular press, the accusation of Kharijism consisted of a primal moral identification of a rebel as a rebel or a terrorist as a terrorist. For the Brothers, by contrast, the label identified the militant sinners and drew attention to the legitimate social and political concerns that led these sinners astray. In short, the Brothers made extremism a more complex, political issue in Egypt. And that complexity created moral ambiguity about Islamist recourse to violence that was not present in the discourses of official Islam. Indeed, without that moral ambiguity, without stretching the symbolic meaning of the Kharijites, the Brothers would have lost their oppositional edge. The youthful neo-Kharijites were, after all, ideological offspring of the Brothers. So to denounce them completely would require that the Brothers denounce themselves. Al-Hudaybi was willing to sacrifice the radicals for the sake of the Brothers' survival. But this was a prison compromise that others began to retract once the Brothers settled into their role of tolerated opposition under Sadat.

The growing antagonism of the Brothers toward Sadat's regime was evinced in the pages of al-Da'wa. Since its reappearance in 1976, the magazine clashed with government policies on almost every major issue. Sadat's turn to the West, his opening to Israel, economic reforms, government corruption, failure to implement Islamic law, all became grist for al-Da'wa's Islamist critique of secular Egypt. The extent of the Brothers' dissatisfaction became apparent in al-Da'wa coverage of al-Dhahabi's murder. The July issue all but ignored the event, except for an encomium to al-Dhahabi on the back cover. And it was not until September that a story on the Takfir group saw print, which turned out to be an attack on journalistic standards of reporting on the case. A second story provided an occasion to criticize the government's decision to try the case before a military judge.[56] Though the magazine saw fit to condemn the murderers and label al-Dhahabi's assassination an "evil crime," it refrained from whipping up the kind of anti-extremist sentiment found in the popular press. In fact, its editorial priorities during the Takfir affair remained focused on painting Egypt as unfriendly toward Islam and oppressive of Muslim activists, specifically the Brothers. The juxtaposition of articles appearing in *al-Da'wa* expressed the conflicted nature of the Muslim Brothers and provided tacit cover for the young radicals. For every piece written on the need for peaceful Islamic activism, several would appear on the torture endured by the Brothers in Nasser's prisons, suggesting that peaceful means may not be appropriate in Egypt or at least that the radicals are radical for good reason.[57] The moral impact of articles that rejected extremist ideas such as excommunication was mitigated by others that decried the un-Islamic character of society and the lack of Muslim leadership in politics.[58]

Despite the Brothers' public commitment to peaceful proselytism, *al-Da'wa* clearly had a more sympathetic view of militant youth than that of the government, official Islam, or the media. This attitude was just one of the growing signs of tension between Islamists and Sadat. Having defined itself as democratic and pro-Islam, Sadat's government was prepared to accommodate peaceful Islamist opposition. But a series of developments in the late 1970s contributed to the anger and confidence of Islamists and engendered a general politics of confrontation in Egypt. Brotherhood discontent over Sadat's peace overture to Israel escalated dramatically between 1977 and 1981 and convinced other opposition factions to join in.[59] The success of Islamic societies on campuses and the model of the revolutionaries in Iran fanned the hopes of an Islamist "takeover" in Egypt. Upper Egypt witnessed a number of anti-Coptic disturbances, which led to a backlash among Copts who feared the consequences of continued quiescence. The regime attempted to appease Islamists by appointing prominent Muslims to government positions and playing up Islamic symbols. In the end, however, these measures drew the ire of both Islamists who saw them as empty gestures and Copts who saw them as dangerous concessions. When sectarian rioting broke out in Cairo in 1981, Sadat finally lost patience and brought his experiment with (limited) liberal pluralism to an end. Avoiding any semblance of favoritism, he ordered arrests across the social and political spectrum: Brothers, student activists, politicians on the left and right, Coptic leaders, businessmen, journalists, and academics. It was in this atmosphere that Sadat was assassinated and the next phase of extremist politics evolved.

The Killing of a Muslim Ruler

Sadat's murder at the hands of the Jihad organization raised the image of the Kharijites to a new level of public attention. The Jihad assassins seemed ready-made candidates for the label. They had, after all, killed the man known as the "believing president," and a common understanding of a Kharijite was someone who rebels against a legitimate leader. Of course, the question of legitimacy had long been at the heart of the Islamist challenge in Egypt. Since the founding of the Muslim Brothers, Islamists had rejected the secular direction in which, they believed, Egyptian leaders had steered the country; and they had consistently pressed for an Islamic (political) order in Egypt and religious standards for judging political leaders. Every major paroxysm of Islamist extremism in Egypt has been, in some sense, predicated on the "fact" that political leaders, society, or citizens were insufficiently Muslim, even non-Muslim. And the rationale for killing Sadat was no different; a "creed" attributed to Muhammad 'Abd al-Salam Faraj, the leader of the Jihad organization in Cairo, declared all modern Muslim rulers apostates from Islam and therefore subject to jihad.[60]

The Jihad organization was more of an alliance of like-minded Islamists than a single bureaucratic entity. Its two main branches were in Cairo and Asyut, but it had ties with other groups in Middle Egypt and Alexandria. Though Faraj emerged in press accounts as the dominant ideologue, he actually shared authority with Karam Zuhdi and relied on the religious advice of Sheikh 'Umar 'Abd al-Rahman. The plot to kill the president was hatched in Cairo by Faraj and one of his recruits, an army lieutenant named Khalid al-Islambouli whose brother, an Islamist organizer in Asyut, was jailed in the mass arrests ordered by Sadat in September 1981. Angered over the unjust detention of his brother, al-Islambouli decided to take revenge when he was assigned to participate in the military parade commemorating Egypt's victory in the October 1973 war. The plot received strong support from Faraj, who solicited the assistance of other branches of Jihad to use the occasion to stage a popular uprising. The assassination was successfully carried out, but the revolution never materialized.[61]

Sheikh 'Umar 'Abd al-Rahman had given formal religious approval (a fatwa) to kill Sadat, but Faraj made the historical and moral argument in his treatise *The Neglected Duty* (*al-Farida al-gha'iba*). The duty that Muslims have neglected, according to Faraj, is jihad, and it is to be carried out against the rulers of the modern state. Drawing on the writings of Ibn Taymiyya (1268–1328), the medieval scholar who had analyzed the Mongol invasion, he characterizes modern-day Muslim rulers as the moral equal of the Mongols. Like the ancient Mongols, Faraj maintains, the modern ones voice the Islamic confession of faith, passing themselves off as Muslims, even though they remain unbelievers.[62] As a result, they deceive good Muslims and lead the community astray. Faraj is methodical about adducing proofs for the judgment (hukm) to kill these rulers, and his logic includes a reference to the Kharijites. After quoting from a hadith in which Muhammad had warned Muslims to beware of the false faith of Kharijites and to kill them whenever possible, Faraj makes an interesting comparison with the Mongols:

> All Muslim Imams command to fight these [Kharijites]. The Mongols and their likes—the equivalent of our rulers today—are (even) more rebellious against the laws of Islam than those who refused the zakat tax, or the [Kharijites]. . . . Whosoever doubts whether they should be fought is more ignorant of the religion of Islam. Since fighting them is obligatory they have to be fought, even though there are amongst them some who have been forced (to join their pagan ranks).[63]

Modern rulers, then, are more dangerous in Faraj's estimation than the Kharijites who historically served as the model of rebellion in Islam. And so, in a strange twist of comparative reasoning, he uses the image of the Kharijites to thwart the very people who had benefited from it. If Kharijite rebellion is condemned in *The Neglected Duty*, rebellion per se is not, for Faraj calls on Muslims to revolt against an infidel ruler who fails to uphold Islamic teachings or introduces innovations into Islam. Here Faraj communicates the difference between bad rebel and good rebel in a linguistic nuance of the same Arabic root *kh-ra-ja*: *khawarij* or Kharijites and *khuruj* or revolt.[64] Writers critical of Islamist violence often blurred this linguistic distinction.

Although Faraj does not advocate separation from society, as Shukri Mustafa had, he views association with the Mongol state and its institutions as morally corrupting and unwise. For example, he advises Muslims to avoid supporting the state and to emigrate if they find themselves compelled to, though fighting is presented as the best option. Those who lend assistance to the Mongols may or may not be considered hypocrites. In addition, he warns Muslims not to participate in "benevolent societies" or to form a political party, since these acts could be construed as furthering the very system that must be overthrown.[65] Salih Siriyya had an even stronger opinion on this matter, arguing that a person became an unbeliever by joining a society or political party.[66] Perhaps the most dramatic example of the ideological divide separating Jihad members and the state was the issue of Israel. In a by–now-famous passage, Faraj declares that "to fight an enemy who is near is more important than to fight an enemy who is far," which meant that Mongol-Egyptian leaders posed a greater threat inside the country than the Israelis did from outside.[67]

Given the deep-seated resentment of Israel among Egyptians, including Islamists, Faraj's downplaying of the threat of Israel can only be seen as a provocation, a way to emphasize radical discontent by adopting a dramatically different view on sensitive domestic issue. During his trial, Shukri Mustafa had expressed similar indifference about Israel, asserting that, if attacked, his group would flee from both the foreign and local enemy.[68] Such comparative references to Israel, the Mongols, jahiliyya, unbelievers, and even the Kharijites were part of the swirl of symbolic language through which radical Islamists communicated their protest, along with their use of violence. Some of this language was shared with moderates because radical and moderate protest overlapped so closely. But the protest of the radicals was not tempered by the kind of political compromise engaged in by moderates, and this resulted in different rhetorical usage of the Kharijites.

For moderate Islamists such as Hasan al-Hudaybi, Mustafa Hilmi, and Salim al-Bahnasawi, recognizing the reality of Kharijite tendencies was an admission that the extremism adopted by some activists was unhealthy and un-Islamic, even though the causes of this extremism actually, in their minds, indicted the Muslim leaders that the anti-extremist rhetoric commonly served to protect. For radicals such as Salih Siriyya and 'Abd al-Salam Faraj, the threat of Kharijism was absorbed into the rationale for violence, conceding nothing to the authorities. It could also be turned into a radical reproof, as indicated in the court testimony of Sheikh 'Umar 'Abd al-Rahman, the spiritual guide of the Jihad organization. Tried twice for complicity in Sadat's assassination, 'Abd al-Rahman was found not guilty both times, based largely on his convincing defense; he was finally convicted in a third trial held in absentia. His account of his testimony before the court offers a fascinating look at the extent to which the accusation of Kharijism had evolved in Egypt and the dilemma of Muslim politics.[69]

In his opening statement, 'Abd al-Rahman presents what is essentially a defense against the charge of Kharijism for those who killed Sadat. He begins by reviewing the issues of sovereignty, obedience, and revolt as they relate to the Muslim ruler. The shari'a or Islamic law, according to 'Abd al-Rahman, is the greatest contribution of the "Islamic revolution" led by the Prophet Muhammad; and it is the embodiment of God's sovereignty over his creation. Muslim society is the place where God's sovereignty, not that of humans, reigns; and a Muslim ruler is someone who enforces the rule of God, that is, Islamic law. For 'Abd al-Rahman, the epitome of a ruler who fails to enforce God's laws is, not surprising, someone who behaves as Sadat did during his tenure as president. It is a ruler who "institutes non-Islamic personal status laws, aids Zionists, constructs an ecumenical house of worship, establishes relations with the greatest enemy of believers [= the Jews], signs the Camp David accords, and avows that there is no religion in politics and no politics in religion."[70] Not only is such a ruler unworthy of the obedience typically accorded a person ruling over Muslims, argues 'Abd al-Rahman, but people are also obligated to revolt against him. That obligation rests on the fact that a ruler who does not rule according to what God revealed is an unbeliever who has reverted to jahiliyya practices. Thus Muslims, he maintains, must make dire decisions when confronted with an unbelieving ruler: do they choose jahiliyya or Islam, do they submit to man or God, do they obey or revolt?[71]

The accusation of Kharijism seems to have been an important element in the prosecutor's case against 'Abd al-Rahman. In fact, though the charges brought against the sheikh were based on breaches of the civil law, the questions posed to him sometimes suggest that religion, not the state, was the injured party. According to the prosecutor, Jihad members should be classified as Kharijites because, like them, "they promote the slogan of God's judgment, while actually substituting for it their own."[72] For 'Abd al-Rahman, the charge turns truth on its head, for Muslims who call people to Islam and make rulers accountable to God cannot be described as Kharijites. The charge also, he believes, makes nonsense of the historical situation of 'Ali, the caliph against whom the Kharijites first rebelled. Muslim scholars agree, 'Abd al-Rahman points out to the prosecutor, that Kharijites are those who refuse to obey a rightful leader, openly declare their rebellion and plot against him. "But where," he cynically asks, "is the rightful leader against whom to rebel? Where is 'Ali b. Abi Talib today?" His challenging questions to the prosecutor continue with barbs more directly aimed at Sadat and the secular state:

> If we are Kharijites, are you 'Ali and his companions? Did 'Ali borrow the basis of law from the Persians and Romans? Was his rule based on socialism or democracy? . . . Was 'Ali an ally of the Jews, a friend of Begin? . . . Was 'Ali among those who separated religion and politics?[73]

For 'Abd al-Rahman, the determination as to whether someone is or is not a Kharijite rests on an understanding of the character of the ruler. If, he informs the prosecutor, a person rebels against a righteous leader, like 'Ali, who rules according to the Qur'an, then such a person is a Kharijite; but if a person rebels against a leader who commits the kind of frivolous deeds just mentioned—deeds clearly associated with Sadat—then such person is not a Kharijite. Although 'Abd al-Rahman may be setting the bar for Muslim rulers rather high by using 'Ali as the comparative model, his response to the prosecutor is historically and symbolically related to the charge of Kharijism leveled against him. He simply reinterprets the prosecutor's view of the Kharijites, which supposedly lends religious sanction to a Muslim ruler, to delegitimize Sadat's political authority, justify violence against him, and promote the Islamist alternative. A similar example of verbal jousting over the Kharijites and Sadat's political legitimacy occurred when Sheikh Salah Abu Isma'il, an Islamist member of the People's Assembly, testified during the second Jihad trial. Questioned about the relevance of the Kharijites to understanding the Muslim Brothers and other Islamists, Abu Isma'il dismisses them as a "problem of history," not a "problem of Islam."[74] They posed a challenge to the caliph 'Ali, he maintains, but the challenge of today is the application of Islamic law. Sadat stood in the way of instituting Islamic law, according to Abu Isma'il, along with committing other sinful deeds; and to the extent that he refused to repent of these deeds, he became an apostate who could be killed.[75]

The idea of repentance raised a warning flag of Kharijism for five al-Azhar scholars who rebutted Abu Isma'il's testimony. Calling someone to repent, they indicated, was an assumption of God's authority, a custom common to the Kharijites and one that followed from excommunication.[76] Abu Isma'il, not surprising, rejected this association and defended the obligation to call apostates to account. Instead of evoking 'Ali's actions against the Kharijites as the al-Azhar scholars had, he spoke of Abu Bakr's efforts against those who turned away from Islam following the death of Muhammad, the so-called *ridda* wars or wars of apostasy (ca. 632–34). Raising the specter of the Kharijites, according to Abu Isma'il, was simply an attempt to distract people from Sadat's renunciation of Islam and the need to unseat him from power.[77] In the give-and-take of a courtroom exchange between two contending claimants for the mantle of Islamic orthodoxy, such exaggerated reliance on religious discourse—apostasy, repentance, 'Ali, Abu Bakr, Kharijites—to debate the murder of Sadat was to be expected. The same level of discourse, however, came to dominate popular media accounts of the assassins as well. Despite appearances, this was no reversion to medieval thinking but rather the uneasy, and sometimes confusing, process of debating modern politics through religious language and symbols, that is, Muslim politics.

In times of crisis, there is a tendency for participants in Muslim politics to "bid up" the competition over Islamic symbols and ideas in an effort to gain legitimacy.[78] Sadat's assassination at the hands of militant Islamists posed such a crisis for Egyptians. The majority of Muslim officials and public commentators responded by upping the ante of anti-extremist rhetoric, which countered Jihad extremism and, by extension, vindicated Sadat's authority. The importance of the image of the Kharijites for Sadat's political legacy was prefigured in several writings intended to address the sectarian strife that wracked upper Egypt and culminated in the mass arrests in the summer of 1981. In September, one month before the assassination, an article appeared in the magazine *Akhir Sa'a*, linking confessional discord to the ideas and activities of Islamic groups (*al-jama'at al-islamiyya*), such as Jund Allah, the Jihad organization, and Takfir wa'l-Hijra. These groups, which were accused of threatening the social peace and national unity of Egypt, were said to be related to the Kharijites.[79] The Ministry of Waqfs also published a commentary piece the same month that condemned the divisive practice of excommunication by identifying it with the Kharijites.[80] Following Sadat's murder, this concern about the political activism of Islamic groups and the religious intolerance they demonstrated translated into a (religious) defense of Sadat and the political direction in which he was supposedly steering the country.

Days after Sadat's murder, the Mufti of al-Azhar, Sheikh Jadd al-Haqq 'Ali Jadd al-Haqq, hailed the ex-president as "a martyr in the path of God and the nation." Assassinations of this kind, he informed the interviewer, have a history in Islam, and they are carried out by Kharijites, who "in every era ruin the cohesion of the group." Keeping his remarks general, the Mufti refrained from endorsing specific policies of Sadat, but the message was clearly one of religious support for the nation's leader and the need for national unity.[81] Other commentators were prepared to deploy the charge of Kharijism to rescue political developments that they feared would be lost if religious extremists were to have their way. Sadat's government had granted Egyptians more social and economic freedoms and had promised a transition to democratic rule. These ideals reflected a political atmosphere quite different from that of Nasser, and the idea of Kharijism was interpreted accordingly. Thus, in addition to their shared identity as violent extremists and religious rebels, the Jihad assassins and the Kharijites were also said to share a hatred of peace, freedom, and democracy.[82] And since the Kharijites were considered the antithesis of Islam, this new negative image played nicely into attempts to portray the Muslim community as a place where political, civil, and religious freedoms were not only respected but championed.[83]

Though late to join the trend toward Muslim politics in the 1970s, political progressives eventually found their voice, as Fathi Ghanim showed in his weekly opinion column in the magazine *Ruz al-Yusuf*. Starting in September of 1981, after the arrest of Islamic groups, Ghanim wrote critically about those who used religion for political purposes. Such people simply wanted power, he maintained, and they sought this power by projecting problems onto religion that were political in nature. Ghanim advocated a cultural understanding of Islam in his columns, one that he believed was best suited to living as a modern Muslim; and he contrasted this with politicized notions of Islam that led toward violence and terrorism.[84] He drew his model for democracy in Egypt from the modern reformer Muhammad 'Abduh, who gave a Muslim, not a colonialist, reading of the political system. He was also not above citing classical sources such as Ibn Hazm and al-Shahrastani, two of the more well-known medieval writers on sects. For Ghanim, Sadat's assassination was a terrorist crime that had its roots in the sectarian splits that marked early Islamic (political) history, specifically the bloody conflict between the factions of 'Ali and Mu'awiya. And he portrayed this crime as an attack on peace, justice, and democracy.[85] His argument for democracy and against Muslim radicals came together in a fascinating piece that employed al-Shahrastani's account of the origins of crime or sin in his *Book of Sects and Divisions*.

As Ghanim points out, the source of sin, according to al-Shahrastani, was Satan, who gave rise to all further sinful acts; and one of these acts was committed by the Kharijites, who rebelled against 'Ali and set the stage for further rebellion. This idea, Ghanim believes, can provide Egyptians with an historical and moral framework for understanding acts of religious violence and overcoming them. His concern here is with having Egyptians take responsibility for evil in both their individual lives and society at large. Too often, he writes, crimes are explained away as arising from "social conditions," an explanation that tends to take human accountability out of the picture. Knowing that Satan fosters evil in our lives and in the world obliges people to root it out. That can best be done, Ghanim asserts, in a democracy, which, though not perfect, allows and encourages citizens to take responsibility. A dictatorship, by contrast, deprives individuals of both responsibility and freedom of thought. His concluding hope is that Egyptians see the "voice of Satan" behind the religious fanatics who "monopolize opinion, accuse society of unbelief, commit assassination and shed blood."[86]

For Ghanim, the interpretive use of a medieval heresiography is an intellectual act of cultural empowerment, not irrational obscurantism. He has adapted the image of the Kharijites to his search for authenticity and progressive political modernization. With different political ends in view, Islamists, both moderate and radical, also participated in this process. Radicals, on the one hand, had their opportunity to defend their deed and refute the charge of Kharijism in court, as seen above. Moderates, on the other hand, appeared in the mainstream press, after their propaganda outlet, *al-Da'wa*, fell victim to government suppression. 'Umar al-Talmasani, the new leader of the Muslim Brothers, was interviewed extensively about the assassins, the role of religion in Egypt, and the agenda of his movement; and he also contributed articles of his own.[87] He, too, mentioned the Kharijites in his assessment of the Jihad organization, and he reiterated what had become the common refrain of the post-Qutb Brothers: that they were not a political party. Of course, political party or not, when al-Talmasani argued for the institution of Islamic law and articulated religious conditions for the ruler, he was being political. But he had to deny the Brothers' political ambitions formally in order to remain a tolerated opposition movement. In Egypt's Muslim politics, where tolerance and democracy were still under negotiation, Islamist activists who wanted openly to participate in society had to practice a degree of dissimulation, not of faith but of interest in power based on faith. Even al-Azhar felt compelled to reassure Egyptians and the government that official Islam was not seeking political authority.[88]

Beneath this thicket of Islamic cultural discourse and hidden meanings, some scholars have detected a circuitous path toward secularization. Mohammed Arkoun has described this subtext of Muslim societies in the following manner:

> Forced to foreswear colonial domination, the West has since the 1960s launched a search for new expressions of modernity, while the Muslim world has, quite to the contrary, turned away from these opportunities and proposed instead an "Islamic" model, which is beyond all scientific investigation. This notion constitutes the triumph of a social imaginary that is termed "Islamic" but that in fact sacralizes an irreversible operation of political, economic, social, and cultural secularization. Analysts have barely noticed this new role of Islam used at the collective level as an instrument of disguising behaviors, institutions, and cultural and scientific activities inspired by the very Western model that has been ideologically rejected.[89]

The Kharijites in particular and Muslim politics in general are part of the Islamic "social imaginary" of which Arkoun wrote. Yet it remains unclear whether they have contributed, in their own way, toward secularization or some other Islamically acceptable form of modernization.[90] The problem lies in the ongoing ambiguity between political and religious authority.

The outpouring of anti-extremist rhetoric after Sadat's assassination indicated that religious authority was divided in Egypt and that this division reflected unresolved political differences. To the extent, however, that these differences were being argued through Islamic discourse, it appeared as though political authority in Egypt depended on the religious authority being invoked by various factions. Sadat himself had contributed toward the general confusion by insisting upon a separation of religion and politics in response to the Islamist challenge,[91] while at the same time engaging in the same game of Muslim politics as his opponents.[92] He did not try to dominate the discourse or the institutions as Nasser had, but he certainly relied on them and, up to a point, benefited from them. The Jihad organization operated under the assumption that religion and politics were one, and its logic for excommunicating and killing the president was based, at least in part, on Sadat's attempt to separate the two spheres. As deployed by representatives of official Islam, political progressives, the popular press, and moderate Islamists, the charge of Kharijism anathematized the use of religiously justified violence against Sadat. But it did so by reaffirming his bona fides as a (good) Muslim. Thus, despite the fact that the Egyptian constitution required no religious test of the president,[93] the importance of the image of the Kharijites indirectly confirmed that Sadat did indeed pass the religious test that Islamists claimed he had failed. Even in death, Sadat continued to blur the distinction that he and his predecessor had never effectively sharpened in life.

5

The New Politics of
Anti-Extremist Rhetoric

Kharijite Essentialism and Beyond

Despite its persistent use in Egyptian public discourse, beginning in
the mid-1960s and continuing into the 1990s, the image of the
Kharijites neither tempered extremism nor resolved ideological ten-
sions between Islamists and the Egyptian state. Islamist violence remained a threat to Egypt's social and economic stability, and Hosni
Mubarak, like his two predecessors, continued to use this violence
to justify emergency measures that restrict civil society and thwart
meaningful political participation.[1] Did Egyptians blame Islamists
more than the ruling regime for this impasse? Was the regime, despite suspicions of its commitment to democracy, empowered by Islamist violence because Egyptians feared an Islamist "reign of virtue
and terror" more than they resented the political and economic status
quo?[2] Such questions test the effectiveness of the Kharijite image
on Egyptian public opinion, but they remain largely unanswered, like
many questions relating to Egypt's political future, stalled at the bal-
lot box.

In the absence of meaningful election results or accurate social
science data, it is difficult to know the extent to which the perceived
threat of Kharijism and other aspects of the Islamic idiom have influenced Egyptian attitudes toward Islamists, whether moderate or
radical, and the state.[3] Of course, there is no denying the polemical
uses to which the label "Kharijte" was put. And, to the extent that
deploying "Kharijite" was effective, it defended the political establishment against the Islamist challenge, even if the establishment

was authoritarian and undemocratic. Thus, much as critics of culture-talk claim, it tended to obfuscate political realities behind an essentialist image of primitive rebellion. But Kharijism was never a stagnant, uncontested image. In fact, its mythic quality allowed it to communicate the traditional Islamic moral sanction against Muslim rebels and to facilitate debate about the modern conditions that provoke extremist tendencies. The control exercised by the Nasserist state, along with the cult-like support the president enjoyed, initially thwarted serious disagreement over mainstream interpretations of Kharijism and its identification with militant Islamism. This situation began to change under Sadat, when Islamists were again permitted to voice openly their dissatisfaction with the "un-Islamic" character of the secular state and thus provide mitigating reasons for their radical wing's resort to violent (supposedly Kharijite) methods. But it was not until after Sadat's assassination that a spectrum of concerned Egyptians addressed the problem of Kharijism and its meaning for the nation. This is not to say that, once a more open exchange of ideas was tolerated, Egyptians came to think better of the Kharijites. Rather, they thought about them differently, in ways that diverged dramatically from traditional characterizations of the first heterodox sect.

This rethinking of Kharijism paralleled a more critical examination of the causes of modern extremism. It is important to remember that the label "Kharijite" was itself intended as an explanation of the cause of militant Islamism. In simplest terms, which is how it was commonly deployed by religious and political commentators, the image of the Kharijites posited a medieval paradigm of illegitimate rebellion to account for modern cases of religiously justified violence. However, Islamist violence in Egypt was anything but simple, a fact of which Egyptians grew increasingly aware during the eras of Nasser and Sadat. Faced with continued paroxysms of Islamist rage, Egyptians began to consider the political, social, and economic realities that contributed to extremist ideas and actions, and they did so through the very cultural symbol that had initially served to mask these realities—Kharijism. The traditional image of Kharijites, then, continued to receive attention throughout the 1980s and 1990s even as Egyptians tried to get behind the essentialism it communicated.

As the evidence in this chapter will show, the Kharijism reinvented in this period facilitated an understanding of the political, social, and economic roots of Islamist extremism. Instead of concealing the underlying processes of change, it helped reveal them. Here the method of revealing should also draw our attention, for it points to the hybrid style of knowledge that has emerged in modern Muslim societies. The reinvention of tradition proceeds by re-mythologizing, by recreating orthodoxy, in the context of a Muslim world transformed by modern social and empirical sciences. Thus, when Muslims "represent the present within an authoritative narrative that includes positive [and negative] evaluations of past events and persons,"[4] their representations have been influenced by these new forms of knowledge. Though traditional Muslim thinkers may hesitate to integrate this knowledge into their analyses, others are more accommodating. More important, the audiences with which established and would-be authorities must collaborate to achieve this instrumental orthodoxy have been educated into, or at least exposed to, these modern sciences. The knowledge produced by such cultural collaboration is not that of the modern social scientist, but neither is it a case of religious essences winning out over the forces of modernization. In fact, more often than not, this collaborative process produces a popular orthodoxy that draws on and subsumes other knowledge bases, including that of traditional religion.

An example of this hybrid cultural style appeared in a series of articles in the popular weekly magazine *al-Musawwar* soon after the assassination of Anwar Sadat.[5] The Jihad attack had demonstrated a blatant disregard for the legitimacy of the presidential office and the political foundation of the modern state. It had also threatened Egypt's image as a progressive, developing nation, one whose citizens were politically mature enough to sustain a democratic system of government. Much of the anti-extremist rhetoric, including the accusation of Kharijism that was initially deployed in response to this situation, had a conservative, establishment content: it undermined the motives and actions of the Jihad assassins, defended Sadat as a legitimate leader, and, by logical extension, confirmed the authority of the state. But in the *al-Musawwar* articles, this same discourse also began to merge with other explanations of Islamist violence, explanations offered by a range of professional experts and opinion makers: representatives of official Islam weighed in with pronouncements about the un-Islamic nature of militancy, including the dangers of Kharijism; politicians commented on the subversive political motivation of the Islamists, on their desire to undermine the democracy in Egypt; a sociologist pointed to the social and economic factors that transform otherwise good people into radicals; a psychologist emphasized the impact of the environment on people's mental state; and public commentators drew attention to the history of political violence in Egypt. These insights presented a complex picture of Islamist violence, but one with no clear focus or perspective, leaving readers with the responsibility of sorting it all out, to determine which insight was most convincing and authoritative. And sorting it all out became increasingly difficult to do as the range and depth of knowledge on extremism expanded.

This new knowledge that was brought to bear on extremism did not advocate tolerating extremists. It did, however, tend to humanize them and make the violence that they perpetuated seem more "normal." Nowhere was this trend more evident than in the discussions of youth (shabab) that came to parallel discourse on extremists and Kharijites. Young people dominated the ranks of Islamist organizations, and they comprised that segment of society most susceptible to the lure of extremist ideas, to becoming neo-Kharijites. Thus the more Egyptians came to know about extremism, the more they came to understand the problems facing the nation's youth and the thin line that separated them from the radical path. In the post-Sadat era, then, public discourse on Kharijite-like extremism became a narrative of national self-discovery, of coming to terms with the limitations and failures of modern Egyptian society and the state that governed it. Such a dramatic shift in public discourse attests to the emergence of new anti-extremist politics. Under Nasser and the old anti-extremist politics, acts of Islamist violence were occasions for valorizing the ruler and the state; under Mubarak and the new politics, acts of Islamist violence were occasions to interrogate the state and society for their complicity in the phenomenon of extremism. Under the old anti-extremist politics, Islamist radicalism was portrayed as a fundamental threat to the values and progress of modern Egypt; under the new politics, radicalism was interpreted as a symptom of larger political, social, and economic problems affecting the nation. This is not to say that the old politics faded from the scene. Instead, both the old and the new contributed to the public discourse on extremism and, in a sense, complemented each other. For while the old nurtured the Egyptian polity in times of crisis, the new insisted that the system was seriously flawed; and, more important, while the old tolerated no compromise with extremism, the new exhibited a critical understanding of it and a noticeable measure of empathy toward those who became caught up in it.

New Knowledge about Extremism

This shift in anti-extremist politics was brought about by historical experience and self-criticism, the culmination of a learning process in which Egyptians came to realize that state authoritarianism and Islamist violence were intertwined elements of the same political culture and that social and economic problems contributed directly to the extremist trend. In other words, Egyptians came to see Islamist extremism as a problem related to the unfinished business of modernization: the formation of a legitimate nation-state and the development of a viable economy. These insights into the nature of the problem received attention in the public discourse during the 1980s and into the 1990s, but the groundwork for this kind of critical analysis of extremism was initially laid in the 1970s, when the politics were ripe for self-criticism. Of course, the kind of political, social, and economic analyses that emerged in the post-Sadat period was not new to Egyptian society. It was, however, newly applied to the phenomenon of extremism.[6] It is important to remember that radical Islamism only emerged in mid-century, with the rising conflict between the Muslim Brothers and Nasser's regime. But putting this conflict into historical perspective, and gleaning lessons from it, took several decades and the effort of a president, Sadat, bent on carving out his own place in Egyptian history.

Throughout the 1950s and 1960s, articles about the rise and development of the Muslim Brothers appeared in the official press on a regular basis, particularly after confrontations with the state. The Brothers, according to the story line of these articles, were a continuation of the great Muslim reformers who had reinterpreted Islam to meet the challenges of the modern age, and who had laid the groundwork for a cultural defense against imperialist aggression. In the photo spread that accompanied these stories, Hasan al-Banna's picture would commonly appear alongside those of Jamal al-Din al-Afghani and Muhammad 'Abduh. Nasser and the Free Officers were also cast in the same historical light as descendents of the reformist tradition. But the violence adopted by some Brothers and justified by many created a breach in the historical consciousness of the time. As popular opinion had it, and as the official press made clear, Nasser and the Free Officers had liberated Egypt from colonial rule and set the nation on a progressive historical course. The 1952 revolution marked a new beginning and, like all revolutions, an end to the need for political violence. For this reason, the militant activities of the Brothers did not comport with Egyptian national self-understanding in the postrevolutionary period, a self-understanding that the Nasser regime itself helped construct and reinforce.

Perhaps this accounts for the historically disjunctive appeal to the Kharijites. Egyptians were too near the actual events of Nasser's rule to judge them clearly, and they were too convinced of the regime's potential, either through hope or fear, to question its version of reality. In a very real sense, the image of the Kharijites filled an intellectual gap by providing a deep historical perspective that had inherent explanatory power. The process by which religion in general and the image of the Kharijites in particular came to serve the state was outlined in chapters 2 and 3. What is important to emphasize here is the extent to which the perceived threat of Kharijism played into the state's desire to separate Islamists from the social and political context of modern Egypt. For Nasser, a politicized Islamic opposition had no role to play in the modern, progressive history of the postrevolutionary nation. The Islamic tradition seemingly assisted in this political critique of Islamism by locating the causes of religious militancy in the transhistorical threat of Kharijism, not the everyday life of Egypt. Though effective while it lasted, the historical disconnect between Islamist politics and the Nasserist state ended with the transfer of power.

In contrast to Nasser's method of dealing with the Islamist opposition, Sadat freed those Brothers who had been imprisoned through legal and extralegal means and allowed the movement to operate with surprisingly little government interference. Moreover, he welcomed their participation, along with that of other previously suppressed groups and the wider public, in a cultural critique of the ex-president's legacy. By promoting a critical assessment of Nasserism, Sadat breathed new life into Egyptian political culture and furthered his own political agenda. He also inadvertently helped foster a more historically informed understanding of Islamist extremism, for as the amount and depth of commentary and analysis grew, the role and responsibility of the Nasserist state in the event-driven history of Islamist militancy became apparent.

By the late 1970s, Islamists had reestablished their activist role in society, including publishing, and they were only too eager to recount their treatment under Nasser's rule. In fact, the memoir, especially the prison memoir, became something of a minor literary genre among Islamists and one of their most potent polemical weapons. After all, what better way to indict the secular state than to detail the tortures it inflicted on the minds and bodies of pious Muslims and their families? One of the more well-known and best-selling memoirs was that of Zeinab al-Ghazali, founder of the Muslim Women's Association and close associate of Hasan al-Banna and Sayyid Qutb. Her life story, which she recounted in *Days of My Life*, epitomized the dedication and sacrifice of Islamists who worked toward the religious and political transformation of Egypt.[7] It also provided a stark witness to the government's systematic harassment and suppression of the movement, both inside and outside of prison. Arrested in the 1965 crackdown under Nasser and released by Sadat in 1971, Zeinab al-Ghazali voiced the experience of a generation of Islamists who viewed themselves as victims of a corrupt and corrupting regime. She expressed many of the same sentiments that Sayyid Qutb had written of earlier in *Signposts* (a work that al-Ghazali helped smuggle out of prison). Her style of criticism, however, was more direct, and she was not tainted by the stigma of extremism. Indeed, Zeinab al-Ghazali skirted the issue of radical politics in her memoir. As one scholar has noted, she "consciously depicts the Brotherhood as a peaceful and peace-loving association of pious Muslims, with no reference to its numerous conflicts or to the Brotherhood's violent tendencies."[8]

Though certainly biased, Zeinab al-Ghazali's memoir left little doubt that Islamists operated in a political context in which their decisions were often reactions to the policies and pressures of the state, and that state-sanctioned violence contributed to the frustration and alienation of Islamists. A similar message emerged in Hasan al-Hudaybi's *Preachers ... Not Judges*, a memoir-like account of the prison debates that split the Islamist movement into radical and moderate factions.[9] Although al-Hudaybi clearly rejected the radical path, he recognized that both radicals and moderates were responding to the realities of life under Nasser. After participating in the revolution, the Brothers had hoped to gain a place of prominence in Egypt's political establishment. Instead, their voices were trivialized by the Free Officers and then suppressed when Nasser sought to consolidate his power. In prison, according to al-Hudaybi, the Brothers debated the best means of dealing with the situation in which they found themselves, with Nasser's treachery and the state-imposed impediments to Islamize society. A faction came to see violence as the only way to counter the threat posed by the secular state and to bring about immediate change, while the majority decided that gradual change through preaching and peaceful social activism was the best course. Al-Hudaybi's narrative, along with that of Zeinab al-Ghazali and of other Islamists, integrated the life of the Islamist movement with the political life of Egypt; and in such narratives, radicalism, though typically condemned, came across as a product of the times, not a throwback to seventh-century sectarian infighting. More scholarly treatments of Nasser's relationship with the Muslim Brothers confirmed the authoritarian setting in which extremism emerged.[10]

But it was not just the work of Islamists that put Nasser's regime and political violence into critical historical focus; other victims of the regime, on the right and left, contributed. The newspaper editor Mustapha Amin, for example, wrote of his imprisonment and torture; and he, along with other journalists, decried the failure of the press under Nasser to see beyond "censorship and nationalization" and fulfill its professional mission.[11] Figures on the left, such as Louis Awad and Fathi 'Abd al-Fattah, also recounted their mistreatment by the regime. Even the literary figure Tawfiq al-Hakim, who had enjoyed Nasser's favor for many years, turned on his benefactor, publishing a scathing and deeply personal reappraisal of Nasser's leadership. By the mid- to late 1970s, these writings had established a clear picture of the authoritarian nature of Nasser's regime. Nasser did have his defenders, but the tide of criticism seemed in agreement that Egypt had become a police state under his rule.[12]

Nasser's victims, then, produced a convincing body of evidence that implicated the state in political violence and helped relativize the idea and practice of extremism. The impetus for this reassessment of the state's role in political violence grew out of Sadat's "corrective revolution," which the new president set in motion in order to secure his hold on power and eliminate challenges from Nasserist loyalists. The corrective revolution began on the dramatic note of a coup attempt, but actual change was far more subtle than the word "revolution" connotes. During the early years of his rule, Sadat was careful to frame his new policies as consistent with Nasser's, even when they were clearly not. Over time, however, he became more openly critical of his predecessor's poor record on both political openness and economic development. Sadat typically empowered others to express concerns about his predecessor's authoritarian politics, but he spoke more openly and bluntly about Nasser's economic development plan. In a 1977 al-Ahram interview, he told reporters, "It was clear to me in 1970 that what we called the socialist experiment and which we carried out in the 1960s was a 100 percent failure."[13] Following the nakba or disaster of the 1967 war, Nasser himself recognized the need to reform his previous economic policies, and he appointed a new minister of finance, Dr. 'Abd al-Aziz Higazi, to oversee the reform process. Sadat kept Higazi in the position and instituted a series of new economic and political policies that undid much of what Nasser had put in place: reversal of the sequestration of property, overhaul of industry, cutting ties with the Soviet Union, and peace overtures toward Israel.

What is important to note here is the general atmosphere of critical reassessment that pervaded both government offices and public discourse at the time. And by the end of the Sadat era, Egyptians had another set of political and economic experiences to evaluate: added to the failures of Nasser's autocratic politics and socialist development plans were Sadat's more liberal political experiment—which was never all that liberal and in the end collapsed—and his capitalist-oriented open-door policy—which filled stores with foreign goods that many desired but only a minority of the population could actually afford. In his October Paper of 1974, Sadat laid out his plan to reinvigorate the economy through a free-market infusion of capital and a modest cutting-back of the welfare program. Once institutionalized, the plan met with dramatic popular resistance: massive strikes of industrial workers (1975–76), bread riots (1977), and increasing Islamist criticism. Egyptians, so it seemed, and so Islamists were quick to point out, had tried two Western programs of modernization and development, and neither had proved successful at creating political and economic stability. Thus, some thirty years after the revolution, Egyptians still found themselves struggling to give birth to a modern state and economy. Sadat's assassination, combined with the rising critical trend in public discourse, triggered a period of national soul-searching that addressed this ongoing struggle and linked it with the continuing threat of Islamist violence.

Egyptians, then, used the occasion of Sadat's assassination to apply what they had learned about Islamist extremism; and they had learned a great deal. Egyptians had clearly become aware of the role of the state in perpetuating the very activities that it purported to oppose. Moreover, with the new historical perspective they had gained on extremism—through the production of personal memoirs, historical studies, and political analysis—Egyptians could see the way the politics of violence played out between the state and Islamists, the way that violence was negotiated. These negotiations began when the Free Officers elicited the aid of the Muslim Brothers during the revolution, when violent street protests were useful to the cause; they continued under Sadat, when he sought to consolidate his hold on power by releasing imprisoned Islamists to oppose Nasserist holdovers; and they have been essential to the survival of Mubarak, whose concessions to Islamists have allowed him to maintain power without democratizing. As Gehad Auda has argued, Mubarak's need to negotiate has exceeded that of his predecessors because Egypt's problems have multiplied and the state has become more vulnerable to criticism. Through his "social contract" with the Muslim Brothers, Mubarak has agreed "to allow an ideologically hostile force to penetrate publicly the institutions of the professional middle class." In return, the Brotherhood:

> agreed it would not politicize the socio-economic hardships that accompanied economic reforms, but would channel the quest for political reform and liberalization of the political system through state political institutions . . . and not through demonstrations, violence and strikes. It agreed, moreover, that its control of substantial influence in state political institutions would not lead it to try to transform these institutions into a power base hostile to the government, and that it would never seek political gains as a result of its control or influence over social resources.[14]

These agreements were not formal accords, signed in public, but rather tacit compromises worked out in the undertones of official statements, voiced by a state that tolerated no real opposition and an illegal organization that desperately needed access to Egypt's limited public square. Such political accommodation, according to Auda, signaled a normalization of relations between the Brothers and the state. In effect, these ideological opponents agreed to live and, when necessary, even cooperate with one other according to established rules. Underlying the political accommodation negotiated between the state and Brothers, however, was the cultural accommodation of political violence taking place in the public discourse on extremism. For while Mubarak and the Brothers in the 1980s were ironing out a modus vivendi, the developing discourse made it clear that Egypt had a history of political violence, that the state was an active participant in it, and that Egypt's political and economic system contributed directly to Islamist extremism. The normalized relations between the state and Islamists, then, coincided with the public's more critical attitude toward political violence and its complex roots. And the main object of the public's concern, as the debate about the problem and causes of extremism proceeded, was the youth of the nation.

Rebellious Youth and Popular Public Sentiment

In his study of the education system in modern-day Egypt, Gregory Starrett argues that religion has become a mainstay of the modern public curriculum, used to inculcate moral values deemed necessary for national development and for combating the Islamist political tide.[15] Reliance on religion to educate the young is a long-standing tradition in Egypt, as it is elsewhere in the Muslim world. Writing in the mid-nineteenth century, Edward Lane, author of the famous *Manners and Customs of the Modern Egyptians*, indicated that the Qur'an was the primary means by which schoolmasters taught young boys basic skills in reading and writing. Lane also noted the chaotic atmosphere of the schools: boys reading their various lessons aloud at the same time and schoolmasters, untrained and poorly paid, exercising nominal supervision.[16] This situation began to change over the course of the nineteenth century as the modern reforms of Muhammad 'Ali, governor of Egypt, and his son and political successor, Isma'il, took effect. These reforms had their inspiration in scientific techniques of bureaucratic and institutional organization formulated in Europe, techniques that would, as Timothy Mitchell has documented, facilitate the colonial project in Egypt and elsewhere. For political leaders seeking to transform and modernize their societies, the utility of these disciplinary methods was obvious: they "produce the organized power of armies, schools, and factories, and other distinctive institutions of modern nation-states. These also produce, within such institutions, the modern individual, constructed as an isolated, disciplined, receptive, and industrious political subject."[17]

Such disciplinary methods were gradually institutionalized in Egypt during the twentieth century, and the national system of education, like other public institutions, sought to generate the kind of "political subject" just cited. Religion was essential to this mission because of its deep cultural roots and its consequent potential to either contribute to or interfere with the disciplinary authority of the modern state. It was not traditional religion, however, that the youth of Egypt were to experience in their modern classrooms. Rather, as Starrett makes clear, it was a religion that had been "objectified" into a subject that needed to be taught by the state and then "funtionalized" into a set of instructive iconic and discursive messages. Put differently, to tame religion to its national institutional will, the state transformed religion from a general cultural influence to a means of shaping "the public"; and the school system was just one sign of the changing importance of religion in Egyptian public life. The institutional direction of modernization, according to Starrett, has made religion relevant in a number of new ways, including the public's reliance on religious discourse.[18]

Religious discourse in Egypt's public schools reflects a state-mandated vision of the Muslim ethical requirements incumbent on the nation's youth. But there is more than just one public in Egypt, as there is more than just one religious discourse. The "public" of the school system is dominated by state authorities, though this control has never been absolute, for teachers are drawn from the same citizen pool that fills the ranks of the Islamist movement and other opposition groups. The "public" of the media and publishing industry reflects a broader range of opinion. By its nature, this popular public is polyphonic and discordant, which is to say that it is composed of multiple discourses, including multiple religious discourses. Moreover, it is constrained, as is all communication in Egypt, by direct and indirect state-oversight. The current government, of course, claims to speak on behalf of this popular public, but contenders for this right exist; and the search to identify contenders, to impact the domestic political process in Egypt, is sometimes furthered by the very popular public that is so difficult to isolate and clarify.[19] Unlike identifiable factions such as Islamists, secularists, traditionalists, and the state, the Egyptian mainstream is more amorphous and difficult to represent. Its views and interests are communicated in the interstices of formal factional debates, in the concessions made by ideologues to popular public sentiment, in state appeals to the masses, and, as I attempt to show, in the popular public discourse on religious extremism. Indeed, extremism in a very real sense gave impetus to the formation and expression of mainstream views, since extremism and its underlying causes most threatened Egyptians' ability to secure a good life.

What is most distinctive and hopeful about mainstream opinion found in public discourse is its critical approach, an attitude often lacking in public debates. For some observers, one of the biggest impediments to reform within Muslim societies has been this lack of critical self-analysis:

> The intelligentsia are as confused as before, and their main preoc-
> cupation is finding culprits abroad, such as the Elders of Zion and
> the Western imperialists, for the misery of their society. The precon-
> dition for any real change is self-criticism, an honest and pitiless
> search for the deeper reasons why things went wrong in the Islamic
> world, why others are strong and Islam is weak, why its societies have
> become cultural deserts. Such critics have existed in the Muslim
> world, but so far they have been voices calling in the wilderness.[20]

In Egypt during the 1980s, the popular discourse on extremism met these preconditions, generating one of the most critical and insightful debates that Egypt has seen; and the voices calling out represented a wider segment of society than is typical in such debates. To be sure, there were those who sought an explanation for Muslim radicalism in Zionist conspiracies and Western intrigues. But the dominant trend was to look for reasons within Egyptian society, reasons informed by the knowledge addressed in the previous section.

Throughout the 1980s, reports in the popular press made it clear that young people were frustrated in general with the world that their parents had created. The youth of the nation loved their country and their religion, but they regarded their lives as constrained by the political status quo, the lack of economic opportunities, and a society that expected conformity and com-promise. Articles about the political situation in Egypt painted a grim portrait. Young people had been raised in an atmosphere where assassinations, vio-lence, and crisis were the norm, where their political opinion was discounted, and where their civic participation was severely curtailed. They came of age when Nasser used prison and the state security apparatus for his own political purpose.[21] And such abuses of state power did not end with the Nasser period. They continued unabated through successive regimes, especially at the hands of the Ministry of Interior, which was charged with domestic security. In fact, in the confrontation of extremist terrorism, the brutal methods of one min-ister, Zaki Badr, were described as part of the problem, not the solution.[22] Not surprising, the same state that strictly policed the nation's youth also failed to reach out to them, to offer them a vision of a meaningful political future. The Wafd Party in particular came in for criticism regarding its inability to attract young people. In sum, according to the opinions expressed in these articles, the youth had certainly lost their way and committed errors, but the larger failure was that of a harsh and unresponsive political system. Lacking positive models of political leadership, and practical models for peaceful and effective political participation, the young had become susceptible to the voices of radical Islam.[23]

Social and economic factors also weighed heavily upon young people. Analysis articles and published discussions with representative groups of youth, including jailed Islamists, highlighted the intense anxiety that dominated the thoughts of young people. Much of this anxiety centered on concerns about the potential for personal success, such as access to university, finding a job, and starting a family. For some, anxiety led to despair; for others, it resulted in anger and resentment. Young people, it seems, were in a delicate psychological state—a fact that professional mental health workers confirmed in their public diagnoses of the radical condition. Almost all discussions about the causes of extremism acknowledged the sensitive psychological nature of youth. Nowhere was this more evident than in the debates about the destructive potential of television. From the early 1980s and throughout the 1990s, television was commonly cited as a contributing cause, sometimes the driving force behind, the youthful turn toward violence. In the 1980s, the debate tended toward the therapeutic, with observers decrying the harmful effects of television on individuals whose mental and moral faculties were not fully formed. By the 1990s, in the wake of Islamist attacks on Naguib Mahfouz and Farag Fowda, the debate had become more politically charged, with factions lining up to assert control over the media.

Of the various causes of extremism debated in public discourse, it was the economic plight of youth that drew the most intense and sustained attention. Young people themselves attested to their frustration with the limited economic opportunities available in Egypt, and media commentators noted that terrorist organizations preyed upon this frustration, leading youth down a destructive path and further sapping the productive potential of the nation.[24] But the economic link with extremism was most clearly established by academic researchers, such as Saad Eddin Ibrahim, who conducted interviews with Islamist radicals. Ibrahim, a professor of sociology at the American University in Cairo, had received government permission to interview imprisoned members of the Military Academy group and al-Takfir wa'l-Hijra, two militant organizations active in the 1970s. The results of his study were published, in English, in 1980,[25] but they received prominent attention in the Egyptian media following Sadat's assassination.[26]

The profile that Ibrahim created of the militants highlighted their class expectations, not their seeming atavistic attitudes and preoccupation with scrupulous piety, which he regarded as distractions from the underlying causes of extremism. According to the profile, the militants were, for the most part, educated, high achievers, the kind of people who "would normally be considered model young Egyptians."[27] They had bought into the dream of modernization and success that Nasser and then Sadat had fostered. They had worked hard as students and they had played by the political rules, despite the restrictions. But when their expectations exceeded the opportunities made available by the state-run economy, these model Egyptians turned to an alternative means of establishing social status—militant Islam. This profile, or variations of it, became a standard theme in the debate about extremism in Egypt, taken up by various factions, including Islamists. It also has had a profound impact on the study of Islamism, moderate and radical, in the Western academy, a critical point to which we shall return later in the chapter.

The twofold assumption behind much of this discourse was that the Egyptian youth who had joined militant Islamist organizations were as much victims as they were victimizers, and that society at large had contributed to this situation, in whole or in part, and was responsible for remedying it. This attitude of collective social accountability was nicely captured in the title of an article that appeared in 1987 in the weekly magazine *Ruz al-Yusuf*: "Extremism Continues and We Are Responsible."[28] In the article, the minister of endowments (*awqaf*), Dr. Muhammad 'Ali Mahjoub, elaborated on the economic, political, and psychological pressures under which young people were forced to live and which drove them down the path of extremism. In light of the Islamist violence that was to unfold in Egypt in the 1990s, especially the 1997 Luxor massacre, and the September 11, 2001, attacks in the United States, such empathetic understanding of young people's recourse to militancy may seem out of place. But in the mid- to late-1980s, a time of relative calm, this message was well received in Egypt. Indeed, it appealed to and even benefited the wider public. After all, most Egyptians were subject to the same political, social, and economic pressures that so adversely affected the young. Granted, the vast majority did not resort to violent means of protest, but frustration was not an uncommon sentiment among people of the lower and would-be middle class. Thus, although the young might be viewed as impetuous and irresponsible, their concerns and complaints were well known to many Egyptians on an experiential level. In fact, wider public interests were served by the media focus on young rebels, for through an open, sympathetic discussion of the challenges facing Egyptian youth, the problems facing all Egyptians achieved public attention and respect.

In the 1980s, public discourse on the social causes of extremism did not translate into condoning Islamist violence or blatant hostility toward the government. Many commentators acknowledged the rightful concerns of the state for order and authority and the need for the state to act resolutely when violence occurred. Moreover, the government was also given credit for trying to resolve many of the economic and social problems that hindered individual success and national development. Public opinion, then, seemed to sympathize with the responsibilities and challenges faced by the state. At the same time, however, the discourse witnessed an unprecedented display of public soul-searching and a tacit accommodation of rebellious youth. Reading Egyptian newspapers and magazines of the period is reminiscent of public responses to chronic social problems in other countries, such as drugs in the United States or organized crime in Italy. The leading contributors to the problem earn little sympathy from the wider public, but many who become caught up in it seem more like confused victims. Some politicians and social commentators opt for the tough approach: crackdowns, public trials (in military courts), and jail. Others prefer a gentler approach: social programs, public awareness campaigns, and therapy. In the end, the nature of the problem is so confusing and the political pressures of ending it are so acute that various, and opposing, approaches are adopted. Indeed, different branches of the same administration's government may be fighting the war in very different ways.[29] The costs of the problem—to the economy, to families and communities, and to the nation as a whole—are constantly played out in the media. The public is up in arms for a period, and then they lose interest. But with each new upsurge in the problem, public attention is again refocused. Over time, people begin to view the problem as not just intractable but incurable, something that they will simply have to accept because the individuals and the institutions involved are the way that they are. To be sure, public officials, politicians, and opinion makers still rail against the problem, but most people learn to live with it as a normal part of their existence.

What are we to make of the array of causes put forth to explain Islamist extremism? Why are Islamist youth both denounced and defended? Why is the state both soundly criticized and highly praised for its actions? One way to answer is to point back to the complexity of the problem. After all, given the various possible contributing factors and their interconnection, some amount of confusion was bound to prevail. For mainstream Egyptians, however, the fundamental problem was not so much confusion as it was a decided ambivalence toward both the state and Islamists, an ambivalence that led to ambiguity in interpreting the meaning of political violence. Egyptians could no longer blindly support the state and criticize Islamists, because the lines between moderation and extremism, between justified and unjustified violence, between innocence and guilt, had been blurred. As experience had shown, and as the public discourse about this experience had reinforced, the state engaged in and perpetuated political violence; and, just as important, the state had failed to make good on its promises of political, economic, and social development. In response, public discourse began to cast doubt on the image of Islamist militants as irredeemable enemies of society, emphasizing instead the factors that drove them to adopt radicalism.

In Egypt of the 1980s, then, discourse on extremism took the debate over political violence in a direction that furthered popular public interests rather than those of the state or Islamists. That direction was one of reform—reform of politics, the economy, and society at large. And the vehicle for promoting such reform was the interpretation of violence. The Egyptian state typically used occasions of Islamist violence to reaffirm its authority and demonstrate its power. Moderate Islamists used such occasions to emphasize the level of righteous, though misdirected, anger among Egyptians and to call for a return to Islamic values. Both of these views found individual expression in the larger public discourse of the 1980s and 1990s; both also contributed to a transvaluation of the discourse on violence, forming a new moral standard based on security and reform. The desire for law and order and the fear of an Islamist reign of terror were unmistakable themes in the discourse of the time. But just as evident, if not more so, was the theme of cautious sympathy for those who may resort to violence as an instrumental means of protest and reform.

The instrumental violence being vindicated here, however, was not for Islamist ends, not for the implementation of Islamic law or the formation of an Islamic state. Instead, it was for practical reforms that the youth and majority of Egyptians, including many Islamists, seemed to support: an opening of the political system, an improvement in economic opportunity, and the development of workable social institutions. The new anti-extremist politics reflected a popular public imaginary that had grown fearful of both an Islamist reign of terror and the state's incompetence and authoritarianism. Resignation toward the realities of political violence was evident in this new politics, but so, too, was the hope that violence had a greater purpose. As one student of political violence has observed, "violence...is a much more effective weapon of reformers than revolutionists."[30] The hope expressed in the new anti-extremist politics was that Egypt's youth were in fact reformers, not revolutionists, and that the violence they perpetuated signaled the dramatic need for change.

When Nature Meets Nurture: The New Kharijites

In the new anti-extremist politics that emerged in the 1980s, the interpretive tendency was to view extremism as a political and social problem that demanded political and social answers. Islamist radicals, simply put, were nurtured within the body politic and the fabric of society. This new insight into the problem of Islamist extremism, along with the new knowledge that supported it, stood in stark contrast to the view fostered by the old politics and the traditional Islamic sources on which it depended. In the old politics, Islamist violence was consistently equated with Kharijism, a demonic force rooted in the original activities of Satan and his ongoing efforts to bring about the downfall of humankind. As a result, Islamist radicals were not portrayed as victims of society's failures, as the new politics would have it, but rather as predators upon society; and in carrying out their rebellions, these modern radicals, these neo-Kharijites, were following their evil nature.

Of course, the argument from nature comports with the traditional image of the Kharijites and seems to obviate the need to provide reasons for why Muslims rebel. Thus, according to the nurture argument, Kharijites rebel simply because they are Kharijites, people who, in a deep ontological sense, are perennial rebels against legitimate authority. Here, however, we must be cautious about attributing to Egyptians under Nasser and Sadat, under the old anti-extremist politics, a naive, uncritical acceptance of the past. The image of the Kharijites was intentionally deployed to counter a perceived threat, and, through a combination of state-control and community-acceptance, it came to hold sway in the discourse. In short, the argument from nature was, and is, only viable to the extent that those participating in the discourse think such a view is useful. The same observation is true for the argument from nurture that emerged in the 1980s.

What is intellectually intriguing, and powerful proof that historical context shapes the symbolic content of discourse (not the other way around), is that the image of the Kharijites remained an integral part of the debate over Islamist extremism, even as the debate shifted focus from the essentialist nature of extremists to the social conditions that nurtured them. References to the Kharijites—their origins, views, and violent actions—appeared in a variety of stories and reports. In some cases, these references occurred in thematic contexts in which references to the Kharijites could be expected, such as discussions about the problem of declaring someone an unbeliever (takfir) and the proper method of calling people to the faith (daʻwa).[31] Religious authorities and public commentators commonly evoked the Kharijites in stage-set prison discussions with select militant youth, whose violent deeds demanded public condemnation but whose hearts and minds were seemingly inclined toward reeducation.[32] And specific acts deemed radical also drew comparisons with Kharijism. For example, when Sheikh ʻUmar Abd al-Rahman reaffirmed Ayatollah Khomeini's death warrant against Salman Rushdie for becoming an apostate (*murtad*) for writing *The Satanic Verses* and extended it to apply equally to Egypt's Nobel Prize winner Naguib Mahfouz, a commentary piece in *Ruz al-Yusuf* accused Sheikh 'Umar of Kharijite-like behavior that jeopardized artists and writers in Egypt.[33]

Still, even in cases in which Kharijism was invoked to condemn extremism, it was clear that the context for understanding radical behavior had changed dramatically and that the traditional anti-model of Kharijism no longer set the standard for judging radicals. A good example is a series of articles that appeared in early 1982 in the government-sponsored religious newspaper *al-Liwa' al-islam*. Part of a government effort to reach out to the nation's youth, the articles provide a fascinating insight into the tension that divided people on the question of extremism. In one article, recounting an "open intellectual dialogue" between al-Azhar scholars and university students on the question "What is extremism and why does it appear in society?" a diverse and contradictory set of responses emerged.[34] For one scholar, the problem of extremism was a matter of right knowledge; for another, extremism was linked to state oppression in prison; for another, extremism had it roots in the Kharijites; for still another, there were different kinds of extremism that needed to be addressed: political extremism, religious extremism, and social extremism. One business student from Port Said wanted to know why they were not talking about economic and social repression, instead of extremism, since repression is what drove young people toward God and extremist ideas. Another student spoke of the fear engendered in the nation's youth from hearing about the treatment of the Muslim Brothers in prison during the Nasser and Sadat periods of rule. This fear, according to the student, has left its mark on the Islamic Group organizations (*al-Gama'a al-Islamiyya*); it is a "sickness" that is mistaken for extremism and for which there is currently no adequate treatment.

Prison dialogues with members of the Islamic Group gave rise to a similar array of opinions about extremism. Once again, radical ideas and behavior were sternly condemned, and sometimes linked to Kharijism, but participants in the dialogues, both members of the Islamic Group and al-Azhar representatives, took the discussion in a variety of social, economic, and political directions that belied any simplistic understanding of extremism or easy solution to the problem. These dialogues with the nation's youth, in and out of prison, reflected the same nurture-based interpretations of extremism that were driving the larger public discourse. For young and old alike, extremism had grown into a far more complex issue, and Kharijism had by association grown along with it. This is not to say that a new definition of Kharijism emerged. In fact, the traditional story line about the rise of Kharijism continued to be told,

and references to medieval heresiographers such as al-Shahrastani still found
their way into print. Yet, however static Kharijism seemed from a historical-
cultural perspective, its meaning experienced subtle shifts when introduced
into specific modern contexts. In the course of the 1980s, as part of the standard cultural backdrop against which extremism was compared, Kharijism was
pulled along on the wave of public interest in the new knowledge about the
social, economic, and political factors that contributed to, if not caused violent
rebellion among the nation's youth. And, as a result, by the end of the decade,
just as the word "extremism" (tatarruf) could no longer be evoked without
drawing attention to these factors, so, too, the name "Kharijites" came with
similar connotations.

This shift in the symbolic meaning of the Kharijites was typically neither
intentional nor intellectually coherent. It occurred in the dynamic exchange of
ideas and opinions in public discourse, and it gave rise to odd interpretive
blends that communicated mixed messages. An example from the mid-1980s
will help make the point. In a weekly column in Ruz al-Yusuf, the subtitle
accuses the Islamic Group of "intellectual laziness" and "political oppor-
tunism."[35] The article goes on to discuss the problem of takfir—its divisive-
ness, its un-Islamic character, and its potential for violence. This problem, so
the article states, has its origin in the actions of the Kharijites, and the modern
heirs of this practice are the Muslim Brothers, most notably Sayyid Qutb. So
far, this reads like one of the many articles that one might have encountered
in the press in the 1960s or '70s. But then a further bit of information is
given: what is called religious extremism developed during the Nasser period
in the furnace-like conditions of military prisons, which inflicted torture on
pious Muslims and produced the idea of takfir.

Here the image of the Kharijites has expanded to implicate and thus
challenge not just the militant Islamists who resort to the practice of takfir—
Muslim Brothers and the Islamic Group—but also the state system of oppression. Here also a further link in the Kharijite chain of causation seems to
mitigate the responsibility of Islamist radicals, for without the corrupting
influence of the state the seeds of takfir may never have taken root. Not all
examples of the new anti-extremist politics, like the one above, lay out a causal
timeline that allows the proximate extremist factor to be clearly identified. But
all imply, with differing degrees of narrative efficiency and effectiveness, that
Kharijsm itself is not the real problem of extremism. Instead, Kharijism is
merely a sign that something else has gone wrong—with society, the economy, or politics—and the only way to eliminate Kharijism is go beyond the
sign and address the underlying problem. In the new politics, then, Kharijism has been reinvented to prioritize the underlying material causes of

extremism over the spiritual manifestation of extremism in misguided ideas and behavior.

In public discourse, a debate over the meaning of extremism pitted the new politics against the old, the argument from nurture against the argument from nature. The most obvious beneficiary of the old politics was the state, which looked to al-Azhar to make the case about the sinful and criminal behavior of the radicals. As it turned out, however, al-Azhar weighed in on both sides of the debate, in part because scholars were divided in their ideological commitments, and in part because the institution itself tried to pander to all sides in order to further its own interests.[36] In the end, neither the state nor the public at large could depend upon al-Azhar for a clear response to extremism. The range of debate on the meaning of extremism can, perhaps, best be captured by the two intellectual antipodes that framed it—the secularist and the Islamist; and no two figures represent these two extremes better than Muhammad Sa'id al-'Ashmawi and Yusuf al-Qaradawi. Both wrote seminal books in the 1980s on the problem of religious extremism, and both drew extensively on the idea of Kharijism to make their case. Their thinking on the problem of extremism reflects the factional politics at work in the discourse and the impact of popular opinion on these factions.

Muhammad Sa'id al-'Ashmawi: Kharijism and the Nature of Extremist Politics

A lawyer by training, al-'Ashmawi served as assistant district attorney in Alexandria and was eventually appointed a judge in Egypt's High Court. He began writing about Islamic law and the relationship between religion and politics in Islam midway into his career. After his retirement in 1993, he dedicated himself to countering the Islamist political agenda in Egypt and presenting a tolerant, enlightened view of Islam to both Muslim and non-Muslim audiences. His writing on religion and politics has been compared to 'Ali 'Abd al-Raziq's *Islam and the Basis of Rule* (*al-Islam wa usul al-hukm*), which raised a firestorm of protest in the 1920s and was banned for a period.[37] Like al-Raziq, al-'Ashmawi has argued for the separation of religion and politics in Muslim societies by reinterpreting Islamic origins against the grain of accepted Muslim understanding. As a result, al-'Ashmawi, like al-Raziq, has been subject to a good deal of intellectual criticism, in addition to physical threats. Al-'Ashmawi's religiously infused method of reasoning about legal and political issues has led one author to cast him as a cross between a Muslim secularist and a reformer.[38] Others have described him more broadly as a universalist and humanist because of his comparative approach to religious morality and meaning.[39] In truth, he does not fit comfortably within any of the categories that have been used to map out modern Muslim thought. One thing seems certain: although al-'Ashmawi's universalist and gnostic-like ideas of religion may lie outside the Egyptian mainstream, his agenda for a rational approach to politics and for institutional separation of religion and politics does not.[40]

Al-'Ashmawi's case against Islamism and the fusion of religion and politics appears most forcefully in *Political Islam (al-Islam al-siyasi)*, a work in which Kharijism plays an important role.[41] For al-'Ashmawy, politics is a limited human enterprise, restricted by group association and by time periods, through which people "search for prestige, positions of power, and financial gain"; religion, by contrast, is a universal phenomenon that expresses peoples' highest aspirations.[42] Thus, when politics takes control of religion, as it has throughout Islamic history, religion is reduced in scope and becomes a reflection of the baser human instincts. The Prophet Muhammad, al-'Ashmawi claims, created a society where religious and civic morality fused, where religion and politics blended seamlessly. But Muhammad's death ended this unique period in Islamic history. Thereafter, without continuing prophetic council, Muslims lost the ability to maintain such a holistic, theocratic society. The rule of the first two caliphs, Abu Bakr and 'Umar, managed to uphold Muhammad's mandate. Their successors, however, began to rely on religion to legitimate their "uninspired" political decisions. And when political disputes arose, as they inevitably do among people, they became difficult, if not impossible, to resolve because terms of religious reprobation, such as infidel, were used to label political opponents. As a result, a series of sectarian conflicts came to divide Muslim against Muslim. Indeed, according to al-'Ashmawi, "All the great political and historical conflicts of Islam have been formulated in a religious manner which hides their essentially political character."[43]

By uncovering this pattern in early Islamic history, al-'Ashmawi hopes to demonstrate the dangerous and un-Islamic character of the modern perpetuators of political Islam, such as Sayyid Qutb of Egypt and Abu 'Ala Mawdudi of Pakistan. The political Islam that these figures promote leads naturally to extremism, in al-'Ashmawi's estimation, because those who advocate the blending of religion and politics lose their capacity for rational thought and become tyrants in the name of God. The prime example of this irrational and tyrannical attitude throughout history has been the slogan "Sovereignty belongs only to God." It was first expressed by the Kharijites, when they rebelled against 'Ali; and it is repeated by modern Islamists, when they rebel against ruling authorities and turn against their fellow Muslims. The slogan itself,

according to al-'Ashmawi, is a verbal sleight of hand. For, although it appears
to promote the rule of God, the real intent of Kharijites old and new is to seize
power under the guise of sacred authority. Moreover, these Kharijites have
deluded themselves into thinking that they have a built-in sanction to use
violence against their (political) opponents, since all those who oppose them
are by definition enemies of God's rule or infidels. The threat posed by the
Kharijites is great, al-'Ashmawi maintains, because "in their hands Islam, a
religion of tolerance and mercy, is transformed into an instrument of terror."[44] The way to avoid this terror is to eliminate religious interference in
politics, to eliminate political Islam.

Attributing the cause of Islamist extremism to the Kharijites both
strengthened and weakened al-'Ashmawi's argument. The image of Kharijites
was certainly part of the overall religious discourse that lent authority and
legitimacy to modern public debates about politics in general and extremism
in particular. But in order to advance a specific political perspective such as
secularism, al-'Ashmawi had to go further than a simple evocation of the
name "Kharijite." After all, everyone in Egypt came out against the Kharijites,
with the notable exception of a few leftist historians in the 1970s.[45] Thus it
was not whether but how people framed their argument against the Khar-
ijiites that revealed their political agenda. Al-'Ashmawi's agenda came
through clearly in the transhistorical definition that he proposed:

> the term Kharijite is less a name designating a group of sects than a
> qualifier for all those who, by manipulating language and exploit-
> ing religion in order to arrive at their political ends, place them-
> selves outside Islam and its law.[46]

This definition, which casts Islamists as heterodox Muslims and the
primary impediments to an institutional divide between religion and politics,
bridged the gap between past and present and put the present situation in
Islamic terms that were easily understood. The Islamic terms, however, put al-
'Ashmawi at cross-purposes with his secular agenda. Al-'Ashmawi wanted to
create a modern political culture in which religion and politics are separate,
in which rationality prevails. As a Muslim secularist, however, he argued this
case by claiming that the institutional separation is inherently Islamic. In
short, al-'Ashmawi tried to use Islam to limit Islam's purview in the political
sphere—an act that leaves him open to the same Kharijite charge that he levels
against Islamists. Indeed, all the participants in public political discourse engaged, to some extent, in the kind of manipulation of language and religion
that al-'Ashmawi characterizes as Kharijite-like.

Relying on religion to further civic-secular ends was nothing new in Egypt or other countries, including those of the West. In the United States, for example, religious organizations and religious debates played an important role in creating the (largely) secular framework that came to dominate public political life.[47] In Egypt, however, the debate in which al-'Ashmawi participated was not taking place at the founding of the republic. Rather, it evolved after a period in which secular governments had tried and failed to meet the political demands and the social and economic needs of their citizens. The seeming ineffectiveness of the secular political alternative was what elevated religious discourse to such prominence. Al-'Ashmawi, then, did not appeal to the existing civil laws of the state or political science theory to justify the separation of religion and politics, because these lacked the cultural legitimacy on which the discourse depended. So, in order to make his case for a separation of religion and politics, he was forced to ignore the very political institutions and ideals that he wished to empower and to empower the very religious influence that he hoped to limit.[48]

The interpretive strain on al-'Ashmawi's analysis of Islamic extremism is most evident when he attempts to address the multiple factors that contribute to it. In his definition of Kharijites and, by extension, their modern Islamist progenitors, it is the unmitigated and un-Islamic drive to political power that leads to extremism. But al-'Ashmawi also writes of extremism as a "universal phenomenon," of which Islamic extremism represents only one facet; and while citing politics as the key determinant of Islamic extremism, he recognizes "other essential factors of a cultural, social and intellectual or psychological order."[49] Specifically, he offers the following list of causal explanations for extremism in Egypt: (1) The inability of uneducated and uncouth rural immigrants (what he terms the "neo-bedouin") to adjust to the more open and sophisticated urban environment leads some to revert to crude pre-Islamic practices. (2) The socioeconomic frustration of those Egyptians who have, due to their limited abilities, been left out of the rising middle class compelled some to assert their claims and seek justice through aggressive religious means. (3) Some Middle Easterners, having been subjected to the political oppression and obscurantist jahiliyya-thinking of the Ottomans for so long, have come to adopt these ways and loose sight of their progressive, enlightened Islamic past. (4) The psychological pressures of living in a complex and confusing modern society lead some of the more spiritually weak and intellectually unreflective members to lash out and resort to terrorism.[50]

Al-'Ashmawi regarded these other factors as tangential to his political assessment of the cause of extremism. Still, he included them in his book because they had already begun to receive public attention by the early 1980s, when he wrote *Political Islam*, and he wanted his analysis to pertain to the debate underway. What is apparent, however, is that he did not take the problems underlying these factors seriously. Instead of presenting them as real-life challenges that effected many Egyptians, and challenges that society would do well to address and resolve, al-'Ashmawi treats them as evidence of the multiple levels of deviancy and backwardness driving the radicals. So, certain Muslims turn to extremism not only because of Kharijite political views, but also because of personal failures and tough-luck experiences in other areas of their life. After weighing all the factors involved with extremism, al-'Ashmawi reached a simple and uncompromising conclusion: neo-Kharijite radicals were all-around losers.

It seems here as though al-'Ashmawi fears that showing sympathy for the conditions that contributed to extremism might strengthen the Islamist position in Egypt. As a result, his critique of political Islam comes across as not just a condemnation of Islamist political activism, but also a staunch defense of the educated, urban, Western-oriented, upper middle class—the segment of the population that is most secularized and most threatened by a potential Islamist-dominated society. In the end, the meaning of extremism most relevant to al-'Ashmawi is one that furthers the interests of the very socioeconomic class that he accuses Islamists of trying, but failing, to enter. Many Egyptians, however, were interested in improving their socioeconomic condition, and they were suspicious of, and sometimes angry about, the political system that they perceived as standing in the way of change. Interestingly enough, these mainstream Egyptians found a more sympathetic voice in Yusuf al-Qaradawi, perhaps the preeminent moderate Islamist of the late twentieth and early twenty-first centuries.

Yusuf al-Qaradawi: The Corrupt Conditions that Nurture Kharijism

Yusuf al-Qaradawi was born in Egypt and earned a Ph.D. at al-Azhar in 1973. He worked for a time at Dar al-Awqaf (the Ministry of Endowments) and taught at al-Azhar, but he later accepted a position in Qatar, where he has lived since. Currently, he serves as dean of the College of Shari'a and Islamic Studies and as director of the Center for Sunna and Sira Studies at the University of Qatar. Al-Qaradawi has been named to the board of many Islamic organizations, and he serves as a consultant in a number of Muslim and non-Muslim countries. He has published numerous books and pamphlets on a wide range of Islamic issues, and he is currently the host of his own talk show on al-Jazira television, the Qatari-based network that has gained a

THE NEW POLITICS OF ANTI-EXTREMIST RHETORIC

popular following in the Arab and wider Muslim world.[51] A firm supporter of
the Islamist politics and policies of Hasan al-Banna, the founder of the Society
of Muslim Brothers, al-Qaradawi has emerged as a moderate thinker who can
bridge the divide between Muslim activists and their respective Muslim and
non-Muslim governments. Although his efforts at mediation have not always
been successful, he has managed to convince factions of radical Islamists in
Egypt of the fruitlessness of violence and the need for gradual, peaceful reform.[52] In fact, his well-known book on the causes of and cures for Islamist
extremism, *Islamic Awakening Between Rejection and Extremism (al-Sahwa al-
islamiyya bain al-juhud wa'l-tatarruf)*, has become something of an instruction
manual for those radicals wanting to confess the error of their ways and (re-)
enter Muslim civil society.

First published in 1982, in the aftermath of Sadat's assassination, *Islamic
Awakening* has gone through several printings and has been translated into
English.[53] Of all al-Qaradawi's writings, this work represents his best effort to
argue the Islamist perspective on a pressing current problem; and of the
various Islamic analyses of extremism, this one is perhaps the most subtle
and insightful ever published. No one who reads *Islamic Awakening* can deny
that al-Qaradawi rejects the extremist violence adopted by some Muslim
youth, but neither could one mistake his sympathy and concern for the
challenges facing them. Thus, although the book serves as a challenge and
corrective to the youth who take up extremism, it is also a devastating critique
of the Egyptian social milieu in which they grow up. And the responsibility for
addressing the problem, in al-Qaradawi's estimation, lies clearly with the
entire community:

> What we actually need is the unflinching courage to admit that our
> youth have been forced to resort to what we call "religious extrem-
> ism" through our own misdeeds...in order to rectify this situation,
> we need to begin by reforming ourselves and our societies accord-
> ing to Allah's decree before we can ask our youth to be calm, to
> show wisdom and temperance.[54]

Again, such remarks may seem overly tolerant, if not radical, in light of
post-September 11 international concerns about the dangers posed by Muslim
extremists. But al-Qaradawi was addressing the needs of a different time and
place. He was participating in a wide-ranging examination of the causes of
extremism with an Egyptian public that was bent on reform. *Islamic Awakening*, then, was not an interpretive exception to the rule but rather a mirror of
society. Still, it was unique in its all-encompassing approach. Unlike most
thinkers who proposed a particular primary cause of extremism, such as

al-'Ashmawi's political and politicized study, al-Qaradawi maintained that extremism had "complex and interrelated" origins. Indeed, for him, "[t]he causes of extremism may be religious, political, social, economic, psychological, intellectual, or a combination of all of these."[55] Of course, al-Qaradawi's complex and interrelated approach was just as politicizied as al-'Ashmawi's, for many of the causes he cites became a further defense of misguided Islamist youth and thus of Islamism itself; and each of these causes also became another count in his indictment of secular government and secular society in Egypt. Islam or, more accurately, moderate Islamism, then, was al-Qaradawi's answer to the problem of extremism, but it was an answer tempered by an astute understanding of the fears and desires of the vast majority of Egyptians.

Egyptians had good reason to fear extremists, according to al-Qaradawi, because their attitudes and behavior clearly impact the life of the mind and life on the streets. Extremists exhibit a decided tendency toward bigotry, intolerance, compulsive excessiveness in personal piety and the judgment of others, coarseness, harshness, suspicion, and even cruelty.[56] Individually, these characteristics lead to oppressive and hostile conditions that are both intolerable and un-Islamic. However, if these characteristics come together in an organized fashion, then "[e]xtremism reaches its utmost limit when a single group deprives all people of the right to safety and protection, and instead sanctions their killing and the confiscation of their lives and property."[57] This kind of organized extremism, al-Qaradawi maintains, emerged with the formation of the Kharijites in early Islam, and Kharijism manifested itself once again in recent times in the form of al-Takfir wa'l-Hijra, the Egyptian group that abducted and executed Sheikh Dhahabi in 1977. For al-Qaradawi, the Kharijites represent the extreme end of extremism, the point that few Muslims actually reach—seemingly even those who killed Sadat did not fall into Kharijism since he fails to mention them—but which stands as the ultimate symbol of what can come of extremist tendencies.

With the fears of Egyptians duly validated, and the taboo image of the Kharijites firmly in place, al-Qaradawi proceeds to address the various causes that push youth toward that ultimate extreme. Here again, he is careful to begin his analysis with an acknowledgment of the errors of Muslim youth, which he, in keeping with his training, attributes primarily to a lack of religious knowledge. If the youth had sufficient knowledge, they would not become preoccupied with marginal or minor matters of the faith, they would not overly extend the lawful prohibitions, they would not read allegorical texts literally, and they would not misunderstand the essentials of the faith. The ignorance of Muslim youth is compounded, according to al-Qaradawi, by their suspicion and subsequent disregard of the 'ulama'.[58] These errors arising from a lack of knowledge are the inspiration for the extremist characteristics cited above, but they represent only half the story and not the most important part of it. For al-Qaradawi, the more dangerous causes of extremism are those that lie beyond the control of Muslim youth, those that go to the root of the culture war that was pitting Muslim against Muslim.

This culture war, al-Qaradawi maintains, has been instigated by the corrupting influence of Western powers on Muslim societies, especially the corrupting influence of secularism. Despite the fact that it is contrary to Islamic teachings and the psychology of Muslim culture, secularism has been imposed throughout the Muslim world by corrupt governments and supported by a few Muslim intellectuals who mistakenly equate modernization with westernization. The result has been a perversion of Muslim societies and the subsequent alienation of Muslim youth. And it is no surprise that so many have become alienated, according to al-Qaradawi, for secularism has had a devastating effect on the lives of Muslim youth. Young people have witnessed the immorality of loose women and alcohol taking over their streets; they have seen the proliferation of political and economic corruption; they have seen the rich grow richer at the expense of the poor; they have seen foreign ideologies and laws replace Islamic law; they have seen their political leaders sell out their own populations in order to curry the favor of Western governments; they have seen Israel defeat and humiliate Muslim nations; and they have seen Western powers provide unlimited support to Israel and undermine Palestinian rights.[59] Traditional Islamic morality, al-Qaradawi points out, informs Muslim youth that they should try to address these problems, but they have limited options for bringing about change:

> They cannot change things by physical force or by voicing their
> concern and opinion. The only way for them is to condemn these
> practices in their hearts. ... But this internal tumult cannot be suppressed forever, and must eventually explode.[60]

In addition to these social, economic, and political factors that lead youth to explode, al-Qaradawi cites religious factors. Muslims are prohibited from freely expressing their religious beliefs and convictions in their own lands. Governments restrict Muslim activists from calling people to Islam and implementing the faith in a meaningful way, and this is occurring even while secularism is being officially promoted. Moreover, governments, especially that of Egypt, have resorted to the use of force against activists, imprisoning and torturing the very people who are committed to reforming and improving their nations. It was such blatant suppression of Muslim identity and freedom that incited some activists to label rulers unbelievers and call for their overthrow—the interpretive act and behavior associated with Kharijism.[61] When Muslim youth face such anti-Islamic agendas in their home countries, al-Qaradawi concludes, it is little wonder that they turn away from peaceful preaching, deciding instead to "meet force with force and violence with violence."[62]

In the end, even though al-Qaradawi condemns extremism throughout the book, his sympathetic analysis of the various pressures affecting Muslim youth winds up weakening his critical stance. He is careful never to sanction violence, but his insistence on a balanced approach to the phenomenon of extremism at places creates the impression that violence is a natural product of the current Egyptian environment. Of the two types of extremism that al-Qaradawi juxtaposes in his balanced approach, the religious and the irreligious, the former has a rather significant measure of justification because the latter ultimately causes it.[63] The state, then, which is irreligious by virtue of its secularism, never receives the same sympathetic interpretation as the radical actions of Egypt's youth. And because he recognizes some justification for religious extremism, al-Qaradawi urges his readers to appreciate the circumstances that Muslim youth find themselves in and to treat them with love and respect. His special pleading here takes an interesting turn when he once again invokes the Kharijtes. This time, however, they do not serve as a symbol of the most extreme of the extremists. Rather, al-Qaradawi recalls how 'Ali dealt fairly with the original Kharijites, never anathematizing them as unbelievers, always treating them as brothers in Islam, and only taking up arms against them as a last resort.[64] Thus to rescue radicalized youth from the punishment inflicted by the secular state, al-Qaradawi is even willing to suggest that (neo-) Kharijites should be dealt with in a softer, gentler manner.

For al-Qaradawi, and Islamists in general, it was first and foremost the culture war—between Islamic and secular ideals—that gave rise to social and economic problems and that led to Kharijite-like extremism on the part of youth. For the Egyptian mainstream, by contrast, it was the social, economic, and political problems that drove the culture war and its related extremism. Both readings of extremism softened the Kharijite image because both concerned themselves with the underlying factors that motivated extremists, and factors provided a degree of mitigation for the crime and the criminals. Islamists, such as al-Qaradawi, used social and economic despair as evidence against secular regimes, but their solution to this problem concentrated on winning the culture war. That is, they provided an ideological response—return to Islam, institute Islamic law and morality, form an Islamic state—to what many regarded as practical problems of governance and development.

Still, the very fact that Islamists recognized the problems and integrated them into their ideological interpretation of extremism shows the extent to which middle-class concerns influenced Islamist thinking.[65]

Of course, the class interests of upwardly mobile Egyptians were not the direct concern of Islamists, as we have seen above. Indeed, socioeconomic class was itself anathema within Islamist teachings, since class, like nationalism, was thought to divide Muslims. But Islamism has served as a "vehicle for class aspirations" by providing a more culturally authentic framework through which political and social protest could be expressed.[66] It is open to question whether Islamism itself can become a permanent, centrist, or middle-class option; whether it can move beyond its current role as a populist movement challenging the authoritarian status quo to become a responsible political actor, capable of fostering a tolerant, workable society. Certainly, the rejection of extremist violence is an indispensable condition for Islamists to achieve broad popular support. And by the end of the 1990s, this condition seemed to have been met. After perhaps Egypt's most violent decade of Islamist attacks on public personalities, government officials, and tourists, imprisoned members of the Islamic Group called for a halt to armed opposition to the regime, ushering in what many have hailed as the end of Islamist violence in Egypt.[67] The end of violence, however, came with no assurance that the factors that nurtured it were being addressed, which means that another round of violence could be in the offing.

The End of Violence?

It was the dramatic and bloody killings at Luxor in November 1997 that pushed Egyptians, both Islamist insiders and public commentators, to insist upon an end to violence. The attackers, members of the Islamic Group, went on a spree at the ancient temple of Hatshepsut, hunting down their victims and executing them with guns and swords. Fifty-eight tourists and four Egyptians were killed. The Egyptian public was shocked by this display of wanton violence and embarrassed by the impression it gave of the nation to the international community. Egypt's tourist industry, already suffering financially from previous public attacks, went into a tailspin. And the Islamist movement itself, as one headline read, fell into a crisis after Luxor, with government pressure mounting and factions arguing about the need to renounce violence.[68] In light of the Luxor attack, then, Gilles Kepel's conclusion about the potential for armed jihad to further Islamist political success seems apt: "[V]iolence has proven to be a death trap for Islamists as a whole, precluding any capacity to hold and mobilize the range of constituencies they need to seize political power."[69]

The primary constituency to which Kepel refers is that of the "ordinary Muslims," the middle and would-be middle classes who had grown disenchanted with Islamist "utopian ideals."[70] Ordinary Muslims in Egypt, however, had come to distrust extremists and the state in equal measure long before Luxor; and no single extremist attack, however offensive to cultural norms, could rescue the state's reputation in the public mind. As one astute journalist has written, "Egypt's militants may have lost the war, but the state has certainly not emerged victorious."[71] This observation, which connects violence with winners and losers, bears further scrutiny, for it highlights the way discourse about violence becomes politicized, not just by the perpetrators of violence and their victims (in this case, Egyptian citizens), but also by those who "objectively" analyze contexts of violence (including the author).

We saw that, in the 1980s, Egyptians reinvented extremism and the idea of Kharijism, using the argument from nurture, to address widely recognized social, economic, and political problems. This was a political act with potential political consequences. By the 1990s, this new anti-extremist politics was firmly entrenched in Egyptian society, and it began to be taken up by journalists, human rights organizations, and academics in the West. The result was a confluence of diverse political interests—revolving around calls for state reform—that interpreted the meaning of extremism in very similar ways. In Egypt, two political perspectives as disparate as those of the Deputy General Guide of the Muslim Brothers, Muhammad M. al-Hudaybi, and the mainstream, semiofficial al-Ahram Center for Political and Strategic Studies reached similar conclusions about problem of extremism:

> the present atmosphere of suppression, instability, and anxiety has forced many young men of this nation to commit acts of terrorism which have intimidated innocent citizens and threatened the country's security, as well as its economic and political future.[72]
>
> As the political system fails to provide unrestricted legal channels for participation in public work, violence would find a nurturing environment in the resulting frustration.[73]

These insights were published in 1997, the same year as the Luxor attack, after seven years of snowballing violence whose origins became part of the debate and discourse on extremism. Radical Islamists no doubt carried out a number of symbolic attacks: the murder of the speaker of the People's Assembly, Dr. Rif'at al-Mahjub, in 1990, followed by a series of deadly strikes, in 1992, against Egyptian Christians (Copts), tourists, and the secular intellectual

Farag Foda. But these events, and others like them, were viewed against the backdrop of growing state pressure to eliminate, preemptively and violently, the Islamist challenge. Domestic and international human rights organizations alike attested to the blatantly aggressive policies of the state and the resulting tit-for-tat cycle of the political violence.[74] Dr. al-Mahjub, for example, was killed in reprisal for the earlier state-sanctioned assassination of Dr. 'Ala Muhi al-Din, a medical doctor and spokesman for the Islamic Group. And, in keeping with authoritarian practice, a new law was passed that sanctioned the harsh measures already being implemented against Islamists and, over time, anyone else who might interfere with state policy.

State operations against Islamists and their families, notes one observer, were characterized by "indiscriminate repression," a lashing out in all directions against an enemy that was never clearly defined.[75] Public perception of such operations was understandably harsh:

> The logical consequence of the randomness in applying security measures in some areas was to create tensions between the public and police agencies. In the midst of conducting a sharp confrontation with some of the Islamic groups, these agencies did not receive the sympathy of the public, which did not provide them a truly helping hand.... The politics of arresting the wives and relatives of fugitives and taking them as hostages aided in inculcating the spirit of revenge between security agents and [the Islamic] groups.[76]

Islamists tried to maintain their organizational base and mount an opposition, but, in the final analysis, the power and extent of state repression—mass arrests, torture, executions, and hostage-taking—in combination with the backlash against Luxor, quieted the Islamist storm that had raged in Egypt for six years. The number of Islamists jailed or killed from 1991 to 1997 was staggering.[77]

For Egyptians, there were no victors in this confrontation, just a steady decline in the political, social, and economic quality of life. Any public credit that Mubarak might have gained for managing the crisis was offset by the widespread understanding that he, like his predecessors Nasser and Sadat, was forced to address, in harsh and unforgiving terms, a problem of Islamist political violence that was largely of his own making. In the West, however, analysts sometimes conferred an inverse victory onto the militants in order to make a political point. For example, Geneive Abdo, the journalist cited above, wrote,

> The militants may have failed to overthrow the state, but they indirectly pushed the government toward totalitarianism. In this way,

the militants have achieved a victory in discrediting the state in the eyes of its own people.[78]

And the Middle East scholar, Fawaz Gerges made a similar point in his analysis of the situation:

> It should be stressed that al-Jama'a [the Islamic Group] and Jihad's continuing importance lies not in endangering the survival of the Egyptian state but in exposing the weakness, rigidity, and closeness of the political system and highlighting the pervasiveness of corruption, the government's dependence on foreign handouts, and its inept micoeconomic policies.[79]

The militants, of course, did not intend to succeed by default, by losing the military battle and winning the war of images. But, for these two analysts, and others, granting the defeated militants a symbolic victory prevented the militarily triumphant Egyptian state from appearing to occupy the moral or political high ground. The message here was clear: the real end of violence cannot be measured by the number of militants dead, imprisoned, or on the run but rather by effective changes in the operation of the state and growth in the economy. Much the same conclusion about the meaning of Islamist violence was reached by many Western scholars, suggesting that Egyptian discourse on extremism in the 1980s has played an unacknowledged role in shaping the direction of discourse in the Western academy in the 1990s and beyond.[80]

In Egypt, Luxor came to mark the end of violence because, in the aftermath of the bloody event, a public consensus on the futility of Islamist extremism seems to have emerged. That consensus depended in part on the Islamic Group's decision to reject the use of violence. It also depended on broad acceptance of the claim underlying the new anti-extremist politics: that Islamist violence was driven more by political and economic frustrations than by ideological commitments. The image of the Kharijites, as we saw, accommodated this new politics, and the Islamic Group made good rhetorical use of this image in its public confession. In four booklets published in 2002, though written earlier, eight imprisoned leaders of the Islamic Group, who had been convicted of participating in Sadat's assassination, explained their shift away from extremist tactics.[81] The four volumes created a minor news sensation and led to a public discussion with the authors that raised questions about whether they were scheming or actually revising their positions.[82]

Whatever their ultimate motives, the al-Gama'a leaders viewed *Islamic Awakenings* as the best analysis of the manifestations and causes of extremism in Egypt, for they drew extensively on al-Qaradawi's work. (And, in this view, they were not alone; a number of Islamist works on extremism adopted important features al-Qaradawi's argument.[83]) Al-Qaradawi, it seems, provided militants with the proper framework in which they could confess the error of their ways and still maintain the ideals that motivated them. They could even admit their descent into Kharijism, with the full knowledge that it meant something quite different than it had to a previous generation of Egyptians.[84] Under al-Qaradawi's pen, and those who followed his lead, neo-Kharijites were not simply pious fanatics, bent on destroying Muslim society; they were, instead, confused victims of a secular, anti-Islamic, and repressive government that was unable to meet the basic needs of its Muslim citizens.

To give the final word on the meaning of Kharijism to Islamists, however, even a moderate such as al-Qaradawi, is not to proclaim the triumph of Islamism. Rather, it is to acknowledge the power of public discourse and the concessions that moderate Islamists have made to it. Ideology may have been the main factor driving al-Qaradawi's analysis of extremism, as it was for most Islamists, but he also emphasized the social, political, and economic conditions that impacted youth—conditions that were central to the reformist agenda of mainstream Egyptians. Ideology may also have motivated al-Qaradawi, and other Islamists, to address the mainstream concerns expressed in the new anti-extremist politics, for Islamism's totalizing worldview asserts authority over all aspects of life, even those that it currently has limited power to influence. Such a totalizing impulse, however, implicates Islamism in details of public life that many regard as practical and secular, not ideological.

By participating in the new anti-extremist politics, and the debate over the meaning of Kharijism that accompanied it, Islamists were no doubt trying to win over the public and make a stronger case against the existing regime. But, in the process, they conceded the importance of the very middle-class demands that informed the new politics; and those demands were not for a religious transformation of Egypt—the creation of an Islamic government or the implementation of Islamic law—but rather for workable social institutions, a more open political process, and a healthy economy. In the political discourse of late–twentieth-century Egypt, then, the end of violence, the end of the problem of Kharijism, entails a new political beginning shorn of absolutist politics of any kind. That new beginning has yet to dawn.

Conclusion

As I was putting the final touches on this manuscript, I received an e-mail communication from an Army officer in the Military Intelligence Readiness Command. The officer, who shall remain nameless, had come across my name while researching information about Islamic radicalism, and he wanted to discuss with me his "idea to spark an anti-jihadist backlash against al-Qaʿida by Sunnis and Shiʾites in all the countries where that group operates by painting them as Kharijites." He requested that I read the short abstract included in the email, and then he hoped to meet in order, as he put it, "to discuss how we might operationalize it."[1] It was unclear to whom the "we" in his message referred, but I began to imagine that I had, without knowing it, been inducted into the Army's Military Intelligence Readiness Command and thus the government's war on terror. The officer and I eventually arranged a meeting, during which I offered the following simple advice: Kharijism is not the sure-fire propaganda tool that it may seem. Labeling Muslim extremists as Kharijites had already been tried in various Arab-Muslim countries, and it had been tried by better-informed and more legitimate authorities (at least in the Muslim world) than the Military Intelligence Readiness Command. Despite these efforts, there was little evidence that the stigma of Kharijism prevented radical behavior or inspired an anti-radical backlash.

The point that I tried to make in the meeting—drawing on my research into the use and evolution of the Kharijite image in

Egypt—is that although cultural symbols such as the Kharijites matter in Muslim societies, they are not fixed in the mind of believers, compelling them to think and behave in specific ways. The meaning of such symbols may be informed by a historical tradition that weighs heavily on individuals and the larger society, but individuals and institutions refract this tradition through the multifaceted and ever-changing prism of a living material environment. Indeed, even the traditional image (or more accurately images) of Kharijism imbedded in medieval sources has material origins, for the anti-model of Muslim political violence emerged directly from the triumph of Sunni rule and its will to maintain power. In modern Egypt, the idea of Kharijism was reawakened to deal with a new environment, one driven by the modernizing forces of the nation-state and the global economy. Over time, however, this environment produced different interpretive readings of Kharijism.

During one period (under Nasser and Sadat), the image of the Kharijites was used in a seemingly traditional way: to defend established political leaders against illegitimate, religiously inspired rebellion. During another period (under Mubarak), it became part of a very different political agenda: to hold the authoritarian state accountable for its role in fostering Islamist violence. Throughout both periods, the underlying pattern of the modernizing forces remained the same. What changed was how these forces impacted the lives of Egyptians and how Egyptians, in turn, responded. In the ongoing discourse on Islamist violence, a shift in the idiom—in the usage of Kharijism—opened up an exploration into the causes of extremism, and the resulting debate led to an outpouring of public concern about the arrogance of state power and the failure of the state to use this power to improve the lives of citizens.

Thus the culture-talk surrounding Kharijism clearly has material origins. Less apparent is the fact that it also has intentional material ends: to control and manage an environment that is itself a by-product of modernizing material forces. Those Egyptians who participated, and still participate, in the new politics of extremism may draw on the image of the Kharijites, but they do so to get beyond the culture-talk and to address the raw material concerns that impact their lives. Some Egyptians, in keeping with notions of what it means to be modern, are no doubt fully conscious of their role in using culture-talk for materialist ends. Conscious or not, however, those living in Muslim societies are engaged in a continuous feedback loop of influence between culture and material forces.

By focusing on the Kharijites, and the traditional negative image they communicated in Muslim society, the Army intelligence officer was searching for a cultural quick fix (=moral propaganda) to a far more complex problem. In this, he was not alone. Egyptians, after all, viewed Islamist violence as the cultural problem par excellence, at least until they came to see the problem differently. Western scholars, too, have long been drawn to analyzing Muslim societies in cultural terms. A good example is the challenge of Islamic fundamentalism, which prompted some Western academics to argue that all Muslims need to do is "think differently"—which meant think more like a liberal Western Christian—and backward attitudes would cease interfering with the process of modernization.[2] There were, to be sure, good reasons for thinking that culture was in the ascendant. Everywhere one turned in Egypt, and other countries in the Muslim world, evidence of its importance seemed apparent: the popularity and growth of the Islamist movement, the public prominence of official religious scholars, the government's dependence on religious legitimacy, and the widespread use of the Islamic idiom in popular discourse. Cultural solutions, then, were proffered for what were perceived as cultural problems and for a society steeped in culture.

For advocates of materialist explanation, attention to culture distracts from or confuses the real issues at work in Muslim societies. Although this is no doubt true to an extent, much the same could be said of many intellectual systems that attempt to capture the complex workings of material forces in history. The real problem in Egypt, and in other Middle Eastern Muslim societies, is not the importance of culture per se. Rather, it is that culture has become an abstract substitute for meaningful civic action and participation in the political system. Islamists rely on Islamic culture to challenge an authoritarian, secular system of government that tolerates no challenge; the state uses the same culture to defend its policies and maintain its absolute hold on power, but it respects no challenge based on the same culture; and the larger public, caught in the political middle, looks to Islam for consolation and to give voice to long-standing and unaddressed concerns for social and political justice.

All the attention to culture no doubt heightens awareness of its importance and spurs on creative uses of it. "Culture," as one observer of Muslim societies has noted, "continues to show a vitality and distinctiveness which contrasts with the official surface of paralysis and domination."[3] But this vitality in Egypt is itself connected to "the official surface of paralysis and domination," signaling a flaw in the relationship between culture and environment. Egyptians try to control and manage their environment through culture-talk, and the paralysis of the modernizing forces enlivens that talk because people are genuinely worried. This culture-talk, however, has no impact on the environment because of state-domination. Simply put, culture-talk in Egypt has grown rampant, almost manic, the more it has become effectively disengaged from the interactive reality that it should reflect and try to influence.

A National Public Radio interview with the Egyptian author Alaa Al Aswany about his recent novel, *The Yacoubian Building*, nicely captured this disengagement between culture-talk and political realities in Egypt.[4] During filming of the movie version of the book, Al Aswany was interviewed by Robert Siegal, one of the hosts of the program *All Things Considered*. While summing up the book, which is a meditation on the current Egyptian condition told through the lives of the building's inhabitants, Siegal said: "[Egypt] is an undemocratic place, a place where power is entrenched, unchecked and often violent, where terrorists are not born but made." The exchange continued from there:

AL ASWANY   I mean, there is some social—very, very heavy social problems which are pushing them to be terrorists. And I try to explain this, and I have very big experience, in my life, seeing these kind of stories. I have seen . . .

SIEGEL   People you know.

AL ASWANY   Yes, I know, yes, because as you read the book, that's exactly what's happening, . . . This is a—we have a whole bunch of complications of lack of democracy.

SIEGEL   . . . So how undemocratic is a society that tolerates such scathing criticism?

AL ASWANY   There is an equation in Egypt which is the government, the regime, is saying now to the writers, "You write whatever you want, but I'm going to do whatever I want." And that's why we don't have the freedom of speech; we have a freedom of talk. And there is a difference.

SIEGAL   The freedom of talk?

AL ASWANY   Yes, because you talk. You talk and you write whatever you want, but this will never be influencing the decisions of the regime.[5]

The irony here is that Al Aswany's novel just adds to the kind of talk that is the root of his complaint—talk that goes nowhere, talk that does not lead to real democracy. The hope, of course, is that such talk will, despite the factors weighing against it, make a difference. After all, what is the alternative? Extremism has certainly not improved the situation. It has only increased official paralysis and domination. So Egyptians continue to talk about Islamist violence, about political reform, about the lackluster economy, and about the end-of-talk and the beginning of meaningful change. Hopeful signs are present. The Islamic Group's call for an end to violence is one. Whatever the leaders' ulterior motives might be, and however divided members are about relinquishing violence, a public admission that enough-is-enough bodes well for the future. The other hopeful sign is Mubarak's recent decision to order the constitution amended (Article 76) to permit multi-candidate elections. The decision only came after increasing pressure from Egyptian opposition parties and the Bush administration, but Mubarak has publicly committed himself, and now political groups at home and governments' abroad will hold him to it.

What is the future of the anti-extremist image of the Kharijites in Egypt? Has it run its course? Public discourse in the 1990s, before the Islamic Group's public confession, had already seen a decline in the frequency of references to the Kharijites. Perhaps Egyptians, exhausted from the cycle of political violence and debates about its causes, have also grown weary of highly charged religious name-calling. It didn't matter whether one was labeled a "Kharijite" or "apostate" (murtadd); both accusations resulted in anger, resentment, and continued conflict. Some analysts have already drawn on the Kharijites to frame the discussion about the meaning of September 11, 2001. But, for Egyptians, the Kharijite label, traditionally understood, is no more likely to stick cleanly to bin Laden and al-Qaʻida than it has to home-grown extremists. There will always be questions about why he turned to violence, about the corruption of the Saudi system that produced him, about the legitimacy of the causes that he claims to defend (however cynically), and about his willingness to stand up to the West (unlike the current band of Arab leaders).

In short, there is a political point to be made by not recognizing him as a neo-Kharijite and by debating the terrorist violence that he perpetuates, and that's what the politics of extremism is all about: using the hated image of extremism to shape hearts and minds on the meaning of violence and, sometimes, on matters wholly unrelated to the extremism but of utmost importance to the interpreters of it. Playing politics with extremism is not a new phenomenon, though its intensity and global extent have increased noticeably since September 11, 2001. It is always, however, a volatile one, hovering as it does between the desire to bring about reform by "reading" extremism and the fear that in the process extremism will be legitimated.

Perhaps the best possible future for the Kharijite image in Egypt is one that I dismissed in the introduction.[6] In her examination of human rights in the Islamic tradition and Muslim societies, Anne Elizabeth Mayer suggested that the Kharijites might serve as a democratic model. Despite their rebellion and unorthodox views, the Kharijites maintained that a leader should be elected by the community, which, Mayer argued, justifies the existence of a democratic principle in early Islam and thus a cultural basis for modern reform.[7] This historical insight about the Kharijites, as I noted earlier, is not how Kharijites are remembered today, at least by the vast majority of Muslims. But, as the history of the debate over Kharijism shows, perceptions can change, and culture can facilitate that change. The challenge in Egypt is to arrange the material conditions to warrant such a dramatic reinvention of culture.

Notes

INTRODUCTION

1. Andrew Rippin, *Muslims: Their Religious Beliefs and Practices*, vol. 2, *The Contemporary Period* (London and New York: Routledge, 1993), 124.

2. Liah Greenfeld, "The Modern Religion?" *Critical Review* 10, no. 2 (Spring 1996): 174.

3. Roy Mottahedeh, *The Mantle of the Prophet: Religion and Politics in Iran* (New York: Simon and Schuster, 1985), 9.

4. Dale F. Eickelman and James Piscatori, *Muslim Politics* (Princeton, N.J.: Princeton University Press, 1996), chap. 2; Robert D. Lee, *Overcoming Tradition and Modernity: The Search for Islamic Authenticity* (Boulder, Colo.: Westview Press, 1997).

5. Sami Zubaida, *Islam, the People and the State* (London and New York: I. B. Tauris, 1993), passim, especially chap. 6; Ghassan Salamé, "Introduction: Where Are the Democrats?," in *Democracy without Democrats?: The Renewal of Politics in the Muslim World*, ed. Ghassan Salamé (London and New York: I. B. Tauris, 1994), 3–6.

6. My thinking here has been influenced by Sami Zubaida, *Islam, the People and the State*; and by Salwa Ismail, *Rethinking Islamist Politics: Culture, the State and Islamism* (London and New York: I. B. Tauris, 2003).

7. On this point, see R. Scott Appleby, *The Ambivalence of the Sacred: Religion, Violence, and Reconciliation* (Lanham, Md.: Rowman & Littlefield, 2000).

8. Ernest Gellner, *Muslim Society* (Cambridge: Cambridge University Press, 1981), 217.

9. See Bruce Lincoln, *Discourse and the Construction of Society* (New York and Oxford: Oxford University Press, 1989); James C. Scott, *Domination and the Arts of Resistance* (New Haven, Conn. and London: Yale University Press, 1990).

10. Aside from the particulars of the cultural overlay, the very notion that there is something identifiable as a "Muslim society" has been called into question; see Sami Zubaida, "Is There a Muslim Society? Ernest Gellner's Sociology of Islam," *Economy and Society* 24, no. 2 (May 1995): 151–88.

11. Talal Asad, *Genealogies of Religion: Discipline and Reasons of Power in Christianity and Islam* (Baltimore and London: Johns Hopkins University Press, 1993), 210.

12. This point and these categories were proposed by William E. Shephard, "Islam and Ideology: Towards a Typology," *International Journal of Middle East Studies* 19 (1987): 307–36.

13. Eickelman and Piscatori, *Muslim Politics*, chap. 1.

14. Emmanuel Sivan, *Radical Islam*, enlarged ed. (New Haven and London: Yale University Press, 1990), x.

15. Kenneth Burke, *A Grammar of Motives* (Berkeley, Los Angeles, London: University of California Press, 1969), 57.

16. Scott, *Domination and the Arts of Resistance*, 206.

17. H. H. Gerth and C. Wright Mills, trans. and eds., *From Max Weber: Essays in Sociology* (New York: Oxford University Press, 1946), 78.

18. On the importance of understanding the modern Middle East experience in terms of the universal processes of nation-state formation and the global economy, see James L. Gelvin, *The Modern Middle East: A History* (New York and Oxford: Oxford University Press, 2005), chap. 3; Simon Bromley, *Rethinking Middle East Politics* (Austin: University of Texas Press, 1994), chap. 1.

19. See Gellner, *Muslim Society*, 216–18; Bromley, *Rethinking Middle East Politics*, 29–30.

20. For an insightful analysis of this phenomenon, see Steve Coll, *Ghost Wars: The Secret History of the CIA, Afghanistan, and Bin Laden, from the Soviet Invasion to September 10, 2001* (New York: Penguin, 2004).

21. See Mahmood Mamdani, *Good Muslim, Bad Muslim: America, the Cold War, and the Roots of Terror* (New York: Pantheon Books, 2004).

22. *The 9/11 Commission Report*, authorized ed. (New York and London: W. W. Norton, n.d.), 362.

23. It's important to note that there was a brief window of criticism, when "many people did seize on September 11th as an opportunity to look into the American soul," but this effort was short lived; see Louis Menand, "Faith, Hope, and Clarity," *The New Yorker*, 16 September 2002, 98.

24. Paul Berman, *Terror and Liberalism* (New York and London: W. W. Norton, 2003), 18.

25. Ibid., 21.

26. Ibid., 120.

27. "Ban on Head Scarves Takes Effect in France," *New York Times*, 3 September 2004, Online edition.

28. G. C. Anawati, "Une résurgence du Kharijisme au xxe siècle: 'l'obligation absente,'" *Mélanges Institut dominicain d'études orientales du caire* 16 (1983): 191–228;

Malise Ruthven, *Islam in the World* (New York and Oxford: Oxford University Press, 1984), 129, 185; Johannes J. G. Jansen, "The Early Islamic Movement of the Kharidjites and Modern Moslem Extremism: Similarities and Differences," *Orient* 27 (1986): 127–35; Hamied Ansari, *Egypt: The Stalled Society* (Albany: State University of New York Press, 1986), 213.

29. An interesting online exchange about Muslim extremists, involving cross-cultural references, including the Kharijites, developed out the comments of Professor David Forte: see Franklin Foer, "Blind Faith," *The New Republic Online*, 22 October 2001, <http:www.tnr.com.102201/foer102201.html> (accessed 22 July 2002); David F. Forte, "Religion Is Not the Enemy," *The National Review Online*, 19 October 2001, <http:www.nationalreview.com/comment/comment-forte101901.shtml> (accessed 22 July 2002); Stephen Schwartz, "Seeking Moderation," *The National Review Online*, 25 October 2001, <http:www.nationalreview.com/comment/comment-schwartz102501 .shtml> (accessed 22 July 2002); David F. Forte, "War for Civilization," *The National Review Online*, 1 November 2001, <http:www.nationalreview.com/comment/ comment-forte110101.shtml> (accessed 22 July 2002). Other evocative references to the Kharijites were voiced by policy experts. One linked Saddam Hussein to the Kharijites; see R. James Woolsey, "America's New War: Should Iraq Be Next?" *New Democrats Online*, May/June 2002, <http:www.ndol.org/blueprint/2002_ may_jun/14_iraq_point.html> (accessed 22 July 2002). British Foreign Office Minister Mike O'Brien gave a speech to the Royal United Services Institute for Defense Studies (London, 22 November 2002), entitled "The Threat of the Modern Kharijites."

30. Ann Elizabeth Mayer, *Islam and Human Rights: Tradition and Politics*, 3rd ed. (Boulder, Colo.: Westview Press, 1999), 46. My criticism here is not leveled at attempts to highlight universal values shared by Muslim and Western societies. Indeed, the image of the Kharijites may be viewed as a particular cultural manifestation of a universal concern to reject extremism. It is important, however, to locate universal trends in the context of living, not theoretical, Muslim discourse.

31. Emmanuel Sivan, *Interpretations of Islam: Past and Present* (Princeton: Darwin, 1985), 62.

32. Peter L. Bergen, *Holy War, Inc.: Inside the Secret World of Osama bin Laden* (New York: Touchstone, 2001); Gilles Kepel, *Jihad: The Trail of Political Islam*, trans. Anthony F. Roberts (Cambridge, Mass.: Belknap Press, 2002); Daniel Benjamin and Steven Simon, *The Age of Sacred Terror: Radical Islam's War against America* (New York: Random House, 2002); *The 9/11 Commission Report*.

33. Quoted in David Remnick, "Letter from Cairo: Going Nowhere," *The New Yorker* (July 12, 19, 2004), 75–76.

CHAPTER 1

1. *al-Ahram*, 15 February 1993. The opinion expressed in the piece was actually that of Nasr Hamid Abu Zaid, though his views were represented by the author of the article, Sheikh Khalil 'Abd al-Karim.

2. Edward Shils, "Tradition," *Comparative Studies in Society and History* 13 (1971): 125. My discussion of tradition has also benefited from Marilyn Waldman, "Tradition as a Modality of Change: Islamic Examples," *History of Religions* 25, no. 4 (1986): 318–40; R. J. Zwi Werblowsky, *Beyond Tradition and Modernity: Changing Religions in a Changing World* (London: Athlone, 1976); and S. N. Eisenstadt, "Post-Traditional Societies and the Continuity and Reconstruction of Tradition," *Daedalus* 102 (1973): 1–27.

3. For outlines of early Kharijite history, see Julius Wellhausen, *The Religio-Political Factions in Early Islam*, trans. R. C. Ostle and S. M. Walzer, ed. R. C. Ostle (New York: American Elsevier, 1975) [original German *Die religios-politischen Oppositionsparteien im alten Islam*, Abhandlung der Konigenlichen Gesellschaft der Wissenschaften zu Gottingen 5, no. 5 (1901)]; Michael G. Morony, *Iraq after the Muslim Conquest* (Princeton, N.J.: Princeton University Press, 1984); and *Encyclopaedia of Islam*, 2nd ed., s.v. "Kharidjites."

4. Ira M. Lapidus, "The Separation of the State and Religion in the Development of Early Islamic Society," *International Journal of Middle East Studies* 6 (1973): 363–85.

5. Rudolf Ernst Brunnow, *Die Charidschiten unter den ersten Omayyaden* (Leiden: E. J. Brill, 1884).

6. Ibid., 11.

7. Ibid., 1–2.

8. Julius Wellhausen, rev. ed. of *Die Charidschiten* by Rudolf Ernst Brunnow, *Deutsche Litteraturzeitung* 23 (1884): 838–39.

9. Wellhausen, *Religio-Political Factions*.

10. M. A. Shaban, *Islamic History: A New Interpretation*, vol. 1, A.D. 600–750 (Cambridge: Cambridge University Press, 1971).

11. Martin Hinds, "Kufan Political Alignments and Their Background in the Mid-Seventh Century A.D.," *International Journal of Middle East Studies* 2 (1971): 346–67; and "The Siffin Arbitration Agreement," *Journal of Semitic Studies* 1 (1972): 93–129.

12. See R. Stephen Humphreys, *Islamic History: A Framework for Inquiry*, rev. ed. (Princeton, N.J.: Princeton University Press, 1991), chap. 3.

13. John Wansbrough, *The Sectarian Milieu: Content and Composition of Islamic Salvation History* (Oxford: Oxford University Press, 1978); Patricia Crone, *Slaves on Horses: The Evolution of the Islamic Polity* (Cambridge: Cambridge University Press, 1980).

14. Bernard Lewis, "Some Observations on the Significance of Heresy in the History of Islam," *Studia Islamica* 1 (1953): 62.

15. al-Bukhari, *istitaba al-murtaddin*, 7; Muslim, *al-zakat*, 2336. [Here I am following the citation system of A. J. Wensinck et al., eds, *Concordance et indices de la tradition musulmane*, 2nd ed., 8 vols. (Leiden: E. J. Brill, 1933–48).]

16. Muslim, *al-zakat*, 2338.

17. al-Bukhari, *istitaba al-murtaddin*, 6; Muslim, *al-zakat*, 2328.

18. Muslim, *al-zakat*, 2325.

19. Ibid., 2318.

20. Morony, *Iraq after the Muslim Conquest*, 239–50, 468–78; *Encyclopaedia of Islam*, 1st ed., s.v. "Tamim."

21. Abu Ja'far Muhammad b. Jarir al-Tabari, *Ta'rikh al-rusul wa'l-muluk*, ed. M. J. de Goeje et al. (Leiden: E. J. Brill, 1879–1901), II, 459–65.

22. I. Goldziher, "Le dénombrement des sectes mohamétanes," *Revue l'histoire des religions* 26, no. 2 (1892): 129–37.

23. [Abu'l-Fath] Muhammad [b. 'Abd al-Karim] al-Shahrastani, *Kitab al-milal wa'l-nihal* (*Book of Religious and Philosophical Sects*), ed. William Cureton (Leipzig: Otto Harrassowitz, 1923). Partial English translation, *Muslim Sects and Divisions*, trans. A. K. Kazi and J. G. Flynn (London: Kegan Paul International, 1984).

24. See Kazi and Flynn's introductory remarks, *Muslim Sects and Divisions*, 4–7.

25. al-Shahrastani, *al-Milal*, 7.

26. Ibid., 7–8.

27. Ibid., 9.

28. Ibid., 10.

29. Ibid., 85.

30. 'Abd al-Qadir Ibn Tahir al-Baghdadi, *al-Farq bayna al-firaq* (Cairo: Madbuli, n.d.), 73; [Abu'l-Fath] Muhammad [b. 'Abd al-Karim] al-Shahrastani, *Kitab al-milal wa'l-nihal* (Beirut: Dar al-Mashriq, 1970), 58.

31. 'Ali b. Ahmed Ibn Hazm, *Kitab al-fasl fi al-milal wa'l-ahwa' wa'l-nihal* (Beirut: Maktaba Khayyat, n.d.), 2:111–17, 4:188–92.

32. Translation from *The Koran Interpreted*, trans. Arthur J. Arberry (New York: Macmillan, 1955), 135.

33. Elie Adib Salem, *Political Theory and Institutions of the Khawarij* (Baltimore: Johns Hopkins Press, 1956), 51.

34. For an insightful challenge to the common understanding of this hadith, see Bernard Lewis's remarks in Ignaz Goldziher, *Introduction to Islamic Theology and Law*, trans. Andras and Ruth Hamori (Princeton, N.J.: Princeton University Press, 1981), 171 n. e

35. Ann K. S. Lambton, *State and Government in Medieval Islam* (Oxford: Oxford University Press, 1981), 24.

36. This does not mean that Muslims at the time did not disagree on issues but rather that, despite their differences, they did not question one another's status as Muslims.

37. Toshihiko Izutsu, *The Concept of Belief in Islamic Theology* (Yokohama, Japan: Yorindo, 1965), 6–10.

38. See W. Montgomery Watt, "Conditions of Membership of the Islamic Community," *Studia Islamica* 21 (1964): 5–12.

39. Izutsu, *Concept of Belief*, chap. 3. Al-Shahrastani, *Milal*, 10; *Muslim Sects*, 120.

40. Richard J. McCarthy, *The Theology of al-Ash'ari* (Beyrouth: Imprimerie Catholique, 1953), 104.

41. Abu'l-Hasan 'Ali ibn Isma'il al-Ash'ari, *al-Ibana 'an usul ad-diyanah* (*The Elucidation of Islam's Foundation*), trans. Walter C. Klein (New Haven, Conn.: American Oriental Society, 1940), 52.

42. Ibid., 52.

43. Ibid., 54.

44. For an analysis of contrasting views of authority among early Islamic factions, see Hamid Dabashi, *Authority in Islam: From the Rise of the Muhammad to the Establishment of the Umayyads* (New Brunswick, N.J.: Transaction Publishers, 1989). Note that Dabashi uncritically assumes that the Kharijites can be analyzed as a coherent protest movement and that Sunni representations of Kharijite views are accurate.

45. A. J. Wensinck, *The Muslim Creed* (London: Frank Cass & Co., 1965), 192.

46. Ibid., 104.

47. For an analysis of letters attributed to Ibn Ibad, see Michael Cook, *Early Muslim Dogma: A Source-Critical Study* (Cambridge: Cambridge University Press, 1981).

48. 'Amr K. Ennami, *Studies in Ibadism* (Benghazi: University of Libya, 1972), 12; *Encyclopaedia of Islam*, 2nd ed., s.v. "Ibadiyya."

49. Ennami, *Studies in Ibadism*, 14.

50. Abu 'Abdullah Muhammad b. Sa'id al-Azdi al-Qalhati, *al-Kashf wa'l-bayan*, vol. 2, ed. Isma'il al-Kashif (Oman: Wazarat al-Turath al-Qawmi wa'l-Thaqafa, 1400/ 1980).

51. Charles Rieu, *Supplement to the Catalogue of the Arabic Manuscripts in the British Museum* (London: Longman & Co., 1894), 122.

52. al-Qalhati, *Kashf*, 240.

53. Ennami, *Studies in Ibadism*, 5.

54. al-Qalhati, *Kashf*, 233–41.

55. Ibid,, 422.

56. Ibid., 422.

57. Ibid., 471, 480.

58. Ibid., 471.

59. For a parallel case of Ibadi conformity to Sunni dominance, see J. C. Wilkinson, "Ibadi Hadith: An Essay on Normalization," *Der Islam* 62 (1985): 231–59.

60. L. Veccia Vaglieri, "Le vicende del harigismo in epoca abbaside," *Revista degli Studi Orientali* 24 (1949): 34; G. E. von Grunebaum, *Classical Islam: A History, 600 A.D.–1258 A.D.* (Chicago: Aldine, 1970), 69.

61. Clifford Edmund Bosworth, *Sistan under the Arabs, from the Islamic Conquest to the Rise of the Saffarids (30–250/651–864)* (Rome: Instituto Italiano per il medio ed estremo Oriente, 1968), 87.

62. *The Abbasid Caliphate in Equilibrium*, trans. C. E. Bosworth, vol. 30, *The History of al-Tabari* (Albany: State University of New York Press, 1989), 265 n. 915.

63. E. W. Brooks, ed., *Corpus Scriptorum Christianorum Orientalium*, vol. 62, *Eliae Metropolitae Nisibeni*, (Louvain: Impremerie Orientaliste, 1954), 104. This reference was kindly brought to my attention by Chase F. Robinson.

64. Another example of the corruption of the name occurs in a work of 'Ali b. Muhammad al-Jurjani (d. 1413), in which the Kharijites are defined as "those who seize the *'ushr* without permission of the sultan" [=*al-Ta'rifat* (Beirut: 'Alam al-Kutub, 1987), 136]. The precise meaning here is unclear, though it appears as if the form of rebellion has come to define Kharijism. Another explanation of this definition might lie in the

observation that in writing *al-Ta'rifat* Jurjani "was not afraid to be simple"; see *Encyclopaedia of Islam*, 2nd ed., s.v. "al-Djurdjani, 'Ali b. Muhammad."

65. al-Tabari, II, 252–53.

66. Ibid., II, 1050.

67. Ibid., III, 59.

68. Ibid., II, 1944.

69. Ibid., II, 987ff., 1386–387.

70. For an astute analysis of Kharijism in Northern Mesopotamia, see Chase F. Robinson, *Empire and Elites after the Muslim Conquest: The Transformation of Northern Mesopotamia* (Cambridge: Cambridge University Press, 2000), chap. 5.

71. Wellhausen, *Religio-Political Factions*, 114, 119 n. 30.

72. Lewis, "Some Observations," 62.

73. al-Tabari, II, 40–41.

74. For a discussion of thematic patterns, such as *fitna* or revolt, in early Islamic literature, see Albrecht Noth, in collaboration with Lawrence I. Conrad, *The Early Arabic Historical Tradition: A Source-Critical Study*, 2nd. ed., trans. Michael Bonner (Princeton, N.J.: Darwin 1994).

75. This is not to say that Kharijites never come in for praise in the sources. Their pride, valor, military prowess, and horsemanship are often noted, especially in poetry; see Ihsan 'Abbas, *Shi'r al-khawarij* (Beirut: Dar al-Thaqafa, 1974).

76. al-Hasan b. 'Ali al-Mas'udi, *Muruj al-dhahab*, 4 vols., ed. Yusef As'ad Daghir (Beirut: Dar al-Andalus, 1965), 3:325.

77. Ibid., 3:325.

78. "Saadiah (Ben Joseph) Gaon," in *Encyclopaedia Judaica*, vol. 14 (Jerusalem, Israel: Keter Publishing House Ltd., 1971), 543–55; Edward L Greenstein, "Medieval Bible Commentaries," in *Back to the Sources: Reading the Classic Jewish Texts*, ed. Barry W. Holtz, (New York: Summit Books, 1984), 217–26.

79. See the discussion of Anan and excerpts from his writings in *Karaite Anthology*, trans. Leon Nemoy (New Haven, Conn.: Yale University Press, 1952), 3–20.

80. This information is developed in Michael Cook, "'Anan and Islam: The Origins of Karaite Scripturalism," *Jerusalem Studies in Arabic and Islam* 9 (1987): 182 n. 98.

81. Lambton, *State and Government in Medieval Islam*, 158–160.

82. Ibn Khaldun, *The Muqaddimah: An Introduction to History*, vol. 2, trans. Franz Rosenthal (New York: Pantheon Books, 1958), 114.

CHAPTER 2

1. Robert Paine, "When Saying Is Doing," in *Politically Speaking: Cross-Cultural Studies of Rhetoric*, ed. Robert Paine (Philadelphia: Institute for the Study of Human Issues, 1981), 9.

2. See Paul Salem, *Bitter Legacy: Ideology and Politics in the Arab World* (Syracuse, N.Y.: Syracuse University Press, 1994); and Martin Kramer, *Arab Awakening and Islamic Revival: The Politics of Ideas in the Middle East* (New Brunswick, N.J.: Transaction Publishers, 1996).

3. P. J. Vatikiotis, *The Modern History of Egypt* (New York: Frederick A. Praeger, Publishers, 1969), chap. 4.

4. Dale F. Eickelman and James Piscatori, *Muslim Politics* (Princeton, N.J.: Princeton University Press, 1996), 5.

5. The phrase "political Islam," for example, has been adopted by some scholars to classify Islamists. See Olivier Roy, *The Failure of Political Islam*, trans. Carol Volk (Cambridge, Mass.: Harvard University Press, 1994); and Nazih Ayubi, *Political Islam: Religion and Politics in the Arab World* (London and New York: Routledge, 1991). In the context of the modern debate, however, this term often seems to prejudge Islamists as outside their element because of their involvement with politics. The problem is evident in Egypt, where a secularist like Muhammad Sa'id al-Ashmawi deploys "political Islam" as a weapon against Islamists.

6. See Edward Shils, "The Concept and Function of Ideology," in *International Encyclopedia of Social Sciences*, ed. David L. Sills (New York: Macmillan, 1968), 7:66–76.

7. Gabriel Baer, *Studies in the Social History of Modern Egypt* (Chicago: University of Chicago Press, 1969), chap. 12.

8. Afaf Lutfi al-Sayyid Marsot, *Egypt's Liberal Experiment* (Berkeley and Los Angeles: University of California Press, 1977).

9. Richard P. Mitchell, *The Society of Muslim Brothers* (London: Oxford University Press, 1969), 105–6.

10. Ibid., 328.

11. H. H. Gerth and C. Wright Mills, *From Max Weber: Essays in Sociology* (New York: Oxford University Press, 1946), 78.

12. David E. Apter, "Political Religion in the New Nations," in *Old Societies and New States: The Quest for Modernity in Asia and Africa*, ed. Clifford Geertz (London: Collier-Macmillan Ltd., 1963), 61.

13. Ibid., 82.

14. Gamal Abdul Nasser, *Egypt's Liberation: The Philosophy of the Revolution* (Washington, D.C.: Public Affairs, 1955).

15. Ibid., 81–114.

16. Guenther Lewy, "Nasserism and Islam: A Revolution in Search of an Ideology," in *Religion and Political Modernization*, ed. Donald Eugene Smith (New Haven, Conn. and London: Yale University Press, 1974), 259.

17. Leonard Binder, *In a Moment of Enthusiasm: Political Power and the Second Stratum in Egypt* (Chicago: University of Chicago Press, 1978), 305.

18. John Waterbury, *The Egypt of Nasser and Sadat: The Political Economy of Two Regimes* (Princeton, N.J.: Princeton University Press, 1983), 307–32.

19. Raymond William Baker, *Egypt's Uncertain Revolution under Nasser and Sadat* (Cambridge, Mass.: Harvard University Press, 1978), 101–8.

20. Anwar el-Sadat, *In Search of Identity: An Autobiography* (New York: Harper Colophon, 1979), 195.

21. Derek Hopwood, *Egypt: Politics and Society, 1945–1981* (London: George Allen & Unwin, 1982), 88.

22. Tawfiq al-Hakim, *The Return of Consciousness*, trans. Bayly Winder (New York: New York University Press, 1985), 28.

23. Nasser, *Philosophy of the Revolution*, 112.

24. Ibid., 113.

25. Morroe Berger, *Islam in Egypt Today* (Cambridge: Cambridge University Press, 1970), 44.

26. See Anwar Sadat, *Nahwa ba'th jadid* (Cairo: Islamic Conference, n.d.).

27. Berger, *Islam in Egypt Today*, 47.

28. Ibid., 47–48. See also A. Cris Eccel, *Egypt, Islam and Social Change: al-Azhar in Conflict and Accommodation* (Berlin: Klaus Schwarz Verlag, 1984), 502–3.

29. Ministry of Waqfs, United Arab Republic, *Wizarat al-awqaf fi ithna 'ashara 'amman, 1952–64* (Cairo, 1964), 115; quoted in Berger, *Islam in Egypt Today*, 48.

30. Daniel Crecelius, "Al-Azhar in the Revolution," *Middle East Journal* 20 (Winter 1966): 35–36.

31. Ibid., 36–37.

32. For a survey of some of this material, see Wolfgang Ule, *Bibliographie zu Fragen des arabischen Sozialismus, des Nationalismus und des Kommunismus unter dem Gesichtspunkt des Islams* (Hamburg: Deutsches Orient-Institut, 1967).

33. See note 46, chapter 3, for a full citation of this work.

34. For a dating of this shift, see Donald E. Smith, "Religion and Political Modernization: Comparative Perspectives," in *Religion and Political Modernization*, ed. Donald Eugene Smith (New Haven, Conn. and London: Yale University Press, 1974), 14.

35. Shepard, "Islam and Ideology," 308.

36. See Ernest Gellner, *Nations and Nationalism* (Oxford: Basil Blackwell, 1983); and Anthony Giddens, *A Contemporary Critique of Historical Materialism*, vol. 2, *The Nation-State and Violence* (Berkeley and Los Angeles: University of California Press, 1985).

37. Benedict Anderson, *Imagined Communities*, rev. ed. (London and New York: Verso, 1991), 5–7.

38. Albert Hourani, *Arabic Thought in the Liberal Age 1789–1939* (Cambridge: Cambridge University Press), 341–43.

39. Roy, *Failure of Political Islam*, 32–34.

40. John L. Esposito, *Islam and Politics* (Syracuse, N.Y.: Syracuse University Press, 1984), 44–57.

41. For a discussion of the reification of "Islam" among modern Muslims, see Wilfred Cantwell Smith, *The Meaning and End of Religion* (San Francisco: Harper & Row, 1978), chap. 4; a similar theme is sounded under the term "objectification" in Eickelman and Piscatori, *Muslim Politics*, 37–45.

42. *al-Da'wa*, 20 February 1951; quoted in Mitchell, *Society of Muslim Brothers*, 321.

43. *Akhir Sa'a*, 15 December 1948; quoted in Mitchell, *Society of Muslim Brothers*, 66.

44. Hasan al-Banna, "Ila ayya shay' nad'u al-nass," in *Majmu'at risa'il al-imam al-shahid Hasan al-Banna'* (Cairo: Dar al-Shihab, n.d.), 44–45.

45. Muhammad 'Abduh, *Risalat al-tawhid* (Cairo, 1942–43); English translation, *The Theology of Unity*, trans. Ishaq Musa'ad and Kenneth Cragg (New York: Books for Libraries, 1980).

46. al-Banna, "Risalat al-mu'tamar al-khamis," in *Majmu'at risa'il*, 153.

47. Sayyid Qutb, *al-'Adala al-ijtima'iyya fi al-Islam* (Beirut and Cairo: Dar al-Shuruq, 1975), 28.

48. Here I am following the analysis of William E. Shepard, "Islam as a 'System' in the Later Writings of Sayyid Qutb," *Middle Eastern Studies* 25, no.1 (January 1989): 31–50.

49. Qutb, *al-'Adala al-ijtima'iyya*, 93–94.

50. Sayyid Qutb, *Ma'arakat al-Islam wa al-ra'smailiyya* (Beirut, Cairo, Jedda: Dar al-Shuruq, 1975), 66.

51. al-Banna, "Da'watuna," in *Majmu'at risa'il*, 17.

52. Ibid.

53. al-Banna, "Nahwa al-nur," in *Majmu'at risa'il*, 60–71.

54. Liah Greenfeld, "The Modern Religion?" *Critical Review* 10, no. 2 (Spring 1996): 186.

55. For a cross-cultural analysis of this phenomenon, see Mark Juergensmeyer, *The New Cold War?: Religious Nationalism Confronts the Secular State* (Berkeley, Los Angeles, London: University of California Press, 1993).

56. See Deniz Kandiyoti, "Introduction," in *Women, Islam and the State*, ed. Deniz Kandiyoti (Philadelphia: Temple University Press, 1991), 7–9; and Jeffrey T. Kenney, "Jews, Kharijites and the Debate over Religious Extremism in Egypt," in *Muslim-Jewish Encounters: Intellectual Traditions and Modern Politics*, eds. Ronald L. Nettler and Suha Taji-Farouki (Amsterdam: harwood academic publishers, 1998), 65–86.

57. al-Banna, "Da'watuna," in *Majmu'at risa'il*, 14.

58. Greenfeld, "The Modern Religion?" 182; Liah Greenfeld, *Nationalism: Five Roads to Modernity* (Cambridge, Mass.: Harvard University Press, 1992), 9–11.

59. For more on this, see the informative discussion of Sami Zubaida, *Islam, the People and the State* (London and New York: I. B. Tauris, 1993), chap. 6.

60. Greenfeld, "The Modern Religion?" 183.

61. al-Banna, "Risalat al-jihad," in *Majmu'at risa'il*, 248–49.

62. An excellent source for study of the changes in language and interpretation is William Shepard, *Sayyid Qutb and Islamic Activism: A Translation and Critical Analysis of "Social Justice in Islam"* (Leiden, New York, Koln: E. J. Brill, 1996). Shepard has translated the final edition, which appeared in 1964, and five earlier editions going back to 1949, allowing the reader to trace the link between radicalism and rhetoric.

63. Sami Jawhar, *al-Mawta yatakallimun* (Cairo: al-Maktab al-Misri al-Hadith, 1977), 129, 135.

64. See Qutb, *Ma'arakat al-Islam wa al-ra'smailiyya*.

65. Qutb, *Ma'alim fi'l-tariq* (Cairo: Dar al-Shuruq, 1987), 149–51.

66. Ibid., 5–13.

67. Ibid., 188.

68. See Issa J. Boullata, "The Rhetorical Interpretation of the Qur'an: *i'jaz* and Related Topics," in *Approaches to the History of the Interpretation of the Qur'an*, ed. Andrew Rippin (Oxford: Clarendon Press, 1988), 150–51; and A. H. Johns, "Let My People Go!: Sayyid Qutb and the Vocation of Moses," *Islam and Christian-Muslim Relations* 1, no. 2 (December 1990): 143–70. Qutb presented his analysis of the communicative style of the Qur'an in *al-Taswir al-fanni fi al-Qur'an* (Cairo: Dar al-Ma'arif, 1963).

69. Qutb, *Ma'alim*, 192–95.

70. Emmanuel Sivan, *Radical Islam*, enlarged ed. (New Haven, Conn. and London: Yale University Press, 1990), chap. 2.

71. Eric Hobsbawm, *The Age of Extremes: A History of the World, 1914–1991* (New York: Pantheon Books, 1994), 344–52. See also Robert Malley, *The Call from Algeria: Third Worldism, Revolution and the Turn to Islam* (Berkeley, Los Angeles, London: University of California Press, 1996).

CHAPTER 3

1. Nadav Safran, *Egypt in Search of Political Community* (Cambridge, Mass.: Harvard University Press, 1961), 241; G. C. Anawati, "Une résurgence du kharijisme au xxe siècle: 'l'obligation absente,'" *Mélanges Institut dominicain d'études orientales du caire* 16 (1983): 191–228; Johannes J. G. Jansen, "The Early Islamic Movement of the Kharidjites and Modern Moslem Extremism: Similarities and Differences," *Orient* 27 (1986): 127–35; Hala Mustafa, "The Islamist Movement under Mubarak," in *The Islamist Dilemma: The Political Role of Islamist Movements in the Contemporary Arab World*, ed. Laura Guazzone (Reading, UK: Ithaca Press, 1995), 173.

2. Richard P. Mitchell, *The Society of Muslim Brothers* (London: Oxford University Press, 1969), 320–21.

3. See Sayyid Qutb, *Ma' alim fi'l-tariq* (Cairo: Dar al-Shuruq, 1987), 62–91; and Johannes J. G. Jansen, *The Neglected Duty* (New York: Macmillan, 1986), passim.

4. Mitchell, *Society of Muslim Brothers*, 320 n. 63.

5. Sami Zubaida, *Islam, the People and the State* (London and New York: I. B. Tauris, 1993), xx.

6. The precise dates of Qutb's stay in the United States and his initial membership in the Society of Muslim Brothers are in dispute. Here I have relied on information provided by William Shepard in a personal communication.

7. For a brief overview of Qutb's life, see Yvonne Y. Haddad, "Sayyid Qutb: Ideologue of Islamic Revival," in *Voices of Resurgent Islam*, ed. John L. Esposito (New York and Oxford: Oxford University Press, 1983), 67–98; Ahmad S. Moussalli, *Radical Islamic Fundamentalism: The Ideological and Political Discourse of Sayyid Qutb* (Beirut: American University of Beirut, 1992), 19–38; 'Adil Hamudah, *Sayyid Qutb: min qarya ila al-mishnaqa* (Cairo: Sina l'l-Nashr, 1987).

8. Qutb, *Ma'alim fi'l-tariq*.

9. Sayyid Qutb, *Fi zilal al-Qur'an*, 6 vols. (Beirut: Dar al-Shuruq, 1982; Jidda: Dar al-'Ilm li'Tiba'a wa'l-Nashr, 1986).

10. Qutb, *Ma'alim*, 11.

11. Ibid., 21.

12. Ibid., 101.

13. Ibid., 11–12.

14. Ibid., 40.

15. Ibid., 50.

16. Ibid., 64.

17. Ibid., 72–73.

18. Ibid., 92–102.

19. For an analysis of the origins of Qutb's conflation of *jahiliyya* and unbelief, see Emmanuel Sivan, *Radical Islam*, enlarged ed. (New Haven, Conn. and London: Yale University Press, 1990), chap. 4, especially 94–107.

20. Qutb, *Ma'alim*, 150.

21. Patrick D. Gaffney, *The Prophet's Pulpit* (Berkeley and Los Angeles: University of California Press, 1994), chap. 2. His "types" are derived from Weber's analysis.

22. Gaffney, *Prophet's Pulpit*, 53.

23. Ibid., 42.

24. See Jeffrey T. Kenney, "Enemies Near and Far: The Image of the Jews in Islamist Discourse in Egypt," *Religion* 24 (1994): 253–70.

25. Gaffney, *Prophet's Pulpit*, 52.

26. *Akhir Sa'a*, 15 September and 22 September 1965.

27. *Akhir Sa'a*, 15 September 1965.

28. I cannot locate in my edition the precise passage quoted in the article, but similar phrasing appears in Qutb, *Ma'alim*, 98.

29. Mitchell, *Society of Muslim Brothers*, 131–62.

30. Ibid., 152.

31. Kirk J. Beattie, *Egypt During the Nasser Years* (Boulder, Colo.: Westview Press, 1994), 134–36.

32. Gilles Kepel, *Muslim Extremism in Egypt*, trans. Jon Rothschild (Berkeley and Los Angeles: University of California Press, 1985), 33.

33. For another example of media coverage of terrorism, see *Akhir Sa'a*, 29 September 1965.

34. Richard Falk, *Revolutionaries and Functionaries: The Dual Face of Terrorism* (New York: Dutton, 1988), 27.

35. Sheikh 'Abd al-Latif Sibki, review of *Ma'alim fi'l-tariq*, by Sayyid Qutb, *Minbar al-Islam* (24 November1965): 21.

36. Sibki, 22; Qutb, *Ma'alim*, 28–29.

37. Qutb, *Ma'alim*, 29.

38. Sibki, 22.

39. Sibki, 22.

40. See *Minbar al-Islam* (24 December 1965): 15–18; (23 January 1966): 107–9; (21 February 1966): 97–98.

41. Sibki, 23; Qutb, *Ma'alim*, 74.

42. Sibki, 24.

43. Kenneth Burke, *A Grammar of Motives* (Berkeley, Los Angeles, and London: University of California Press, 1969), 503.

44. Robert N. Bellah et al., *The Good Society* (New York: Vintage, 1992), 13.

45. Sibki, 26.

46. *Ra'y al-din fi ikhwan al-shaytan* (Cairo: al-Majlis al-A'la li-l Shu'un al-Islamiyya, n.d.[1966]).

47. Ibid., 87.

48. Ibid., 14–16.

49. Ibid., 3–4.

50. Ibid., 4.

51. Ibid., 4.

52. Ibid., 46–47.

53. Ibid., 48–49.

54. Ibid., 74.

55. The equation of Kharijites, Muslim Brothers, and terrorists follows a similar pattern of symbolic association in the essays; see, for example, *Ra'y al-din*, 54.

CHAPTER 4

1. Fouad Ajami, "In the Pharaoh's Shadow: Religion and Authority in Egypt," in *Islam in the Political Process*, ed. James P. Piscatori (Cambridge: Cambridge University Press, 1983), 13.

2. See David D. Laitin, "Political Culture and Political Preferences," *American Political Science Review* 82, no. 2 (June 1988): 589–593.

3. Fouad Ajami, "The Summoning," *Foreign Affairs* 72, no. 4 (September/October 1993): 9.

4. Samuel P. Huntington, "The Clash of Civilizations?" *Foreign Affairs* 72, no. 3 (Summer 1993): 22–49. Ajami's comment that "civilizations do not control states, states control civilizations" was a response to Huntington's theory of cultural clashes.

5. Bruce Lincoln, *Authority: Construction and Corrosion* (Chicago and London: University of Chicago Press, 1994), 112–13.

6. P. J. Vatikiotis, *The Modern History of Egypt* (New York: Frederick A. Praeger Publishers, 1969), 406–11; Afaf Lutfi al-Sayyid Marsot, *A Short History of Modern Egypt* (Cambridge: Cambridge University Press, 1985), 124–27.

7. Speech marking the anniversary of the revolution; quoted in Derek Hopwood, *Egypt: Politics and Society, 1945–1981* (London: George Allen & Unwin, 1982), 97.

8. Yvonne Haddad, "Islamists and the 'Problem of Israel': The 1967 Awakening," *Middle East Journal* 46, no. 2 (Spring 1992): 266–85.

9. See Tawfic Farah and Yasumasa Kuroda, eds., *Political Socialization in the Arab States* (Boulder, Colo.: Lynne Rienner Publishers, 1987); and Mark Tessler, ed., *The Evaluation and Application of Survey Research in the Arab World* (Boulder, Colo.: Westview Press, 1987).

10. For an exchange on the value of analyzing Arab politics through the political culture approach, see Michael C. Hudson, "The Political Culture Approach to Arab

Democratization: The Case for Bringing It Back In, Carefully," in *Political Liberalization and Democratization in the Arab World*, vol. 1, eds. Rex Brynen, Bahgat Korany, and Paul Noble (Boulder, Colo.: Lynne Riener Publishers, 1995), 61–76; and Lisa Anderson, "Democracy in the Arab World: A Critique of the Political Culture Approach," in ibid., 77–92.

11. *International Encyclopedia of the Social Sciences*, s.v. "propaganda."

12. Muhammad ʿAbduh and Rashid Rida, *Tafsir al-qurʾan al-hakim* (Cairo: Dar al-Manar, 1346–54 [1927–36]), 6:396–409.

13. Sayyid Qutb, *Fi zilal al-Qurʾan* 2:887–905.

14. Sami al-Jawhar, *al-Mawta yatakallimun* (Cairo: al-Maktab al-Misri al-Hadith, 1977), 135.

15. The debates are outlined in Emmanuel Sivan, *Radical Islam*, enlarged ed. (New Haven, Conn. and London: Yale University Press, 199), 107–29.

16. Scholars of the period have typically exonerated al-Hudaybi from the violence that occurred, portraying him as a victim of the secret organization. A recent work, however, challenges this view of al-Hudaybi's involvement in the plot to kill Nasser, accusing him of "passive acquiescence"; see Joel Gordon, *Nasser's Blessed Movement: Egypt's Free Officers and the July Revolution* (New York and Oxford: Oxford University Press, 1992), 183.

17. Hasan Ismaʿil al-Hudaybi, *Duʿah..la qudah* (Cairo: Dar al-Tibaʿa waʾl-Nashr al-Islamiyya, 1977).

18. Ibid., 14.

19. Ibid., 16–33.

20. Ibid., 38.

21. Ibid., 58–60.

22. Ibid., 161–62.

23. Ibid., 162–64.

24. James C. Scott, *Domination and the Arts of Resistance* (New Haven, Conn. and London: Yale University Press, 199), 102–3.

25. Anwar el-Sadat, *In Search of Identity: An Autobiograpy* (New York: Harper Colophon, 1979), 210.

26. Ibid., 49–50.

27. Saad Eddin Ibrahim, "An Islamic Alternative in Egypt: The Muslim Brotherhood and Sadat," *Arab Studies Quarterly* 4, nos. 1–2 (1981): 81, 93.

28. Muhammad Heikal, *Autumn of Fury: The Assassination of Sadat* (New York: Random House, 1983), 128.

29. Originally published in booklet form, without attribution to Sirriya, by a student association at Dar al-ʿUlum; see Rifʿat Sayyid Ahmed, *Islambouli: ruʾya jadida li-tanzim al-Jihad* (Cairo: Madbouli, 1987), 69 n. 4. Complete text reprinted in Rifʿat Sayyid Ahmed, *al-Nabiy musallah (vol.1): al-rafidun* (London: Riad el-Rayyes Books, 1991), 31–52.

30. Sirriya, "Risalat al-iman," in Ahmed, *al-Nabiy musallah (vol. 1)*, 31–32.

31. My portrait of the group has been informed by ʿAbd al-Rahman Abu al-Khair, *Dhikriyati maʿa Jamaʿt al-Muslimin* (Kuwait: Dar al-Buhuth al-ʿIlmiyya, 1980); ʿAdil

Hamuda, *al-Hijra ila al-'unf: al-tatarruf al-dini min hazima yuniya ila ightiyal oktobir* (Cairo: Sina l'l-Nashr, 1987), 169–223; Gilles Kepel, *Muslim Extremism in Egypt*, trans. Jon Rothschild (Berkeley and Los Angeles: University of California Press, 1985), chap. 3.

32. Hamid Hassan et al., *Muwajahat al-fikr al-mutatarrif fi'l-Islam* (Cairo: Matba'a al-Gabalawi, 1980), 41–48.

33. Ibid., 19–22; Abu al-Khair, *Dhikriyati*, 18–19, 34–35.

34. For a sociological analysis of the members of Takfir and the Military Academy group, see Saad Eddin Ibrahim, "Anatomy of Egypt's Militant Islamic Groups: Methodological Notes and Preliminary Findings," *International Journal of Middle East Studies* 12 (1980): 423–53.

35. *Qabasat min huda al-Islam*, Maktaba al-Imam no. 12 (Cairo: Wazarat al-Awqaf, 1975).

36. Muhammad Hussein al-Dhahabi, *al-Ittijahat al-munharifa fi tafsir al-qur'an al-karim* (Cairo: Dar al-I'tisam, 1976).

37. Abu al-Khair, *Dhikriyati*, 141–47. For Mustafa's view of Dhahabi and al-Azharites in general, see his trial transcripts in Ahmed, *al-Nabiy musallah (vol.1)*, 53–103.

38. *Qabasat*, 24–25.

39. Ibid., 3–4.

40. Ibid., 60–64.

41. al-Dhahabi, *al-Ittijahat al-munharifa*, 7.

42. Ibid., 63–64.

43. Abu al-Khair, *Dhikriyati*, 61.

44. *al-Ahram*, 8 July 1977; *Ruz al-Yusuf*, 18 July 1977.

45. *al-Ahram*, 8 July 1977, *Ruz al-Yusuf*, 29 August 1977; *Oktober*, 28 August 1977, 16 October 1977; *Minbar al-Islam*, August 1977, September 1977.

46. For an interesting account of the confrontation between the Sheikh of al-Azhar, 'Abd al-Halim Mahmud, and the Sadat regime, see Kepel, *Muslim Extremism*, 99–102.

47. *al-Ahram*, 8 July 1977.

48. Mustafa Hilmi, *al-Khawarij: al-usul al-ta'rikhiyya li masalat al-muslim* (Cairo: Dar al-Ansar, 1977).

49. Ibid., 1–3. (Here I have provided actual numbers for the Arabic lettered pages of the introduction to the series, written by Muhammad 'Abd al-Karim Khayal.)

50. Ibid., 50–53.

51. It should be noted that Hilmi assumes familiarity among his readers with the Protocols, since he simply mentions "fifth protocol" without any explanation.

52. Hilmi, *al-Khawarij*, 54. See also Jeffrey T. Kenney, "Enemies Near and Far: The Image of the Kharijites in Islamist Discourse," *Religion* 24 (1994): 265–66.

53. Salim 'Ali al-Bahnasawi, *al-Hukm wa qadiyya takfir al-muslim* (Cairo: Dar al-Ansar, 1977).

54. Ibid., 3–7

55. Ibid., 323–71.

56. *al-Da'wa*, January 1978, 54–55.

57. See, for example, the juxtaposition of articles in *al-Da'wa*, January 1997, 28–29.

58. See, for example, *al-Da'wa*, July 1977, 6–7.

59. Ibrahim, "Islamic Alternative in Egypt," 86.

60. Johannes J. G. Jansen, *The Neglected Duty* (New York: Macmillan, 1986), 169–75, 191–92. First published in *al-Ahrar*, 14 December 1981; see also Muhammad 'Amara, *al-Farida al-gha'iba* (Beirut: Dar al-Wahda, 1983).

61. For an overview of the Jihad organization, see Nemat Guenena, "The 'Jihad': An Islamic Alternative in Egypt," in *Cairo Papers in Social Science*, vol. 9, mono. 2 (Cairo: The American University in Cairo Press, 1986).

62. Jansen, *Neglected Duty*, 172–76.

63. Ibid., 179.

64. Ibid., 191–92.

65. Ibid., 182–84.

66. Sirriya, "Risalat al-iman," in Ahmed, *al-Nabiy musallah (vol. 1)*, 42–43.

67. Jansen, *Neglected Duty*, 192–93.

68. Hassan et al., *Muwajahat*, 63–65.

69. 'Umar 'Abd al-Rahman, *Kalimat haqq* (Cairo: Dar al-I'tisam, 1987).

70. Ibid., 31.

71. Ibid., 59–80.

72. Ibid., 101.

73. Ibid., 105.

74. Salah Abu Isma'il, *al-Shahada* (Cairo: Dar al-Qafila, 1984), 52–53.

75. Ibid., 61–64, 102. The list of sinful deeds cited by Abu Isma'il is almost identical to that given by Abd al-Rahman in his testimony.

76. Ibid., 118–21.

77. Ibid., 170–71.

78. Dale F. Eickelman and James Piscatori, *Muslim Politics* (Princeton, N. J.: Princeton University Press, 1996), chap. 5.

79. *Akhir Sa'a*, 23 September 1981.

80. Wazarat al-Awqaf, *Dirasat fi al-Islam* no. 243 (September 1981), 75, 83.

81. *Oktober*, 11 October 1981; see also *al-Musawwar*, 20 November 1981.

82. *Oktober*, 25 October 1981, 1 November 1981, 8 November 1981; *Mayo*, 2 November 1981; *al-Musawwar*, 30 October 1981.

83. *Oktober*, 17 January 1982; *Ruz al-Yusuf*, 26 October 1981

84. *Oktober*, 21 September 1981, 28 September 1981.

85. *Oktober*, 12 October 1981.

86. *Oktober*, 7 December 1981. For a discussion of this passage in al-Shahrastani's *Milal*, see chap. 1.

87. *al-Musawwar*, 22 January 1982, 5 February 1982, 19 February 1982, 19 March 1982; *Mayo*, 16 November 1981; *Oktober*, 8 November 1981.

88. *Mayo*, 15 November 1982.

89. Mohammed Arkoun, *Rethinking Islam: Common Questions, Uncommon Answers*, trans. and ed. Robert D. Lee (Boulder, Colo., San Francisco, Oxford: Westview Press, 1994), 13.

90. Arkoun doesn't distinguish between secularization and modernization, but given the comparison with the West, he seems to regard them as roughly equivalent, if not synonymous ideas.

91. See his speeches in *al-Ahram*, 2 May 1980 and 16 May 1980.

92. See Ibrahim, "Islamic Alternative in Egypt"; Gabriel R. Warburg, "Islam and Politics in Egypt: 1952–80," *Middle Eastern Studies* 18 (1982): 131–57; Raphael Israeli, "The Role of Islam in President Sadat's Thought," *The Jerusalem Journal of International Relations* 4, no. 4 (1980): 1–12; Norma Salem-Babikan, "The Sacred and the Profane: Sadat's Speech to the Knesset," *Middle East Journal* 34, no. 1 (Winter 1980): 13–24.

93. The rules governing the head of state are elaborated in part five, chapter one of the constitution; see the translation of the 1971 text in "Constitution of the Arab Republic of Egypt," *Middle East Journal* 26 (Winter 1972): 55–68.

CHAPTER 5

1. For a concise analysis of the situation, see Dennis J. Sullivan and Sana Abed-Kotob, *Islam in Contemporary Egypt: Civil Society vs. the State* (Boulder, Colo. and London: Lynne Rienner Publishers, 1999).

2. Fouad Ajami gives this question an affirmative answer in his "In the Pharaoh's Shadow: Religion and Authority in Egypt," in *Islam in the Political Process*, ed. James P. Piscatori (Cambridge: Cambridge University Press, 1983), 12–13.

3. The Egyptian government's fear of popular opinion is evident in the number of questions censored in the global public opinion survey carried out by The Pew Research Center. Clearly half of the survey questions were eliminated, making Egypt the most censored Muslim nation, and putting it in the company of China and Vietnam. See *The Pew Global Attitudes Project: What The World Thinks in 2002* (Washington, D.C.: The Pew Research Center for the People & the Press, 2002).

4. Talal Asad, *Genealogies of Religion: Discipline and Reasons of Power in Christianity and Islam* (Baltimore and London: Johns Hopkins University Press, 1993), 210.

5. *al-Musawwar*, 30 October 1981, 6 November 1981, 20 November 1981.

6. Islamists had in fact drawn attention to the social and political causes of extremism earlier, though their analysis was ideologically driven.

7. *Ayyam min hiyati* (Cairo and Beirut: Dar al-Shuruq, 1987).

8. Valerie J. Hoffman, "An Islamic Activist: Zaynab al-Ghazali," in *Women and the Family in the Middle East*, ed. Elizabeth Warnock Fernea (Austin: University of Texas Press, 1985), 234.

9. Hasan Isma'il al-Hudaybi, *Du'ah . . . la qudah* (Cairo: Dar al-Tiba'a wa'l-Nashr al-Islamiyya, 1977).

10. See 'Abdullah Imam, *'Abd al-Nasir wa'l-Ikhwan al-Muslimin* (Cairo: Dar al-Mawqif al-'Arabi, 1981).

11. Ami Ayalon, "Journalists and the Press: The Vicissitudes of Licensed Pluralism," in *Egypt from Monarchy to Republic: A Reassessment of Revolution and Change*, ed. Shimon Shamir (Boulder, Colo.: Westview Press, 1995), 273.

12. John Waterbury, *The Egypt of Nasser and Sadat: The Political Economy of Two Regimes* (Princeton, N.J.: Princeton University Press, 1983), 338–39.

13. *Al-Ahram*, 27 June 1977; quoted in Waterbury, *Egypt of Nasser and Sadat*, 355.

14. Gehad Auda, "The 'Normalization' of the Islamic Movement in Egypt from the 1970s to the Early 1990s" in *Accounting for Fundamentalisms: The Dynamic Character of Movements*, vol. 4, eds. Martin E. Marty and R. Scott Appleby (Chicago and London: University of Chicago Press, 1994), 388.

15. Gregory Starrett, *Putting Islam to Work: Education, Politics, and Religious Transformation in Egypt* (Berkeley, Los Angeles, London: University of California Press, 1998).

16. Edward William Lane, *Manners and Customs of the Modern Egyptians* (1895 ed.; reprint, The Hague and London: East-West Publications, 1978), 65–68.

17. Timothy Mitchell, *Colonizing Egypt* (Berkeley, Los Angeles, Oxford: University of California Press, 1991), xi.

18. Starrett, *Putting Islam to Work*, 5–10.

19. Amira Howeidy, "Who Can Speak for the Public?" *al-Ahram Weekly* (20–26 January 2005).

20. Walter Laqueur, "A Failure of Intelligence," *The Atlantic Monthly* (March 2002): 130.

21. *al-Musawwar*, 22 June 1982.

22. *Ruz al-Yusuf*, 19 October 1987.

23. *al-Musawwar*, 30 October, 6 November, and 20 November 1981; 22 June 1982

24. *Oktober*, 13 December 1981.

25. Saad Eddin Ibrahim, "Anatomy of Egypt's Militant Islamic Groups: Methodological Notes and Preliminary Findings," *International Journal of Middle East Studies* 12 (1980): 423–53.

26. *al-Musawwar*, 30 October 1981.

27. Ibrahim, "Anatomy of Egypt's Militant Islamic Groups," 440; *al-Musawwar*, 30 October 1981.

28. *Ruz al-Yusuf*, 5 October 1987.

29. It is important to note the contradictory messages communicated by al-Azhar officials and representatives of the state security apparatus.

30. Hannah Arendt, "Reflections on Violence," *The New York Review of Books*, 27 February 1969, 30.

31. *al-Liwa' al-islami*, 11 February 1982, 11 March 1982, 8 April 1982; *al-Musawwar*, 5 February 1982; *Ruz al-Yusuf*, 6 August 1984, 17 April 1989.

32. *Mayo*, 8 November 1982, 6 December 1982, 21 June 1982; *al-Liwa' al-islami*, 11 March 1982, 8 April 1982.

33. *Ruz al-Yusuf*, 1 May 1989.

34. *Al-Liwa' al-islami*, 11 February 1982.

35. *Ruz al-Yusuf*, 6 August 1984.

36. See A. Chris Eccel, "Alim and Mujahid in Egypt: Orthodoxy Versus Subculture, or Division of Labor," *Muslim World* 85 (July 1988): 189–208; Steven Barraclough, "Al-Azhar: between the Government and the Islamists," *Middle East*

Journal 52, no, 2 (Spring 1998): 236–49; Tamir Moustafa, "Conflict and Cooperation between the State and Religious Institutions in Contemporary Egypt," *International Journal of Middle East Studies* 32 (2000): 3–22.

37. William E. Shepard, "Muhammad Sa'id al-'Ashmawi and the Application of the Shari'a in Egypt," *International Journal of Middle East Studies* 28 (1996): 39–42; Carolyn Fluehr-Lobban ed., *Against Islamic Extremism: The Writings of Muhammad Sa'id al-'Ashmawy* (Gainesville: University Press of Florida, 1998), 1–11.

38. Shepard, "al-'Ashmawi and the Application," 51–52.

39. Fluehr-Lobban, *Against Islamic Extremism*, 30; George F. Mclean, "Preface," in *Islam and the Political Order*, by Muhammad Said al-'Ashmawy (Washington, D.C.: The Council for Research in Values and Philosophy, 1994), 1–9.

40. See Fauzi M. Najjar, "The Debate on Islam and Secularism in Egypt," *Arab Studies Quarterly* 18, no. 2 (Spring 1996): 1–21.

41. *Al-Islam al-siyasi* (Cairo: Sina li-l-Nashr, 1987). Two partial translations are available: in French, *L'islamisme contre l'islam* (Paris: Editions La Découverte, 1989); and in English, *Islam and the Political Order*.

42. Al-'Ashmawi, *al-Islam al-siyasi*, 7; *Islam and the Political Order*, 11.

43. Al-'Ashmawi, *al-Isalm al-siyasi*, 10; *Islam and the Political Order*, 13.

44. Al-'Ashmawi, *al-Islam al-siyasi*, 54; *Islam and the Political Order*, 45.

45. Emmanuel Sivan, *Interpretations of Islam: Past and Present* (Princeton, N.J.: Darwin, 1985), 62

46. Al-'Ashmawi, *al-Islam al-siyasi*, 31; *Islam and the Political Order*, 27.

47. See Nathan O. Hatch, *The Democratization of American Christianity* (New Haven, Conn. and London: Yale University Press, 1989).

48. Much the same point has been made about the work of another secular writer, Fuad Zakaria, whose argumentative style [in *al-Haqiqa wa'l-wahm fi'l-harakat al-islamiyya al-mu'asira*, 3rd printing (Cairo: Dar al-Fikr, 1988)] has been likened to a case of "your Islam versus my Islam"; see Salwa Ismail, *Rethinking Islamist Politics: Culture, the State and Islamism* (London and New York: I. B. Tauris, 2003), 54.

49. Al-'Ashmawi, *al-Islam al-siyasi*, 58; *Islam and the Political Order*, 48.

50. Al-'Ashmawi, *al-Islam al-siyasi*, 58–62; *Islam and the Political Order*, 48–50.

51. For a biographical overview, publication record, and list of current activities, see his personal Web site: http://www.qaradawi.net.

52. Gilles Kepel, *Jihad: The Trail of Political Islam*, trans. Anthony F. Roberts (Cambridge, Mass.: Belknap Press, 2002), 165, 199, 234.

53. Yusuf al-Qaradawi, *al-Sahwa al-islamiyya bain al-judud wa'l-tatarruf*, 3rd printing (Cairo: Dar al-Shuruq, 1983); *Islamic Awakening between Rejection and Extremism*, 2nd rev. ed. (Herndon, Va.: American Trust Publication and The International Institute of Islamic Thought, 1991).

54. *al-Sahwa al-islamiyya*, 22–23; *Islamic Awakening*, 15.

55. *al-Sahwa al-islamiyya*, 62–63; *Islamic Awakening*, 49

56. *al-Sahwa al-islamiyya*, 43–54; *Islamic Awakenings*, 33–39.

57. *al-Sahwa al-islamiyya*, 57; *Islamic Awakenings*, 43.

58. *al-Sahwa al-islamiyya*, 61–110; *Islamic Awakening*, 49–83.

59. al-Sahwa al-islamiyya, 110–19; Islamic Awakening, 83–89.

60. al-Sahwa al-islamiyya, 116; Islamic Awakening, 88.

61. al-Sahwa al-islamiyya, 121–29; Islamic Awakening, 90–95.

62. al-Sahwa al-islamiyya, 125; Islamic Awakening, 93.

63. al-Sahwa al-islamiyya, 139–41; Islamic Awakening, 104–6.

64. al-Sahwa al-islamiyya, 148–50; Islamic Awakening, 109–11.

65. My point here is to show that Islamists, despite their ideological views, get drawn into mainstream economic concerns through the power of the discourse; for a comparative assessment, see Ismail, Rethinking Islamist Politics, 56.

66. Graham E. Fuller, The Future of Political Islam (New York: Palgrave Macmillan, 2003), 34–36.

67. See Fawaz A. Gerges, "The End of the Islamist Insurgency in Egypt: Costs and Prospects," Middle East Journal 4 (Fall 2000): 592–612; Geneive Abdo, No God but God: Egypt and the Triumph of Islam (Oxford and New York: Oxford University Press, 2000).

68. Khaled Dawoud, "Islamism in Crisis," Al-Ahram Weekly (31 December 1998–6 January 1999).

69. Kepel, Jihad, 376.

70. Ibid., 240.

71. Abdo, No God but God, 196.

72. Muhammad M. el-Hodaiby, "Upholding Islam: The Goals of Egypt's Muslim Brotherhood," Harvard International Review 19, no. 2 (Spring 1997): 23.

73. Quoted in Gerges, "End of the Islamist Insurgency," 610.

74. Middle East Watch, "Egypt: Arrest and Detention Practices and Prison Conditions" (March 1992); Middle East Watch, "Egypt: Hostage-Taking and Intimidation by Security Forces" (January 1995); Amnesty International, "Egypt: Grave Human Rights Abuses Amid Political Violence" (May 1993). See also François Burgat, Face to Face with Political Islam (London and New York: I. B. Tauris, 2003), 98–101

75. Mohammed M. Hafez, Why Muslims Rebel: Repression and Resistance in the Islamic World (Boulder, Colo. and London: Lynne Rienner Publishers, 2004), 84.

76. Hasanein Tawfiq Ibrahim, "al-Anf al-siyasi fi misr" in Dhahiret al-anf al-siyasi min mandhour muqarin, ed. Navin Abdel Mun'am Mus'ad (Cairo: Markaz al-Bihouth wa'l-Dirasat al-Siyasia, 1995), 412–13; quoted in Hafez, Why Muslims Rebel, 88.

77. For an overview of the statistics, see Hafez, Why Muslims Rebel, 84–88.

78. Abdo, No God but God, 196.

79. Gerges, "End of the Islamist Insurgency," 599.

80. See, for example, Ahmed Abdalla, "Egypt's Islamists and the State: From Complicity to Confrontation," Middle East Reports (July–August 1993): 28–31; Cassandra, "The Impending Crisis in Egypt," Middle East Journal 49, no. 1 (Winter 1995): 9–27; Joel Campagna, "From Accommodation to Confrontation: The Muslim Brotherhood in the Mubarak Years," Journal of International Affairs 50, no. 1 (Summer 1996): 278–304; Eberhard Kienle, "More Than a Response to Islamism: The Political Deliberalization of Egypt in the 1990s," Middle East Journal 52, no. 2 (Spring 1998): 219–35.

81. Karam Muhammad Zuhdi, Najim Ibrahim 'Abdallah, Usama Ibrahim Hafiz, Fu'ad Mahmud al-Dawalibi, Hamdi 'Abd al-Rahman al-'Azim, 'Ali Muhammad 'Ali al-Sharif, and 'Asim 'Abd al-Majid Muhammad (primary authorship changes with each volume, though all names are cited), *Mubarada waqf al-'unf, Hurma al-ghuluw fi 'l-din wa takfir al-muslimin, Taslit al-adawa' 'ala ma waqa'a fi 'l-jihad min akhta', al-Nash wa 'l-tabiyyin fi tashih mafahim al-muhtasabin* (Cairo: Maktaba al-Turath al-Islami, 2002).

82. Makram Muhammad Ahmed, *Mu'amara am muraja'a: hiwar ma'a qada al-tatarruf fi sijin al-'aqrab* (Cairo: Dar al-Shuruq, 2002). The Egyptian government was initially suspicious of the motives of the repentant al-Jama'a leaders, which no doubt accounts for the publication delay of the four books; see Maye Kassem, *Egyptian Poliltics: The Dynamics of Authoritarian Rule* (Boulder, Colo. and London: Lynne Rienner Publishers, 2004), 156–57. Since then, it has promoted the public pronouncements and confessions of these leaders, hoping to benefit both domestically and internationally, especially after 9/11; see Jailan Halawi, "Rethinking Militancy," *Al-Ahram Weekly* (28 August–3 September 2003).

83. See especially, 'Umar 'Abdallah Kamil, *al-Mutatarrifun: al-Khawarij al-judud* (Cairo: Maktaba al-Turath al-Islami, 1998). Al-Qaradawi wrote the preface for this book. The work clearly condemns the perpetrators of the attack and labels them Kharijites, but the various social, political, and economic causes listed in the book suggest that Kharijism is driven by secular, not Islamic, forces.

84. The analysis of Kharijism appears mainly in the booklet *Hurma al-ghuluw*.

CONCLUSION

1. Personal e-mail communication, 29 January 2005.

2. See W. Montgomery Watt, *Islamic Fundamentalism and Modernity* (London and New York: Routledge, 1988); and Niels C. Nielsen, Jr., *Fundamentalism, Mythos, and World Religions* (Albany: State University of New York Press, 1993).

3. Fred Halliday, *Nation and Religion in the Middle East* (Boulder, Colo.: Lynne Rienner Publishers, 2000), 216.

4. Alaa Al Aswany, *The Yocoubian Building* (Cairo: The American University Press, 2005). The novel was first published in Arabic in 2002.

5. NPR, "All Things Considered," 22 February 2005.

6. "Introduction," 18, n. 35.

7. Ann Elizabeth Mayer, *Islam and Human Rights: Tradition and Politics*, 3rd ed. (Boulder, Colo.: Westview Press, 1999), 46.

Bibliography

Abdalla, Ahmed. "Egypt's Islamists and the State: From Complicity to Confrontation." *Middle East Reports* (July-August 1993): 28–31.

'Abdallah, Najim Ibrahim, et al. *Hurma al-ghuluw fi'l-din wa takfir al-muslimin.* Cairo: Maktaba al-Turath al-Islami, 2002.

'Abd al-Rahman, 'Umar. *Kalimat haqq.* Cairo: Dar al-I'tisam, 1987.

Abdo, Geneive. *No God but God: Egypt and the Triumph of Islam.* Oxford and New York: Oxford University Press, 2000.

Abu al-Khair, 'Abd al-Rahman. *Dhikriyati ma'a Jama't al-Muslimin.* Kuwait: Dar al-Buhuth al-'Ilmiyya, 1980.

Abu Isma'il, Salah. *al-Shahada.* Cairo: Dar al-Qafila, 1984.

'Abduh, Muhammad. *The Theology of Unity.* Translated by Ishaq Musa'ad and Kenneth Cragg. New York: Books for Libraries, 1980.

'Abduh, Muhammad, and Rashid Rida. *Tafsir al-qur'an al-hakim.* Cairo: Dar al-Manar, 1346–54 [1927–36].

Ahmed, Makram Muhammad. *Mu'amara am muraja'a: hiwar ma'a qada al-tatarruf fi sijin al-'aqrab.* Cairo: Dar al-Shuruq, 2002.

Ahmed, Rif'at Sayyid. *Islambouli: ru'ya jadida li-tanzim al-Jihad.* Cairo: Madbouli, 1987.

———. *al-Nabiy musallah (vol. 1): al-rafidun.* London: Riad el-Rayyes Books, 1991.

———. *al-Nabiy musallah (vol. 2): al-tha'irun.* London: Riad el-Rayyes Books, 1991.

Ahrari, M. E. "Islam as a Source of Conflict and Change in the Middle East." *Security Dialogue* 25, no. 2 (1994): 177–92.

Ajami, Fouad. *The Arab Predicament.* Cambridge: Cambridge University Press, 1981.

————. "In the Pharaoh's Shadow: Religion and Authority in Egypt." In *Islam in the Political Process*. Edited by James P. Piscatori. Cambridge: Cambridge University Press, 1983.

————. "The Summoning." *Foreign Affairs* 72, no. 4 (September/October 1993): 2–9.

'Amara, Muhammad. *al-Farida al-gha'iba*. Beirut: Dar al-Wahda, 1983.

Anawati, G. C. "Une résurgence du Kharijisme au xxᵉ siècle: 'l'obligation absente'." *Mélanges Institut dominicain d'études orientales du caire* 16 (1983): 191–228.

Anderson, Benedict. *Imagined Communities*. Rev. ed. London and New York: Verso, 1991.

Ansari, Hamied. "The Islamic Militants in Egyptian Politics." *International Journal of Middle East Studies* 16 (1984): 123–44.

————. *Egypt: The Stalled Society*. Albany: State University of New York Press, 1986.

Appleby, R. Scott. *The Ambivalence of the Sacred: Religion, Violence, and Reconciliation*. Lanham, Md.: Rowman & Littlefield, 2000.

Apter, David E. "Political Religion in the New Nations." In *Old Societies and New States: The Quest for Modernity in Asia and Africa*. Edited by Clifford Geertz. London: Collier-Macmillan Ltd., 1963.

Arberry, Arthur J., trans. *The Koran Interpreted*. New York: Macmillan, 1955.

Arendt, Hannah. "Reflections on Violence." *The New York Review of Books* (27 February 1969), 19–31.

Arkoun, Mohammad. *Rethinking Islam: Common Questions, Uncommon Answers*. Translated and edited by Robert D. Lee. Boulder, San Francisco, Oxford: Westview Press, 1994.

Asad, Talal. *Genealogies of Religion: Discipline and Reasons of Power in Christianity and Islam*. Baltimore and London: Johns Hopkins University Press, 1993.

al-Ash'ari, Abu'l-Hasan 'Ali ibn Isma'il. *al-Ibana 'an usul ad-diyanah (The Elucidation of Islam's Foundation)*. Translated by Walter C. Klein. New Haven, Conn.: American Oriental Society, 1940.

al-'Ashmawi, Muhammad Sa'id. *al-Islam al-siyasi*. Cairo: Sina li-l-Nashr, 1987. Partial translation under the title *Islam and the Political Order*. Preface by George F. Mclean. Washington, D.C.: The Council for Research in Values and Philosophy, 1994.

Aswany, Alaa Al, *The Yacoubian Building*. Cairo: The American University Press, 2005.

Auda, Gehad. "The 'Normalization' of the Islamic Movement in Egypt from the 1970s to the Early 1990s." In *Accounting for Fundamentalisms: The Dynamic Character of Movements*. Edited by Martin E. Marty and R. Scott Appleby. Chicago and London: University of Chicago Press, 1994.

Ayalon, Ami. "Journalists and the Press: The Vicissitudes of Licensed Pluralism." In *Egypt from Monarchy to Republic: A Reassessment of Revolution and Change*. Edited by Shimon Shamir. Boulder, Colo.: Westview Press, 1995.

Ayubi, Nazih. *Political Islam: Religion and Politics in the Arab World*. London and New York: Routledge, 1991.

al-'Azim, Hamdi 'Abd al-Rahman, et al. *Taslit al-adawa' 'ala ma waqa'a fi'l-jihad min akhta'*. Cairo: Maktaba al-Turath al-Islami, 2002.

Baer, Gabriel. *Studies in the Social History of Modern Egypt*. Chicago: University of Chicago Press, 1969.

al-Baghdadi, 'Abd al-Qadir Ibn Tahir. *al-Farq bayna al-firaq*. Cairo: Madbuli, n.d.

al-Bahnasawi, Salim 'Ali. *al-Hukm wa qadiyya takfir al-muslim*. Cairo: Dar al-Ansar, 1977.

al-Banna, Hasan. *Majmu'at risa'il al-imam al-shahid Hasan al-Banna'*. Cairo: Dar al-Shihab, n.d.

Baker, Raymond William. *Egypt's Uncertain Revolution under Nasser and Sadat*. Cambridge, Mass.: Harvard University Press, 1978.

Barraclough, Steven. "Al-Azhar: Between the Government and the Islamists." *Middle East Journal* 52, no. 2 (Spring 1988): 236–49.

Beattie, Kirk J. *Egypt during the Nasser Years*. Boulder, Colo.: Westview Press, 1994.

Bellah, Robert N., et al. *The Good Society*. New York: Vintage, 1992.

Benjamin, Daniel, and Steven Simon. *The Age of Sacred Terror: Radical Islam's War Against America*. New York: Random House, 2002.

Berger, Morroe. *Islam in Egypt Today*. Cambridge: Cambridge University Press, 1970.

Bergen, Peter L. *Holy War, Inc.: Inside the Secret World of Osama bin Laden*. New York: Touchstone, 2001.

Berman, Paul. *Terror and Liberalism*. New York and London: W. W. Norton, 2003.

Binder, Leonard. *In a Moment of Enthusiasm: Political Power and the Second Stratum in Egypt*. Chicago: University of Chicago Press, 1978.

———. *Islamic Liberalism*. Chicago: University of Chicago Press, 1988.

Bosworth, Clifford Edmund. *Sistan under the Arabs, from the Islamic Conquest to the Rise of the Saffarids (30–250/651–84)*. Rome: Instituto Italiano per il medio ed estremo Oriente, 1968.

Boullata, Issa J. "The Rhetorical Interpretations of the Qur'an: *i'jaz* and Related Topics." In *Approaches to the History of the Interpretation of the Qur'an*. Ed. Andrew Rippin. Oxford: Clarendon Press, 1988.

Bromley, Simon. *Rethinking Middle East Politics*. Austin: University of Texas Press, 1994.

Brooks, E. W., ed. *Eliae Metropolitae Nisibeni*. Vol. 62, *Corpus Scriptorum Christianorum Orientalium*. Louvain: Impremerie Orientaliste, 1954.

Brunnow, Rudolf Ernst. *Die Charidschiten unter den ersten Omayyaden*. Leiden: E. J. Brill, 1884.

Burgat, François. *Face to Face with Political Islam*. London and New York: I.B. Tauris, 2003.

Burke, Kenneth. *A Grammar of Motives*. Berkeley, Los Angeles, London: University of California Press, 1969.

Campagna, Joel. "From Accommodation to Confrontation: The Muslim Brotherhood in the Mubarak Years." *Journal of International Affairs* 50, no. 1 (Summer 1996): 278–304.

Cassandra. "The Impending Crisis in Egypt." *Middle East Journal* 49, no. 1 (Winter 1995): 9–27.

Coll, Steve. *Ghost Wars: The Secret History of the CIA, Afghanistan, and Bin Laden, from the Soviet Invasion to September 10, 2001*. New York: Penguin Press, 2004.

"Constitution of the Arab Republic of Egypt." *Middle East Journal* 26 (Winter 1972): 55–68.

Cook, Michael. *Early Muslim Dogma: A Source-Critical Study.* Cambridge: Cambridge University Press, 1981.

———. "'Anan and Islam: The Origins of Karaite Scripturalism." *Jerusalem Studies in Arabic and Islam* 9 (1987): 161–82.

Crecelius, Daniel. "Al-Azhar in the Revolution." *Middle East Journal* 20 (Winter 1966): 31–49.

Crone, Patricia. *Slaves on Horses: The Evolution of the Islamic Polity.* Cambridge: Cambridge University Press, 1980.

Davis, Eric. "Ideology, Social Class and Islamic Radicalism in Modern Egypt." In *From Nationalism to Revolutionary Islam.* Edited by Said Amir Arjomand. Albany: State University of New York Press, 1984.

al-Dhahabi, Muhammad Hussein. *al-Ittijahat al-munharifa fi tafsir al-qur'an al-karim.* Cairo: Dar al-I'tisam, 1976.

Eccel, A. Cris. *Egypt, Islam and Social Change: al-Azhar in Conflict and Accommodation.* Berlin: Klaus Schwarz Verlag, 1984.

———. "Alim and Mujahid in Egypt: Orthodoxy Versus Subculture, or Division of Labor." *Muslim World* 85 (July 1988): 189–208.

Eickelman, Dale F, and James Piscatori, *Muslim Politics.* Princeton, N.J.: Princeton University Press, 1996.

Ennami, Amr K. *Studies in Ibadism.* Benghazi: University of Libya, 1972.

Esposito, John L. *Islam and Politics.* Syracuse, N.Y.: Syracuse University Press, 1984.

Falk, Richard. *Revolutionaries and Functionaries: The Dual Face of Terrorism.* New York: Dutton, 1988.

Fluehr-Lobban, Carolyn, ed. *Against Islamic Extremism: The Writings of Muhammad Sa'id al-Ashmawy.* Gainesville: University Press of Florida, 1998.

Fuller, Graham E. *The Future of Political Islam.* New York: Palgrave Macmillan, 2003.

Gaffney, Patrick D. *The Prophet's Pulpit.* Berkeley and Los Angeles: University of California Press, 1994.

Gellner, Ernest. *Muslim Society.* Cambridge: Cambridge University Press, 1981.

Gelvin, James L. *The Modern Middle East: A History.* New York and Oxford: Oxford University Press, 2005.

Gerges, Fawaz A. "The End of the Islamist Insurgency in Egypt: Costs and Prospects." *Middle East Journal* 4 (Fall 2000): 592–612.

Gerth, H. H., and C. Wright Mills, trans. and eds. *From Max Weber: Essays in Sociology.* New York: Oxford University Press, 1946.

al-Ghazali, Zeinab. *Ayyam min hiyati.* Cairo and Beirut: Dar al-Shuruq, 1987.

Goldziher, I. "Le dénombrement des sects mohamétanes." *Revue l'histoire des religions* 26, no. 2 (1892): 129–37.

Gordon, Joel. *Nasser's Blessed Movement: Egypt's Free Officers and the July Revolution.* New York and Oxford: Oxford University Press, 1992.

Greenfeld, Liah. *Nationalsim: Five Roads to Modernity.* Cambridge, Mass.: Harvard University Press, 1992.

———. "The Modern Religion?" *Critical Review* 10, no. 2 (Spring 1996): 169–91.

Guenena, Nemat. "The 'Jihad': An Islamic Alternative in Egypt." In *Cairo Papers in Social Science*. Vol. 9, mon. 2. Cairo: The American University in Cairo Press, 1986.

Haddad, Yvonne Y. "Sayyid Qutb: Ideologue of Islamic Revival." In *Voices of Resurgent Islam*. Edited by John L. Esposito. New York and Oxford: Oxford University Press, 1983.

———. "Islamists and the 'Problem of Israel': The 1967 Awakening." *Middle East Journal* 46, no. 2 (Spring 1992): 266–85.

Hafez, Mohammed M. *Why Muslims Rebel: Repression and Resistance in the Islamic World*. Boulder, Colo. and London: Lynne Rienner Publishers, 2004.

Hafiz, Usama Ibrahim, et al. *Mubarada waqf al-'unf*. Cairo: Maktaba al-Turath al-Islami, 2002.

al-Hakim, Tawfiq. *The Return of Consciousness*. Translated by Bayly Winder. New York: New York University Press, 1985.

Halliday, Fred. *Nation and Religion in the Middle East*. Boulder, Colo.: Lynne Rienner Publishers, 2000.

Hamudah, 'Adil. *Sayyid Qutb: min qarya ila al-mishnaqa*. Cairo: Sina l'l-Nashr, 1987.

———. *al-Hijra ila al-'unf: al-tatarruf al-dini min hazima yuniya ila ightiyal oktobir*. Cairo: Sina l'l-Nashr, 1987.

Hanafi, Hasan. "The Relevance of the Islamic Alternative in Egypt." *Arab Studies Quarterly* 4 (Spring 1982): 54–74.

Hassan, Hamid, et al. *Muwajahat al-fikr al-mutatarrif fi'l-Islam*. Cairo: Matba'a al-Gabalawi, 1980.

Heikal, Muhammad. *Autumn of Fury: The Assassination of Sadat*. New York: Random House, 1983.

Hilmi, Mustafa. *al-Khawarij: al-usul al-ta'rikhiyya li masalat al-muslim*. Cairo: Dar al-Ansar, 1977.

Hinds, Martin. "Kufan Political Alignments and Their Background in the Mid-Seventh Century A.D." *International Journal of Middle East Studies* 2 (1971): 346–67.

———. "The Siffin Arbitration Agreement." *Journal of Semitic Studies* 1 (1972): 93–129.

Hobsbawm, Eric. *The Age of Extremes: A History of the World, 1914–1991*. New York: Pantheon Books, 1994.

Hoffman, Valerie J. "An Islamist Activist: Zaynab al-Ghazali." In *Women and the Family in the Middle East*. Edited by Elizabeth Warnock Fernea. Austin: University of Texas Press, 1985.

Hopwood, Derek. *Egypt: Politics and Society, 1945–1981*. London: George Allen & Unwin, 1982.

Hourani, Albert. *Arabic Thought in the Liberal Age 1789–1939*. Cambridge: Cambridge University Press, 1983.

el-Hodaiby, Muhammad M. "Upholding Islam: The Goals of Egypt's Muslim Brotherhood." *Harvard International Review* 19, no. 2 (Spring 1997): 20–23, 62–63.

al-Hudaybi, Hasan Isma'il. *Du'ah..la qudah*. Cairo: Dar al-Tiba 'a wa'l-Nashr al-Islamiyya, 1977.

Humphreys, R. Stephen. *Islamic History: A Framework for Inquiry*. Rev. ed. Princeton, N.J.: Princeton University Press, 1991.

Huntington, Samuel P. "The Clash of Civilizations?" *Foreign Affairs* 72, no. 3 (Summer 1993): 22–49.

Ibn Hazm, 'Ali b. Ahmed. *Kitab al-fasl fi al-milal wa'l-ahwa' wa'l-nihal*. 4 vols. Beirut: Maktaba Khayyat, n.d.

Ibn Khaldun. *The Muqaddimah: An Introduction to History*. 3 vols. Trans. Franz Rosenthal. New York: Pantheon Books, 1958.

Ibrahim, Saad Eddin. "Anatomy of Egypt's Militant Islamic Groups: Methodological Notes and Preliminary Findings." *International Journal of Middle East Studies* 12 (1980): 423–53.

———. "An Islamic Alternative in Egypt: The Muslim Brothers and Sadat." *Arab Studies Quarterly* 4, nos. 1–2 (1981): 75–93.

———. "Islamic Activism: A Rejoinder." *Security Dialogue* 25, no. 2 (1994): 193–98.

Imam, 'Abdullah. *'Abd al-Nasir wa'l-Ikhwan al-Muslimin*. Cairo: Dar al-Mawqif al-'Arabi, 1981.

Ismail, Salwa. *Rethinking Islamist Politics: Culture, the State and Islamism*. London and New York: I. B. Tauris, 2003.

Israeli, Raphael. "The Role of Islam in President Sadat's Thought." *The Jerusalem Journal of International Relations* 4, no. 4 (1980): 1–12.

Izutsu, Toshihiko. *The Concept of Belief in Islamic Theology*. Yokohama, Japan: Yorindo, 1965.

Jansen, Johannes J. G. "The Early Islamic Movement of the Kharidjites and Modern Moslem Extremism: Similarities and Differences." *Orient* 27 (1986): 127–35.

———. *The Neglected Duty*. New York: Macmillan, 1986.

Jawhar, Sami. *al-Mawta yatakallimun*. Cairo: al-Maktab al-Misri al-Hadith, 1977.

Johns, A. H. "Let My People Go!: Sayyid Qutb and the Vocation of Moses." *Islam and Christian-Muslim Relations* 1, no. 2 (December 1990): 143–70.

Juergensmeyer, Mark. *The New Cold War?: Religious Nationalism Confronts the Secular State*. Berkeley, Los Angeles, London: University of California Press, 1993.

Kamil, 'Umar Abdallah. *al-Mutatarrifun: al-Khawarij al-judud*. Cairo: Maktaba al-Turath al-Islami, 1998.

Kandiyoti, Deniz. "Introduction." In *Women, Islam and the State*. Edited by Deniz Kandiyoti. Philadelphia: Temple University Press, 1991.

Kassem, Maye. *Egyptian Politics: The Dynamics of Authoritarian Rule*. Boulder, Colo. and London: Lynne Rienner Publishers, 2004.

Kenney, Jeffrey T. "The Emergence of the Kharwarij: Religion and the Social Order in Early Islam." *JUSUR* 5 (1989): 1–29.

———. "Enemies Near and Far: The Image of the Jews in Islamist Discourse in Egypt." *Religion* 24 (1994): 253–70.

———. "Jews, Kharijites and the Debate over Religious Extremism in Egypt." In *Muslim-Jewish Encounters: Intellectual Traditions and Modern Politics*. Edited by Ronald L. Nettler and Suha Taji-Farouki. Amsterdam: Harwood Academic Publishers 1998.

Kepel, Gilles. *Muslim Extremism in Egypt*. Translated by Jon Rothschild. Berkeley and Los Angeles: University of California Press, 1985.

———. *Jihad: The Trail of Political Islam*. Translated by Anthony F. Roberts. Cambridge, Mass.: Belknap Press, 2002.

Kerr, Malcolm. *Islamic Reform: The Political and Legal Theories of Muhammad 'Abduh and Rashid Rida*. Berkeley: University of California Press, 1966.

Kienle, Eberhard. "More Than a Response to Islamism: The Political Deliberalization of Egypt in the 1990s." *Middle East Journal* 52, no. 2 (Spring 1998): 219–35.

Lambton, Ann K.S. *State and Government in Medieval Islam*. Oxford: Oxford University Press, 1981.

Lane, Edward William. *Manners and Customs of the Modern Egyptians*. 1895 ed. Reprint. The Hague and London: East-West Publications, 1978.

Lapidus, Ira M. "The Separation of the State and Religion in the Development of Early Islamic Society." *International Journal of Middle East Studies* 6 (1973): 363–85.

Lee, Robert D. *Overcoming Tradition and Modernity: The Search for Islamic Authenticity*. Boulder, Colo.: Westview Press, 1997.

Lewis, Bernard. "Some Observations on the Significance of Heresy in the History of Islam." *Studia Islamica* 1 (1953): 43–63.

Lewy, Guenther. "Nasserism and Islam: A Revolution in Search of an Ideology." In *Religion and Political Modernization*. Edited by Donald Eugene Smith. New Haven, Conn. and London: Yale University Press, 1974.

Lincoln, Bruce. *Discourse and the Construction of Society*. New York and Oxford: Oxford University Press, 1989.

———. *Authority: Construction and Corrosion*. Chicago and London: University of Chicago Press, 1994.

McCarthy, Richard J. *The Theology of al-Ash'ari*. Beyrouth: Imprimerie Catholique, 1953.

Makram-Ebeid, Mona. "Democratization in Egypt: The 'Algeria Complex.'" *Middle East Policy* 3 (Summer 1994): 119–26.

———. "Egypt's 2000 Parliamentary Elections." *Middle East Policy* 8 (June 2001): 32–44.

Mamdani, Mahmood. *Good Muslim, Bad Muslim: America, the Cold War, and the Roots of Terror*. New York: Pantheon Books, 2004.

Marsot, Afaf Lutfi al-Sayyid. *Egypt's Liberal Experiment*. Berkeley and Los Angeles: University of California Press, 1977.

———. *A Short History of Modern Egypt*. Cambridge: Cambridge University Press, 1985.

al-Mas'udi, al-Hasan b. 'Ali. *Muruj al-dhahab*. Edited by Yusef As'ad Daghir. 4 vols. Beirut: Dar al-Anadalus, 1965.

Mayer, Ann Elizabeth. *Islam and Human Rights: Tradition and Politics*. 3rd ed. Boulder, Colo.: Westview Press, 1999.

Menand, Louis. "Faith, Hope, and Clarity." *The New Yorker* (September 16, 2002): 98–104.

Mitchell, Richard P. *The Society of Muslim Brothers*. London: Oxford University Press, 1969.

Mitchell, Timothy. *Colonizing Egypt*. Berkeley, Los Angeles, Oxford: University of California Press, 1991.

Morony, Michael G. *Iraq after the Muslim Conquest*. Princeton, N.J.: Princeton University Press, 1984.

Moustafa, Tamir. "Conflict and Cooperation between the State and Religious Institutions in Contemporary Egypt." *International Journal of Middle East Studies* 32 (2000): 3–22.

Moussalli, Ahmad S. *Radical Islamic Fundamentalism: The Ideological and Political Discourse of Sayyid Qutb*. Beirut: American University of Beirut, 1992.

Mottahedeh, Roy. *The Mantle of the Prophet: Religion and Politics in Iran*. New York: Simon and Schuster, 1985.

Mustafa, Hala. "The Islamist Movement under Mubarak." In *The Islamist Dilemma: The Political Role of Islamist Movements in the Contemporary Arab World*. Edited by Laura Guazzone. Reading, UK: Ithaca Press, 1995.

El-Naggar, Said. "Politics and Economic Reform in Egypt." Washington, D.C.: Center for Contemporary Arab Studies, 1995.

Najjar, Fauzi M. "The Debate on Islam and Secularism in Egypt." *Arab Studies Quarterly* 18, no. 2 (1996): 1–21.

Nasser, Gamal Abdul. *Egypt's Liberation: The Philosophy of the Revolution*. Washington, D.C.: Public Affairs, 1955.

Nemoy, Leon, trans. *Karaite Anthology*. New Haven, Conn.: Yale University Press, 1952.

The 9/11 Commission Report. Authorized Edition. New York and London: W. W. Norton, n.d.

O'Kane, Joseph P. "Islam in the New Egyptian Constitution: Some Discussions in *al-Ahram*." *Middle East Journal* 26 (Spring 1972): 137–48.

Paine, Robert. "When Saying Is Doing: In *Politically Speaking: Cross-Cultural Studies of Rhetoric*. Edited by Robert Paine. Philadelphia: Institute for the Study of Human Issues, 1981.

Piscatori, James P., ed. *Islam in the Political Process*. Cambridge: Cambridge University Press, 1983.

Qabasat min huda al-Islam. Maktaba al-Imam no. 12. Cairo: Wazarat al-Awqaf, 1975.

al-Qalhati, Abu 'Abdullah Muhammad b. Sa'id al-Azdi. *al-Kashf wa'l-bayan*. Edited by Isma'il al-Kashif. 2 vols. Oman: Wazarat al-Turath al-Qawmi wa'l-Thaqafa, 1400/1980.

al-Qaradawi, Yusuf. *al-Sahwa al-islamiyya bain al-judud wa'l-tatarruf*. Cairo: Dar al-Shuruq, 1983. Translation under the title *Islamic Awakening between Rejection and Extremism*. 2nd rev. ed. Herndon, Va.: American Trust Publications, 1991.

Qutb, Sayyid. *al-'Adala al-ijtima'iyya fi al-Islam*. Beirut and Cairo: Dar al-Shuruq, 1975.

———. *Ma'arakat al-Islam wa al-ra'smailiyya*. Beirut, Cairo, Jedda: Dar al-Shuruq, 1975.

———. *Fi zilal al-Qur'an*. 6 vols. Beirut: Dar al-Shuruq, 1982.

———. *Ma'alim fi'l-tariq*. Cairo: Dar al-Shuruq, 1987.

Ra'y al-din fi ikhwan al-shaytan. Cairo: al-Majlis al-A'la li-l Shu'un al-Islamiyya, n.d.

Remnick, David. "Letter from Cairo: Going Nowhere." *The New Yorker* (July 12 & 19, 2004): 74–83.

Rieu, Charles. *Supplement to the Catalogue of the Arabic Manuscripts in the British Museum.* London: Longman & Co., 1894.

Rippin, Andrew. *Muslims: Their Religious Beliefs and Practices.* Vol. 2, *The Contemporary Period.* London and New York: Routledge, 1993.

Robinson, Chase F. *Empire and Elites after the Muslim Conquest: The Transformation of Northern Mesopotamia.* Cambridge: Cambridge University Press, 2000.

Roy, Olivier. *The Failure of Political Islam.* Translated by Carol Volk. Cambridge, Mass.: Harvard University Press, 1994.

Ruthven, Malise. *Islam in the World.* New York and Oxford: Oxford University Press, 1984.

el-Sadat, Anwar. *In Search of Identity: An Autobiography.* New York: Harper Colophon, 1979.

Safran, Nadav. *Egypt in Search of Political Community.* Cambridge, Mass.: Harvard University Press, 1961.

Said Aly, Abd al-Monein, and Manfred Wenner. "Modern Islamic Reform Movements: The Muslim Brotherhood in Contemporary Egypt." *Middle East Journal* 36, no. 3 (1982): 336–61.

Salamé, Ghassan, ed. *Democracy without Democrats?: The Renewal of Politics in the Muslim World.* London and New York: I. B. Tauris, 1994.

Salem, Elie Adib. *Political Theory and Institutions of the Khawarij.* Baltimore: Johns Hopkins Press, 1956.

Salem-Babikan, Norma. "The Sacred and the Profane: Sadat's Speech to the Knesset." *Middle East Journal* 34, no. 1 (Winter 1980): 13–24.

Scott, James C. *Domination and the Arts of Resistance.* New Haven, Conn. and London: Yale University Press, 1990.

Shaban, M. A. *Islamic History: A New Interpretation.* Vol. 1, A.D. 600–750. Cambridge: Cambridge University Press, 1971.

al-Shahrastani, [Abu'l-Fath] Muhammad [b. 'Abd al-Karim]. *Kitab al-milal wa'l-nihal.* Edited by William Cureton. Leipzig: Otto Harrassowitz, 1923. Translated in part by A. K. Kazi and J. G. Flynn under the title *Muslim Sects and Divisions.* London: Kegan Paul International, 1984.

al-Sharif, 'Ali Muhammad 'Ali, et al. *al-Nash wa'l-tabiyyin fi tashih mafahim al-muhtasabin.* Cairo: Maktaba al-Turath al-Islami, 2002.

Shephard, William E. "Islam and Ideology: Towards a Typology." *International Journal of Middle East Studies* 19 (1987): 307–36.

———. "Islam as a 'System' in the Later Writings of Sayyid Qutb." *Middle Eastern Studies* 25, no. 1 (January 1989): 31–50.

———. *Sayyid Qutb and Islamic Activism: A Translation and Critical Analysis of "Social Justice in Islam."* Leiden, New York and Koln: E. J. Brill, 1996.

———. "Muhammad Sa'id al-'Ashmawi and the Application of the Shari'a in Egypt." *International Journal of Middle East Studies* 28 (1996): 39–58.

Shils, Edward. "The Concept and Function of Ideology." In *International Encyclopedia of Social Sciences*. Edited by David L. Sills. New York: Macmillan, 1968.

———. "Tradition." *Comparative Studies in Society and History* (1971).

Sivan, Emmanuel. *Interpretations of Islam: Past and Present*. Princeton, N.J.: Darwin, 1985.

———. *Radical Islam*. Enl. ed. New Haven, Conn. and London: Yale University Press, 1990.

Smith, Donald E. "Religion and Political Modernization: Comparative Perspectives." In *Religion and Political Modernization*. Edited by Donald Eugene Smith. New Haven, Conn. and London: Yale University Press, 1974.

Smith, Wilfred Cantwell. *The Meaning and End of Religion*. San Francisco: Harper & Row, 1978.

Starrett, Gregory. *Putting Islam to Work: Education, Politics, and Religious Transformation in Egypt*. Berkeley, Los Angeles, London: University of California Press, 1998.

Sullivan, Dennis J., and Sana Abed-Kotob. *Islam in Contemporary Egypt: Civil Society vs. the State*. Boulder, Colo. and London: Lynne Rienner Publishers, 1999.

al-Tabari, Abu Ja'far Muhammad b. Jarir. *Ta'rikh al-rusul wa'l-muluk*. Edited by M. J. de Goeje et al. Leiden: E. J. Brill, 1879–1901.

Vaglieri, L. Veccia. "Le vicende del Harigismo in epoca abbaside." *Revista degli Studi Orientali* 24 (1949): 31–44.

Vatikiotis, P. J. *The Modern History of Egypt*. New York: Frederick A. Praeger, Publishers, 1969.

Von Grunebaum, G. E. *Classical Islam: A History, 600 A.D.—1258 A.D.* Chicago: Aldine, 1970.

Wansbrough, John. *The Sectarian Milieu: Content and Composition of Islamic Salvation History*. Oxford: Oxford University Press, 1978.

Warburg, Gabriel R. "Islam and Politics in Egypt: 1952–80." *Middle Eastern Studies* 18 (1982): 131–57.

Waterbury, John. *The Egypt of Nasser and Sadat: The Political Economy of Two Regimes*. Princeton, N.J.: Princeton University Press, 1983.

Watt, W. Montgomery. "Conditions of Membership of the Islamic Community." *Studia Islamica* 21 (1964): 5–12.

———. *Islamic Fundamentalism and Modernity*. London and New York: Routledge, 1988.

Wellhausen, Julius. *The Religio-Political Factions in Early Islam*. Translated by R. C. Ostle and S. M. Walzer. Edited by R. C. Ostle. New York: American Elsevier Publishing Company, 1975.

Wensinck, A. J. *The Muslim Creed*. London: Frank Cass & Co., 1965.

Wensinck, A. J., et al., eds. *Concordance et indices de la tradition musulmane*. 2nd ed. 8 vols. Leiden: E. J. Brill, 1933–48.

Zakaria, Fuad. *al-Haqiqa wa'l-wahm fi'l-harakat al-islamiyya al-mu'asira*. 3rd printing. Cairo: Dar al-Fikr, 1988.

Zubaida, Sami. *Islam, the People and the State*. London and New York: I. B. Tauris, 1993.

———. "Is There a Muslim Society? Ernest Gellner's Sociology of Islam." *Economy and Society* 24, no. 2 (May 1995): 151–88.

Index

Muhammad (prophet of Islam), 20,
   33, 51–52, 84
   and the Kharijites, 26–29
   modern reinventions of, 75, 77–78,
      94, 105, 137, 165
Muhi al-Din, 'Ala, 175
mujahidun, 90
Murji'ites, 35–36
al-Musawwar, 147
Muslim Brothers. *See* Society of
   Muslim Brothers
Muslim politics, 58, 83, 87, 120, 137,
   139, 142
Muslim Women's Association, 150
Mustafa, Ahmed Shukri, 127–128,
   136–137
Mu'tazilites, 35, 41

Nahrawan, 22, 27, 31, 38–40
Nasser, Gamal Abdul, 55–58, 116,
   148, 156
   confrontation with Society of
      Muslim Brothers, 57–61, 77,
      84–87, 92, 97–103, 117–120,
      149–152
   opposition to, 123–124
   political philosophy and action,
      62–72
nationalism, 56–58, 73, 79–82, 85,
   95, 105, 113–115, 173
   Arab nationalism, 63, 65, 105,
      113–116
   religious nationalism, 77, 82–83,
      85–86
nation-state, 5, 10, 57, 71–72, 80–83,
   85, 88, 105, 109, 116, 126,
   148, 180
Neglected Duty, The (*al-Farida al-
   gha'iba*), 135–136
Neguib, General (Muhammad), 61,
   63, 100
9/11 Commision Report, The, 12
Nuqrashi Pasha, (Mahmud
   Fahmi), 60

Pakistan, 73, 165
Pan-Arabism, 66, 85
Pan-Islamism, 68, 74
Piscatori, James, 58
political religion, 62–63, 72, 88
al-Qa'ida, 3, 12, 16, 179, 183

al-Qalhati, Abu 'Abdullah
   Muhammad b. Sa'id al-Azdi,
   39–41
qanun (secular law), 106
al-Qaradawi, Yusuf, 164, 168–173,
   176–177
Qutb, Sayyid, 12, 15–16, 73, 120–122,
   124, 150, 163, 165
   Signposts Along the Road, 71, 91–97,
      99, 104–109, 121, 150
   Society of Muslim Brothers and,
      77–80, 83–86

Ramadan, Sa'id, 99
Revolutionary Command Council,
   65, 100
Rida, Rashid, 75, 120
Rushdie, Salman, 161
Ruz al-Yusuf, 140, 158, 162–163

Sa'adiah Gaon, 49
Sadat, Anwar, 3, 57, 67, 69, 72
   corrective revolution of, 152
   discourse surrounding his
      assassination, 134–143, 153
   Islamist organizations and, 127,
      130, 133–134
   Society of Muslim Brothers and,
      124–125, 149–150
al-Sanadi, 'Abd al-Rahman, 121
Saudi Arabia, 16, 68, 119, 183
secular(ism), 5, 8–9, 14, 72–73, 80,
   83, 91, 95, 114, 135, 146, 155, 164,
   168, 170–172, 177, 181
secularization, 6, 72, 142
September 11, 2001, 3, 11, 12–16, 158,
   169, 183